THE CIVILIZATION OF THE AMERICAN INDIAN

# POPOL VUH

*The Sacred Book of the Ancient Quiché Maya*

# POPOL VUH

*The Sacred Book of the Ancient Quiché Maya*

ENGLISH VERSION BY

*Delia Goetz and Sylvanus G. Morley*

FROM THE TRANSLATION OF

*Adrián Recinos*

NORMAN
UNIVERSITY OF OKLAHOMA PRESS

## *By* Adrián Recinos

*Monografía del Departamento de Huehuetenango.* Guatemala, 1913.
*Lecciones de Filosofía.* Guatemala, 1914.
*Poesías de José Batres Montúfar.* Madrid, 1924.
*Popol Vuh: Las Antiguas Historias del Quiché.* Mexico, 1947.
*Memorial de Solola. Anales de los Cakchiqueles.* Mexico, 1950.
*Popol Vuh: The Sacred Book of the Ancient Quiché Maya.* Norman, 1950.
*The Annals of the Cakchiquels* (with Delia Goetz). Norman, 1953.

International Standard Book Number: 0–8061–0205–5

Copyright 1950 by the University of Oklahoma Press, Publishing Division of the University. Manufactured in the U.S.A. First edition, 1950; second printing, 1950; third printing, 1953; fourth printing, 1957; fifth printing, 1961; sixth printing, 1965; seventh printing, 1969; eighth printing, 1972; ninth printing, 1975.

*Popol Vuh: The Sacred Book of the Ancient Quiché Maya* is Volume 29 in *The Civilization of the American Indian Series.*

*To the memory of Sylvanus Griswold Morley, who with untiring enthusiasm took part in the preparation and publication of an English version of the Sacred Book of the Quiché Maya, this edition of the* POPOL VUH *is gratefully dedicated.*

A. R.

# Foreword

THE *Popol Vuh*, or Sacred Book of the ancient Quiché Maya, as it has been happily subtitled, is, beyond any shadow of doubt, the most distinguished example of native American literature that has survived the passing centuries.

The original redaction of this most precious fragment of ancient American learning is now lost; however, it seems first to have been reduced to writing (in characters of the Latin script), in the middle of the sixteenth century, from oral traditions then current among the Quiché, by some unknown but highly educated, not to say literary, member of that race.

This now lost original was again copied in the Quiché language, again in characters of the Latin script, at the end of the seventeenth century, by Father Francisco Ximénez, then parish priest of the village of Santo Tomás Chichicastenango in the highlands of Guatemala, directly from the original sixteenth-century manuscript, which he had borrowed for the purpose from one of his Indian parishioners.

The *Popol Vuh* is, indeed, the Sacred Book of the Quiché Indians, a branch of the ancient Maya race, and contains an account of the cosmogony, mythology, traditions, and history of this native American people, who were the most powerful nation of the Guatemala highlands in pre-Conquest times. It is written in an exalted and elegant style, and is an epic of the most distinguished literary quality.

Indeed, the chance preservation of this manuscript only serves

to emphasize the magnitude of the loss which the world has suffered in the almost total destruction of aboriginal American
literature.

SYLVANUS G. MORLEY

*Museum of New Mexico*
  *Santa Fé*

# Preface

> Of all American peoples, the Quichés of Guatemala
> have left us the richest mythological legacy. Their
> description of the Creation as given in the *Popol Vuh*,
> which may be called the national book of the Quichés,
> is, in its rude strange eloquence and poetic originality,
> one of the rarest relics of aboriginal thought.—Hubert
> Howe Bancroft, *The Native Races*, III, 42.

THE NATIONAL BOOK of the Quiché, which contains
the mythology, traditions, and history of this remarkable American people, was not known by the scientific world until the past
century, when two European travelers, Carl Scherzer and Abbé
Charles Etienne Brasseur de Bourbourg, published, respectively,
the first Spanish version made in Guatemala at the beginning of
the eighteenth century and a contemporary French translation.
The two illustrious travelers visited the Central American countries almost at the same time, in 1854 and 1855, and both interested
themselves in the study of the aboriginal races of Guatemala,
which were those that had reached the highest degree of civilization in the center of the New World.

In the library of the University of San Carlos in the city of
Guatemala, Scherzer found the manuscript which contains the
transcription of the Quiché text and the first Spanish version of
the *Popol Vuh*, made by Father Francisco Ximénez of the Dominican Order. This first Spanish version of the Quiché document
was published by Scherzer in Vienna in 1857.

The Abbé Brasseur de Bourbourg carried his interest in the

Indian cultures of Guatemala much further. Having lived for some time in the country, he was in contact with the Indians, learned the Quiché and Cakchiquel tongues, and upon his return to Europe he published in Paris, in 1861, a handsome volume entitled *Popol Vuh, Le Livre Sacré et les mythes de l'antiquité américaine, avec les livres héroiques et historiques des Quichés,* which contains the original Quiché text, a translation into French, an extensive introduction, and rather full notes. The publication of this work at once attracted the attention of the public to the native peoples of Central America, whose existence and cultural achievements were at that time completely unknown in Europe and the United States. Since then, the book has been used by historians and ethnologists in their investigations of the native races and civilizations of America.

Brasseur de Bourbourg collected a number of old manuscripts in Guatemala, which he took with him to Europe and used in his writings on the history and the Indian languages of Central America. Among them was the volume which contains the *Arte* or grammar of the three principal languages of Guatemala, the Cakchiquel, the Quiché, and the Zutuhil, written in the eighteenth century by the same Father Francisco Ximénez, who was parish priest of Santo Tomás Chuilá, the present Chichicastenango. The same manuscript volume includes also the transcription and translation of the *Popol Vuh*, composed of 112 folios written in two columns, which has the title *Empiezan las historias del origen de los indios de esta provincia de Guatemala.* This volume, in the handwriting of Father Ximénez, was acquired in Europe by Edward E. Ayer, and today forms part of the valuable linguistic collection which bears his name and is preserved in the Newberry Library of Chicago.

The catalog of the Ayer Collection, however, did not list the manuscript of the *Historias del origen de los indios,* which as has been said, is bound together with that of the *Arte de las tres lenguas* by Father Ximénez. For this reason it was a very pleasant surprise to me to find it at the end of that volume, when I visited the Newberry Library for the first time in 1941. I wish to express here my gratitude to Mary Lapham Butler, in charge of the Edward E. Ayer Collection, for the facilities which she made available to me to complete my research in that center of study.

Comparing the original text transcribed by Ximénez with the text published by Brasseur de Bourbourg, I noticed some differences, important omissions, and other changes which affect the interpretation of the Quiché document. Furthermore, the possibility of clarifying and correcting passages in the existing translations stimulated my desire to undertake a new version direct from the original Quiché into Spanish. Thus, by making use of the work of my predecessors in this field, I would somewhat advance knowledge of the document that Bancroft has called the most valuable heritage which we have received from aboriginal American thought.

When the Spanish version was published in Mexico in 1947, my distinguished friend Sylvanus Griswold Morley, recognized as the highest authority on the Maya civilization, became interested in having an English translation made of this old book of the Quiché. It seems strange, indeed, that while this historical and mythological masterpiece is known in several Spanish, French, and German translations, there is no complete version in English for the use of readers and students of the English-speaking world. Mr. Morley's enthusiasm found generous response in the Rockefeller Foundation, always disposed to lend its support to intellectual pursuits, and with its valuable assistance the present English translation has been carried to a happy conclusion.

In both the Spanish and the English version of the *Popol Vuh*, I have tried to keep to the original text and to adjust myself strictly to the peculiarities of the Quiché language, which is simple and synthetical and yet does not lack elegance of expression. It would have been easy to give the narrative a literary form more pleasing to the modern reader; but this could have been done only by sacrificing the fidelity which must be the translator's guide in a work of this kind. In general I have tried to preserve the original construction, its passive forms and its frequent repetitions. In doing so, I have found very helpful the grammars and vocabularies of the Quiché and Cakchiquel languages compiled by the Spanish missionaries, which may be consulted in various libraries of Europe and the United States. The words of the original manuscript appear in footnotes when they have been omitted or altered in the transcription by Brasseur de Bourbourg. The spelling is that of the original text. Father Francisco de la Parra, in the middle of the sixteenth century, invented four characters to represent certain sounds peculiar to the Indian languages of Guatemala. These phonetic signs sometimes appear in the Ximénez manuscript, but they are not reproduced here because it is not considered necessary. In their place the generally accepted equivalent is given. The sound of *v* is the same as that of *u*, as was the custom in Spanish colonial times. The *h* has the same sound as in English. The initial *x* which occurs in certain Quiché words and proper names is the sign of the feminine and the diminutive and is pronounced like *sh*. For example, *Xbalanqué* and *Xmucané* are pronounced *Shbalanqué* and *Shmucané* respectively.

The original manuscript is not divided into parts or chapters; the text runs without interruption from the beginning until the end. In this translation I have followed the Brasseur de Bourbourg division into four parts, and each part into chapters, because the arrangement seems logical and conforms to the meaning and subject matter of the work. Since the version of the French Abbé is the best known, this will facilitate the work of those readers who may wish to make a comparative study of the various translations of the *Popol Vuh*.

The etymology of the proper names is a difficult matter and lends itself to dangerous conjectures and deceptive suppositions. For this reason, I have accepted only those which seem natural, without entering into an analysis of the components of the ancient names, a work which seldom gives real results. In various places, however, I have pointed out the relation of these names to others of the Maya tongue, to which the Quiché has a close resemblance, and sometimes with the Náhuatl tongue of Mexico, which has greatly influenced the languages of Central America.

I have also proceeded with caution in the use of geographical names. Some of the places mentioned in the text still retain their old names; but many others are known by the Mexican or Spanish names which were given to them after the Conquest. The modern names of the ancient places which it has been possible to identify may be found in the notes.

The map of the Maya-Quiché region, which has been especially prepared for the better understanding of the book, gives an idea of the wanderings of the Guatemala tribes and of their final settlement in the interior of the country. It serves, also, in my opinion, to explain the geographical and ethnical unity which exists among the peoples of southern Mexico and Yucatán and the native races which in pre-Columbian times occupied the land of Guatemala; and shows clearly the course of the large rivers, through which in those days an active intertribal trade was carried on.

I wish to express my gratitude to the Rockefeller Foundation for its valuable help, as well as my appreciation of the brilliant co-operation of my late friend Sylvanus G. Morley and of the able American writer Miss Delia Goetz in the making of the present English version. I wish also to mention the contribution of Isaac Esquiliano in the design of the dust jacket. And last, but not least, I wish to acknowledge the interest and encouragement of the University of Oklahoma Press with regard to the publication in English of the Quiché book.

ADRIÁN RECINOS

*Guatemala, C. A.*

# Contents

# Illustrations

The drawing on the title page is of the Bat God of the Maya

# POPOL VUH

*The Sacred Book of the Ancient Quiché Maya*

# M A P
## OF THE MAYA-QUICHÉ REGION

GULF OF MEXICO

Y U C A T Á N

Mérida • • Itzamal
• Mayapán • Chichén Itzá
• Uxmal

I. Cozumel

• Campeche

QUINTANA
ROO

• Chakanputún

CAMPECHE

Bacalar •

Tuxtla • Zuyva
Xicalanco • Laguna
Nonoalco de Términos
Xulpit •
Acu Cumán

TABASCO

VERACRUZ

Teoazacuancu
(Coatzacoalco)

Belize

• Palenque

Uaxactún •
• Tikal

• Piedras Negras

PETÉN

• Yaxchilán

Tayasal •

• Quen Santo

GULF
OF HONDURAS

CHIAPAS

GUATEMALA
VERAPAZ

Chamá • Carchah
• Cobán

Golfo Dulce

MAM • Nebaj
Zaculeu
Huehuetenango
Tacná • QUICHÉ
Utatlán • S. Cruz
Totonicapán • Chichicastenango
Quezaltenango • Iximché (Tecpán-Quauhtemallan)
Ayutla Solola (Tecpán-Atitlán) Kaminal-juyú
Lago Atitlán (Guatemala)
CAKCHIQUEL Lago Amatitlán
• Escuintla

Quiriguá •

• Copán

HONDURAS

Rabinal •

PACIFIC OCEAN

EL SALVADOR

# INTRODUCTION

1. *The Chronicles of the Indians*

When the conquest of Mexico by the Spaniards was completed, Hernán Cortés, who had heard of the existence of rich lands inhabited by a number of tribes in Guatemala, decided to send Pedro de Alvarado, the most fearless of his captains, to subdue them.

In the sixteenth century, the territory immediately to the south of Mexico, which is now the Republic of Guatemala, was inhabited by various independent nations which were descended from the ancient Maya, founders of the remarkable civilization whose remains are to be found throughout northern Guatemala and western Honduras, in Chiapas, and in Yucatán, Mexico. Of the nations located in the interior of Guatemala, the most important and numerous, without doubt, were the kingdoms of the Quiché and of the Cakchiquel, rival nations which had often made war upon each other for territorial, political, and economic reasons, and which continually disputed with each other for supremacy. At the time of the Spanish Conquest, the Quiché nation was the most powerful and cultured of all those that occupied the region of Central America. In 1524, when Alvarado attacked the Quiché, the Indians offered vigorous resistance, but after bloody battles they were forced to surrender before the superiority of the arms and tactics of the Spaniards. As a last desperate measure, the Quiché kings decided to receive Alvarado in peace at Utatlán, their capital. But once within its walls, the astute Spanish captain suspected that they were trying to destroy him and his army in the

3

narrow streets between the fortifications, and so he withdrew to the surrounding fields and there seized the kings, condemned them to death as traitors, and executed them before their terrorized subjects. Then he ordered the city razed to the ground and the inhabitants scattered in all directions.

In a letter which he addressed to Hernán Cortés, giving an account of the campaign, Alvarado himself describes the motives which he believed were those of the Quiché kings and concluded with these words:

And as I knew them to have such a bad will towards service to His Majesty, and for the good and peace of this land, I burned them and ordered the city burned and levelled to the ground, because it is so dangerous and so strong that it seems more like a house of thieves than [the abode] of people.[1]

When the conquest of the Quiché was completed, it is likely that a part of the inhabitants of Utatlán, especially members of the nobility and the priesthood, who had their houses in the capital and saw them disappear in the devouring flames, moved to Chichicastenango, the next town, which the ancient Quiché called Chuilá, or "place of nettles." Later the Spaniards named this town Santo Tomás and entrusted its pacification to missionaries of the religious orders, who converted the inhabitants to the Roman Catholic faith and introduced them to the civilization of the Old World. In this way, Santo Tomás Chichicastenango, as it is still called, became an important center of the Quiché Indians, which prospered throughout the three hundred years of Spanish rule and which today is still one of the most industrious and extensive Indian communities of Guatemala and the Mecca of foreigners, who are strongly attracted by the natural beauty of the place and the picturesque dress and customs of its people.

At the beginning of the eighteenth century, Father Francisco Ximénez of the Dominican Order lived within the thick walls of the convent of Chichicastenango. Father Ximénez was a wise and

[1] *Carta-Relación de Pedro de Alvarado a Hernando Cortés*, dated at Utatlán, April 11, 1524, *Historiadores Primitivos de Indias* (Vols. XXII, XXVI of *Biblioteca de Autores Españoles*, Madrid, 1852, 1853), XXII, 458.

virtuous man, who knew the languages of the Indians and had a lively interest in converting them to the Christian faith. It is probable that in his dealings with them, and through his help and fatherly advice, he had won their confidence and had succeeded in having them tell him the stories and traditions of their race. Ximénez, as I have said, was an accomplished linguist and, therefore, had the advantage of being able to communicate with his parishioners directly in the Quiché language, concerning which he has left valuable grammatical studies. All of these favorable circumstances helped to overcome the natural distrust of the Indians, and it is probably due to this fact, that, finally, the book which they so jealously guarded, and which contained the ancient histories of their nation, came into the hands of this Dominican friar.

This document, written shortly after the Spanish Conquest by a Quiché Indian who had learned to read and write Spanish, is generally known as the *Popol Vuh, Popol Buj, Book of the Council, Book of the Community,* the *Sacred Book,* or *National Book* of the Quiché, and it contains the cosmogonical concepts and ancient traditions of this aboriginal American people, the history of their origin, and the chronology of their kings down to the year 1550.

The name of its author and the fate of his original manuscript, which remained hidden for more than 150 years, are unknown. Father Ximénez, who found it in his parish at Santo Tomás Chichicastenango, transcribed the original Quiché text and translated it into Spanish under the title *Historias del Origen de los Indios de esta Provincia de Guatemala.* This transcription, in the handwriting of this priest-historian, is still preserved; but no information has survived concerning the original document written in the Quiché tongue, and it is possible that after Father Ximénez had finished copying it, it was returned to its Indian owners and to the obscurity in which it had remained up to then.

Ximénez says in the foreword to his second translation of the manuscript that the lack of information about the ancient history of the Indians is due to the fact that they hid their books in which it was written, and if some of them had been found in some places,

it was impossible to read or to understand them. For this reason—
says the historian—"much has been imagined about these various
peoples and their origin." And he adds:

and so I determined to transcribe, word for word, all of their tales
and translated them into our Spanish language from the Quiché language in which I found they had been written, from the time of the
Conquest, when (as they say there) they changed their way of writing to ours; but it was with great reserve that these manuscripts were
kept among them, with such secrecy, that neither the ancient ministers
knew of it, and investigating this point, while I was in the parish of
Santo Tomás Chichicastenango, I found that it was the doctrine which
they first imbibed with their mother's milk, and that all of them knew
it almost by heart, and I found that they had many of these books
among them. . . . And because I have seen many historians who write
about these peoples and their beliefs, say and touch upon some things
contained in their histories which were only scattered fragments,
since the historians had not seen the actual histories themselves, as
they were written, I decided to put here and transcribe all of their
histories, according to the way they had written them.[2]

In the foreword to his first Spanish version of the Quiché
manuscript, in describing the purpose of his work, Father Ximénez
had previously written:

In addition to bringing to light what had been among the Indians
in olden days, this work of mine attempts to give information on the
errors, which they had in their paganism and which they still adhere
to among themselves. I wanted to transcribe literally all the traditions
of these Indians, and also to translate them into the Spanish language
and put the commentaries, which are at the end, and which are like
annotations to the narrative about the things of the Indians, for I
imagine that there may be many curious people who would like to
know them, and in this manner, even if they do not know the language,
they will be able to learn it.[3]

In the *Relación* of Fray Alonso Ponce's expedition it is said

[2] *Historia de la Provincia de San Vicente de Chiapa y Guatemala*, I, 5.

[3] *Las Historias del Origen de los Indios de esta Provincia de Guatemala*
(1857 ed.), 1–2.

that one of the three things for which the Maya of Yucatán (whom he visited in 1586) were most praised is that:

they had characters and letters, with which they wrote their histories and ceremonies, and the order of the sacrifices to their idols and their calendar in books made of the bark of a certain tree, which were the very long strips of a quarter, or a third [of a Spanish *vara*] width which they folded and brought together and in this way it had the form of a bound book in quarto, more or less. Only the priests of the idols (who in that language are called "*ahkines*") and some principal Indians understood these letters and characters.[4]

The Indians of Mexico and Guatemala also preserved their histories and other writings by means of paintings on cloths, some of which were saved from the general destruction in which the books and Indian documents disappeared. The Bishop of Chiapas, Fray Bartolomé de las Casas, who, from the beginning of the Conquest, gathered extensive information about the life and customs of the Indians, says, in an oft-quoted passage, that among them were chroniclers and historians who knew the origin of everything pertaining to their religion, the founding of villages and cities, how the kings and lords carried out their memorable deeds, how they governed, and how they elected their successors; they knew about their great men and their courageous captains, of their wars, their ancient customs, and all that belonged to their history. And, he adds:

these chroniclers kept account of the days, months, and years [and] although they did not have writing such as ours, they had, nevertheless, their figures and characters,

with which they could represent all that they wanted to, and with them they formed:

their large books with such keen and subtle skill that we might say our writings were not an improvement over theirs. Some of these

[4] *Relación breve y verdadera de algunas cosas de las muchas que sucedieron al Padre Fray Alonso Ponce en las provincias de la Nueva España* (Vols. LVII, LVIII, *Colección de documentos para la historia de España*, Madrid, 1873), II, 392.

books were seen by our clergy, and even I saw part of those which were burned by the monks, apparently because they thought [these books] might harm the Indians in matters concerning religion, since at that time they were at the beginning of their conversion.[5]

The historians Acosta, Clavijero, and Ixtlilxóchitl say that the Indians learned to recite the most notable speeches of their ancestors and the songs of their poets, and that one or another of them taught these to the youths in schools which were connected with the temples, and in this way they were handed down from generation to generation. Bishop Las Casas, writing at the beginning of the Conquest, about 1540, says in the chapter previously cited from his *Apologética* that "in some places they did not use this way of writing, but that the knowledge of the ancient things came down from one to the other, from hand to hand," and that four or five, or perhaps more, of those who devoted themselves to the work of historians were instructed about ancient things, memorizing all that pertained to their history, and reciting it among themselves, while the others corrected them, but this method was naturally defective.

In another passage of the *Apologética*, Bishop Las Casas reports that the Mexican Indians had five books of figures and characters. The first book contained the history and the computation of their time; the second had the days of ceremony and the feast days of each year; the third dealt with dreams, auguries, and superstitions; the fourth with the way in which children were named; and the fifth contained their marriage rites and ceremonies. He adds that besides computing the years, feast days, and days of ceremony, the books of the first class told of their wars, victories, and defeats, the origin, genealogy, and deeds of the principal lords, and public disasters and their conquests down to the arrival of the Spaniards. This book mentions the peoples who in olden times inhabited the territory of Mexico, and of whom it says confusingly that they came from the Seven Ravines. That first book, says Las Casas in conclusion, is called *Xiuhtonalamatl* in the Indian lan-

[5] Las Casas, *Apologética Historia de las Indias* (Vol. I of *Nueva Biblioteca de Autores Españoles*), Chap. CCXXXV, "*De los libros y de las tradiciones religiosas que había en Guatemala.*"

8

guage, or "Story of the Counting of the Years."[6]

Ixtlilxóchitl, on his part, makes the following statement about his Mexican ancestors:

Each tribe had its writers; some wrote annals, arranging in order the things that came to pass during each year, together with the day, month, and hour; others had charge of the genealogy of the descendants of the kings, lords, and persons of lineage, setting down with detailed account those who were born, and in the same manner striking out the names of those who died. Some had the care of the paintings of the boundaries, limits, and landmarks of the lands; whose they were, and to whom they belonged; others had charge of the books of laws, rites, and ceremonies which they followed.[7]

According to Ixtlilxóchitl, Huematzin, the king of Tezcuco, had gathered together all the chronicles of the Tolteca in the *Teoamoxtli*, or "Divine Book,"[8] which contained the legends of the creation of the world, the emigration from Asia of those peoples, the stops on the journey, the dynasty of their kings, their social and religious institutions, their sciences, arts, and so on.

In the well-known passage of the *Relación* by the Oidor Diego García de Palacio, written in Guatemala in 1576, which speaks of the ruins of Copán, one reads the following words:

I have tried to find out from the memory of the ancients what people lived there, what they know and hear of their ancestors. I have not found books of their ancient things, nor do I believe that in all of this district there is more than one, which I have. They say that in olden times a great lord of the Province of Yucatán came here and built these buildings and that at the end of a few years he returned to his home alone, and left them empty. . . . According to this book it seems that in olden times, people from Yucatán conquered and subjected the provinces of Ayajal [Tayasal?], Lacandon, Verapaz, and the land of Chiquimula and this of Copán.[9]

[6] *Ibid.*, Chap. CCXXXIII.
[7] Ixtlilxóchitl, *Obras Históricas*, II, *Prólogo*.
[8] *Ibid.*
[9] García de Palacio, "*Relación hecha por el Licenciado Palacio al Rey D. Felipe II en la que describe la provincia de Guatemala*," in *Colección de documentos inéditos de Indias*, Vol. VI, p. 5.

These facts from the book, or manuscript, which García de Palacio possessed are interesting as proof of the theory that Copán was founded by the Maya of the North and subsequently abandoned. We do not know, however, whether or not this book may have contained other information of interest about the ancient inhabitants of that region.

Herrera, the well-known compiler of the Spanish historical reports of the sixteenth century, repeats the information about these native books which were found "in Yucatán and in Honduras."[10] Oviedo and Gómara, on their part, give an account of the books of the Indians of Nicaragua. "They have," says Gómara, "books of paper and parchment, a hand in width and twelve hands in length, folded like a bellows, on both sides of which they make known, in blue, purple, and other colors, the memorable events which take place."[11]

Bernal Díaz del Castillo, who wrote his *Verdadera Historia de la Conquista de la Nueva España*, in Guatemala, says that the Indians of Mexico had "booklets of a paper made of the bark of a tree which they called *amate* [*Ficus*], and in them made their signs of the times and of past events."

Some of these books were still in existence at the end of the seventeenth century, in the territory which is now the Republic of Guatemala. Father Francisco Ximénez tells that in the province of Petén, to the south of Yucatán, the Spaniards, during their expedition of 1696 against the Itzá, found some books written with characters which resembled Hebrew characters and also those used by the Chinese.[12] Doubtless they were books written in Mayan hieroglyphs, and it is possible that they may even be the same codices which were taken to Europe and are now preserved in Dresden, Paris, and Madrid.

In his *Relación de las dos entradas* in which he describes his journeys in the province of Petén, Father Avendaño y Loyola

[10] Herrera y Tordesillas, *Historia general de los hechos de los castellanos en las islas y tierra firme del mar Oceano*, Dec. III, Book II, Chap. XVIII.

[11] López de Gómara, *Historia General de las Indias, Historiadores Primitivos de Indias* (Vols. XXII, XXVI of *Biblioteca de Autores Españoles*), XXII, 284.

[12] *Historia de la Provincia de San Vicente de Chiapa y Guatemala*, I, 4.

declares that formerly he had seen these books, which he calls *anabtees* (probably derived from the Mexican word *amatles*), which the Indians used, and which this same Franciscan missionary describes as "some books of the bark of trees smoothed and bleached with chalk which, by means of figures and characters painted on them, contained prophecies or prognostications of future events."[13] And, farther on, he adds that these books were "a quarter of a hand in length and about five fingers wide, and were made of the bark of trees, folded back and forth like a screen, each leaf of the fold the thickness of a Mexican piece of eight. These were painted on both sides with a variety of figures and characters which not only gave an account of those days, months, and years, but also gave the ages [their twenty-year periods], and the prophecies which their gods announced to them."[14]

Ximénez also says that the Indians read the horoscopes of the new-born children in books such as the one he possessed,[15] which must have been a *cholquih* (*tzolkin* in Maya, *tonalamatl* in Náhuatl), with the ritual calendar of 260 days and the classification of those days as lucky or unlucky. Father Vicente Hernández Spina found such a calendar in the village of Santa Catarina Ixtlahuacán (Guatemala), and it was published in the magazine of the Sociedad Económica de Guatemala in 1870. Ximénez describes the book in this way:

> And this is seen in a book which they had as a book of prophecy, from the time of their paganism, in which they have all the months and the signs corresponding to each day, and one of which [books] I have in my possession.

The Canon Ordóñez y Aguiar copies a paragraph of the *Constituciones Diocesanas* of the Bishop of Chiapas, Núñez de la Vega, in which he relates the superstitions of the Tzeltal Indians and tells of "a very old historical booklet," written by them, which was in the hands of the prelate. This book, according to the Bishop, clearly shows, by generations, the names of the principal men

[13] Folio 29*v*.
[14] Folio 35*r*.
[15] *Las Historias del Origen de los Indios* (1857 ed.), 160.

and their ancestors. Ordóñez y Aguiar adds that the Indians entrusted him with this same original booklet, which he calls *Probanza de Votán,* and that he had decided to interpret and explain it.[16] This same Votán had written a book about the origin of the Indians and their emigration to those countries, if one can believe what Ordóñez y Aguiar says in a passage of the second volume of his work, which Brasseur de Bourbourg reproduced in the introduction to his edition of the *Popol Vuh.*[17] In that which pertains to the Quiché kingdom we have the priceless testimony of the author of the *Manuscrito de Chichicastenango,* who declares that in olden times there was in his village one of these books, doubtlessly written with the aid of paintings, which described historical events and foretold future happenings which might affect the life of the nation. This statement is corroborated by the contemporaneous testimony of Alonso de Zorita, Oidor of the Audiencia de los Confines, who says that during his visit to the province of Utatlán, between 1553 and 1557, he could, with the help of a Dominican friar [Bishop Las Casas], familiarize himself with the political system of the Quiché "from paintings they had of their ancient times, of more than 800 years and from accounts of very old people."[18]

It was very difficult for the natives of Guatemala to renounce the traditions of their forefathers, and for a long time after the Conquest they continued to perform their dances, during which they sang episodes of their ancient history and recited passages of their mythology. The Spaniards were not pleased with this, and as early as the year 1550, Licenciado Tomás López, Oidor of the Audiencia of Guatemala, less tolerant than his predecessor the illustrious Zorita, requested the King that he not permit the Indians to perform their "old dances, as they do, singing their ancient, idolatrous histories."[19]

[16] Ordóñez y Aguiar, *Historia de la Creación del Cielo y de la Tierra,* Preface.

[17] *Popol Vuh. Le Livre Sacré et les mythes de l'antiquité américaine, avec les livres heroïques et historiques des Quichés,* p. LXXXVIII.

[18] *Breve y Sumaria Relación de los Señores de la Nueva España,* 225-26.

[19] *Colección de documentos inéditos relativos al descubrimiento, conquista*

The American Indian's devotion to his ancient beliefs still persisted in Yucatán in the seventeenth century, according to the following paragraphs from Cogolludo's *Historia de Yucatán:*

They had very harmful legends of the creation of the world, and some (after they knew how) had them written down, kept them and read them in their gatherings, although they had been baptized Christians. Dr. Aguilar says in his *Informe* that he had one of these books of legends which he took from a choir-master of the chapel, by the name of Cuytún, of the town of Zucop, from which he [the choir-master] fled, and he could never reach him in order to learn the origin of their Genesis.[20]

This is also the origin of the *Books of Chilan Balam,* which were found in various places in Yucatán and which contain the chronological story of the ancient deeds of the Maya of the peninsula.

With a very liberal and human understanding, befitting real Christian missionaries, the Spanish priests and friars of Guatemala from the beginning of the Colonial Period undertook to teach the Indians to read and write Spanish. Some of the latter made rapid progress in writing and using the Latin alphabet, and wrote in their own language the chronicles and stories of the ancient times which they had preserved by handing them down by word of mouth, or by means of pictorial characters. The Spanish clergy not only did not oppose this work, but actually encouraged the Indians in it, and thanks to this enlightened policy, valuable documents have come down to us which shed light on the history of the races that inhabited the country many centuries before the Spaniards arrived.

With regard to this policy, the anonymous author of the *Isagoge Histórica Apologética de las Indias Occidentales,* written in Guatemala at the end of the eighteenth century, comments:

At the request of the first Spaniards and the first priests, the Indians wrote down various accounts in which they told of their origin,

*y colonización de las posesiones españolas en América y Oceanía* (Madrid, 1864–84), Vol. XXIV, p. 192.

[20] Page 192.

their kings, their coming to these lands, and other stories which they knew from tales told them by their forefathers, or from the characters and books through which they learned of their past.[21]

And he goes on to mention some of the original documents which the author of the *Recordación Florida* used in writing his history. The chronicler, Fuentes y Guzmán describes, in effect, different manuscripts which he claims to have had in his hands. Unfortunately, most of these documents have been lost. Among others that he had were three Quiché manuscripts. The author of one of them identifies himself in this way:

I, Don Francisco Gómez, first Ahzib Quiché, write here on this paper of the coming of our fathers and grandfathers from the other side of the sea whence the sun rises.[22]

The curious accounts of this author are supplemented by two other documents, the first written by "Don Juan de Torres, son of King Chignauicelut and Don Juan Macario, his son," and the second

which is a notebook of the *calpules*, or noble families of Santa Catarina Istaguacán, written on twenty-eight pages by one of their chiefs, Don Francisco García Calel Yzumpán, who says at the beginning of his narrative that being among the first who learned the meaning of our letters by order of the Reverend Bishop Don Francisco Marroquín, he writes this brief account of his elders, and that he begins this service on the ninth of December, 1561.[23]

Ximénez gave little importance to the documents that Fuentes y Guzmán cites, which, according to his judgment, offer "very little authority because they were written by individual Indians of other towns, many years after the Conquest, and without more information than that which was generally known among them." On the other hand, he says that the histories which he found and translated into Spanish

[21] Book I, Chap. VIII, p. 61 (1935 ed.).
[22] Fuentes y Guzmán, *Recordación Florida* (1933 ed.), Vol. II, Part II, Book 7, Chap. II.
[23] *Ibid.*, Vol. II, Part II, Book 1, Chaps. V–IX; Book 7, Chaps. II–LV.

are the originals of the court and those which their highest priests preserved according to their style of writing; and so, although most of it is wild fancy, they must be regarded as more authentic in all those things in which they show good judgment.[24]

Besides the *Manuscrito de Chichicastenango*, the following are the only original Quiché documents which are preserved:

1. the original manuscript of the *Historia Quiché* by Don Juan de Torres, dated October 24, 1580, which differs from the manuscript which Fuentes y Guzmán cites and which contains the account of the kings and lords, chiefs of the Great Houses, and of the *chinamitales* or *calpules* of the Quiché;
2. the Spanish translation of the *Títulos de los antiguos nuestros antepasados, los que ganaron las tierras de Otzoyá*, written apparently in 1524 and bearing the signature of Don Pedro de Alvarado;
3. the Spanish translation of the *Título de los Señores de Totonicapán*, dated 1554; and
4. the *Papel del Origen de los Señores* included in the *Descripción de Zapotitlán y Suchitepec, año de 1579*.[25]

Despite their brevity, these documents contain interesting accounts of the origin, political organization, and history of the Quiché people, which supplement the information given in the *Popol Vuh*.[26]

Although written in another language, the *Memorial Cakchiquel de Solola*, or *Tecpán-Atitlán*, must be mentioned here not only because of its great historical value, but also because, in the first part, it confirms much of the information given in the *Popol Vuh* concerning the origin and·emigrations of the tribes at the time when they were all united and before they had separated into

[24] *Historia de la Provincia de San Vicente de Chiapa y Guatemala*, I, 54.

[25] For an English translation of this last, see the Appendix at the end of this book.

[26] "*Historia Quiché de D. Juan de Torres*," MS, Gates Collection, preserved in the Institute for Advanced Study at Princeton. "*Títulos de los antiguos nuestros antepasados, los que ganaron estas tierras de Otzoyá antes de que viniera la fe de Jesucristo entre ellos en el año de mil y trescientos.*" In *Anales de la Sociedad de Geografía e Historia de Guatemala*, September, 1941. *Título de los Señores de Totonicapán* (Alencon, 1885).

the different groups into which the territory of Guatemala was divided at the beginning of the sixteenth century. After the Spanish Conquest, Francisco Hernández Arana, grandson of one of the kings of the country and a member of the Xahilá family, began writing the Cakchiquel book and Francisco Díaz of the same family continued it and brought the narrative down to the year 1604.

## II. *The Manuscript of Chichicastenango*

The manuscript which Father Francisco Ximénez found in his parish at Chichicastenango ranks highest among the documents composed by the American Indians after they had learned to write their own languages by means of the Latin letters which the Spanish missionaries had taught them. Its author was undoubtedly one of the first students who learned from the friars the marvelous art of phonetic writing. The Quiché chronicler knew that in olden times there was a book which contained the traditions and accounts of his people, and, knowing them perfectly, he had the happy inspiration of recording them.

Genêt and Chelbatz believe that it is a translation of a manuscript written in hieroglyphs, and declare that no other Maya-Quiché document can be compared with it.[27] Bancroft also believed that the *Popol Vuh* was the translation of a literal copy of a truly original book written by one or more Indians of that race in the Quiché language, using Latin letters, after the occupation of Guatemala by the Christians; and that this copy had been made to replace the original book after the latter's loss or destruction. He adds that of all the American people, the Quiché of Guatemala have left us the richest mythological heritage.[28]

Professor Max Müller, in an excellent summary of this work, classifies it as a literary composition in the true sense of the word,

[27] *Histoire de peuples maya-quichés*, 46.
[28] *The Native Races*, III, 42.

an exposition of the mythology and history of the civilized races of Central America. He believes that it is an authentic document which occupies a very prominent place among the works which the Indians composed in their own language, using the characters of the Latin alphabet. He adds that in it the author recounts, from memory, the incidents and fables which he heard as a child, and that to pretend to take from these memories a consecutive history is simply impossible.[29]

The author of the Manuscript says that he writes it because now the *Popol Vuh*, or the original "Book of the People," as Ximénez calls it, is no longer to be seen. We have no facts by which to identify this original book other than those which its unknown author gives. Nevertheless, from the knowledge that we have of the American Indians' system of writing before the Conquest, it seems doubtful that the ancient Quiché book could have been a document of set form and permanent literary composition. Rather one must suppose that it might have been a book of paintings with hieroglyphs which the priests interpreted to the people in order to keep alive in them the knowledge of the origin of their race and the mysteries of their religion.

Lewis Spence observes that, at the time of the Conquest, writing among the Indians was in a state of transition and that a version of the *Popol Vuh* written in a set literary form could not have been in existence for long, and that it is more likely that it was passed on by word of mouth, a way of preserving literature which was very common among the people of ancient America.[30] Before the invention of writing and printing, all the peoples of the world were accustomed to preserve their legends and traditions by oral transmission. It has been related how the Indians of Mexico had the youth of their race learn the famous orations of their great men and commit to memory the outstanding events of their history. Furthermore, in America, as in the Old World, there were troubadours who preserved the national spirit with the evocation of the glories and legends of the olden times.

[29] *Chips from a German Workshop*, I, 309–337.
[30] Spence, *The Popol Vuh. The Mythic and Heroic Sagas of the Kichés of Central America*, 31.

The Manuscript of Chichicastenango has no title. It begins directly with these words:

This is the beginning of the old traditions of this place called Quiché. Here we shall write and we shall begin the old tales, the beginning and the origin of all that was done in the town of the Quiché, by the tribes of the Quiché nation.

And two paragraphs farther on the same narrator says:

This we shall write now within the Law of God and Christianity; we shall bring it to light because now the Popol Vuh as it is called cannot be seen any more, in which was clearly seen the coming from the other side of the sea, and the narration of our obscurity, and our life was clearly seen. The original book written long ago existed; but its sight is hidden from the searcher and the thinker.

"The truth is," says Ximénez, "that such a book never appeared nor has been seen, and thus it is not known if this way of writing was by paintings, as those of Mexico, or by knotting strings, as the Peruvians: You may believe that it was by painting on woven white cloths."[31] This was the graphic system in use in Mexico and Guatemala, and Father Sahagún, writing in the sixteenth century, says that he was informed of the ancient things of New Spain directly by the Indians, and adds that "all the information that I obtained, they made known to me by means of their paintings."[32]

The influence of the Bible is evident in the description of the creation, although this does not succeed in taking away the indigenous flavor of the Quiché book. Commenting on the edition of the *Popol Vuh* by Brasseur de Bourbourg, Adolf Bandelier observed in 1881 that the first sentences appear to be transcriptions of the Book of Genesis and are not aboriginally American. He argues that in the epoch in which the *Popol Vuh* was written the Indians of Guatemala were already under the influence of the

[31] *Las Historias del Origen de los Indios* (1857 ed.), 161.
[32] Sahagún, *Historia general de las cosas de Nueva España* (1938 ed.), Vol. I, Book II, Preface, p. 80.

paintings, books, and chants which the Spanish missionaries used to instruct them in Christianity. The native author expressly declares, in the Preamble of this work, that he is writing under Christianity. The editor of the Spanish translation of the French text of Brasseur de Bourbourg has carefully noted the concordance of its first chapter with the Book of Genesis. Max Müller had previously (1878) referred to certain similarities between the *Popol Vuh* and the Old Testament, but although admitting that there was Biblical influence in this book, he believes that it must be recognized that its content was a true product of the intellectual soil of America. Bandelier arrives at the same conclusion in another place where he says, commenting again on the Quiché book:

> It appears to be, for the first chapter, an evident fabrication, or, at least, accommodation of the Indian mythology to Christian notions, a pious fraud, but the bulk is an equally evident collection of original traditions of the Indians of Guatemala, and as such the most valuable work for the aboriginal history and ethnology of Central America.[33]

The *Popol Vuh* was also the book of prophecies and the oracle of the kings and lords, according to a reference which the author of the Manuscript makes in another passage, where he states that the kings

> knew if there would be war and everything was clear before their eyes; they saw if there would be death and hunger, if there would be strife. They well knew that there was a place where it could be seen, that there was a book which they called *Popol Vuh*.[34]

And in the final paragraph, the Quiché chronicler adds with a melancholic accent that what he has said in his work is all that has been preserved of the ancient Quiché, "because no longer can be seen [the book of the *Popol Vuh*]_which the kings had in olden times, for it has disappeared."

How and when was the Quiché book lost? The author of the Manuscript says only that already, in his time, it was not to be seen, that it was hidden and had been lost. Probably it disappeared

[33] Peabody Museum *Eleventh Annual Report, 1880,* 391.
[34] *Popol Vuh*, Part IV, Chap. 11.

in the catastrophe which destroyed the Quiché kingdom in 1524; it is possible that it may have been consumed by the flames which destroyed Utatlán.

Professor Max Müller criticized the Abbé Brasseur de Bourbourg for having given the name, *Popol Vuh*, to the Manuscript of Chichicastenango, and because, in translating it into French, he gave it the title of *Le Livre Sacré*, instead of *El Libro Nacional* or *El Libro del Consejo*, as Ximénez proposed.[35] Other writers, following Müller's example, have repeated these same objections; but the fact remains that the name *Popol Vuh* has been generally accepted and continues to be used to designate this book of the Quiché. Furthermore, if the words of the preamble of the Manuscript, which have been quoted above, are carefully read, it will be seen that they clearly indicate the author's purpose in compiling the document—to supply the lack of the ancient book which had been lost; and in this sense, the book written in Christian times, or after the Conquest, may be considered a substitute for the *Libro Nacional*, as a revision and a new version of the accounts which had been preserved in the venerable volume which had already disappeared.

In the words which he uses to describe the ancient book, the unknown author of the Quiché Manuscript reveals that he knew its contents. Doubtless, with the aid of his prodigious memory and his brilliant talent as a writer, he could compose a transcription of the tales and ancient traditions of his race that is possibly clearer and even more complete than the original, because in composing it he used phonetic writing, which as a medium of expression has an infinite advantage over the hieroglyphs and pictography used by his forefathers.

These tales and traditions of the Indians were still common among them at the beginning of the eighteenth century, and Ximénez says that, being in the parish of Santo Tomás Chichicastenango at the time, he found that they were the doctrine which the natives first imbibed with their mother's milk, and that they knew it almost by memory. And he adds that later he discovered "that they had among them many of these books."

[35] *Chips from a German Workshop*, I, 325.

20

In the introduction to his *Historia de la Creación del Cielo y de la Tierra*, written in the last decade of the eighteenth century, Canon Ordóñez y Aguiar says that an Indian who gave him the manuscript of the *Probanza de Votán* also offered to give him the original of that same history, i. e., the book of the traditions of the Quiché Indians which Ximénez translated; but because of the death of the Indian, he could not obtain it.

As was said before, Ximénez believed that the traditions of the Quiché had been preserved in paintings, and that after the Spanish Conquest the Indians had converted them into the Spanish method of writing. This is also the opinion of a modern investigator, Rudolf Schuller, who argues that the greater part of the *Popol Vuh*, or the ancient traditions, must be considered only as an interpretation of one, or perhaps many pictorial writings of the Quiché, the originals of which were lost long ago.[36]

Abbé Brasseur de Bourbourg, who made such a profound study and commentary upon the *Manuscrito de Chichicastenango*, also believed that this document had been copied, in part, from the ancient books; and he observed that the compiler, a well-educated man of distinguished family, had written it in a Quiché of the greatest elegance. Here are the words of Brasseur de Bourbourg, translated into English:

The *Popol Vuh* appears to have been written, in part, from memory, following ancient originals, and in part, copied from the sacred books of the Quichés, to which the name of Popol Vuh, or Book of the Princes was given. Reading it carefully, it may be seen that a great number of passages have been transposed, no doubt unconsciously by its anonymous author. . . . This manuscript, the most valuable about the origins of Central America, is written in a Quiché of great elegance, and the author must have been one of the princes of the royal family, who composed it a few years after the arrival of the Spaniards, when all of their ancient books were disappearing.[37]

Concerning the time in which the Manuscript was composed,

[36] *"Der Verfasser des Popol Vuh," Anthropos,* Vol. XXVI, Nos. 5–6 (September-December, 1931), 930.

[37] *Histoire des Nations Civilisées du Mexique et de l'Amérique Centrale,* Vol. I, p. LXXX.

there are two important facts in the document itself which make it possible to determine its date approximately. The first is the visit that the Bishop of Guatemala made to the city of Utatlán, or Gumarcaah, which place, as one reads in the Manuscript itself, was blessed by Bishop Francisco Marroquín. Ximénez says that Bishop Marroquín gave Utatlán the name of Santa Cruz del Quiché "when in the year 1539 he was at that Court and, blessing the place he fixed and raised the standard of the Faith."[38]

The second important fact mentioned above is found in the final chapter of the Manuscript, which contains the succession of the kings and lords of the Quiché. In it, Tecún and Tepepul, the sons of the kings burned by Alvarado in 1524, are named as the thirteenth generation of kings, and Don Juan Rojas and Don Juan Cortés, the sons of Tecún and Tepepul, are named as the last successors to the dignity, and as of the fourteenth generation of kings. The latter Quiché lords were still living in the middle of the sixteenth century. The Oidor Zorita, previously mentioned, lived in Guatemala from 1553 to 1557, as a member of the Royal Audience, and he says that he traveled through the province several times as inspector and that he met

those, who were at one time Lords of Utatlán, [are] as poor and miserable as the poorest Indian of the village, and their wives made the *tortillas*[39] for their meal . . . and they carried water and wood for their houses. The principal one of them was called don Juan de Rojas, the second don Juan Cortés, and the third, Domingo, all were extremely poor; they left children all of whom were destitute and miserable.[40]

The signatures of Don Juan Cortés, *"Rey Caballero,"* and Don Juan Rojas, together with that of Don Pedro de Alvarado, "Spaniard, judge, captain, and conqueror," appear at the end of the *Títulos de la Casa Ixcuin-Nihaib, señora del territorio de Otzoyá.*

[38] *Historia de la Provincia de San Vicente de Chiapa y Guatemala,* I, 115.

[39] A kind of cake the size of a pancake made of baked corn meal, which constituted in ancient times, as well as today, the staple food of the Indians of both Mexico and Guatemala.

[40] *Breve y Sumaria Relación de los Señores de la Nueva España,* 225–26.

This document appears to have been written many years after the conquest of Utatlán.

The signatures of the Quiché kings also appear on the *Título de los Señores de Totonicapán*, executed September 28, 1554, together with the signature of Don Cristóbal Fernández Nihaib. The *Popol Vuh* mentions "Don Cristóval" as the king of Nihaib, "who reigned in the presence of the Spaniards," and names as his successor "Don Pedro de Robles, Ahau Galel." This reference indicates that the *Popol Vuh* was finished after September 28, 1554, under the reign of Don Cristóbal's successor.

Another Quiché document which belonged to the collection of Brasseur de Bourbourg and which is now in the Institute for Advanced Study at Princeton, New Jersey, is the *Título Real de Don Francisco Izquín, Ahpop-Galel*, dated November 22, 1558, in which it is definitely said that it is executed by "the Kings of the Quiché, Don Juan Cordes Reyes, Caballero" and "Don Martín Ahau Quiché," whose signatures are at the end of this document. The signature of Don Juan de Rojas does not appear on the document, which leads one to believe that he was already dead in 1558 and had been succeeded by Don Martín Ahau Quiché. As this change in the situation of the last Quiché kings is not recorded in the *Popol Vuh*, there is ground for believing that the composition of the Manuscript of Chichicastenango had been finished before November 22, 1558, and that, consequently, this famous Quiché book was written between the years 1554 and 1558.

# T
III. *The Author of the Popol Vuh*

The Manuscript of Chichicastenango is an anonymous document. Father Ximénez, who had the original manuscript in his hands, and transcribed and translated it into Spanish, left no indication whatever of its author. The terms which Ximénez employed in referring to this document lead one to think that he believed there had been various authors, or compilers, of the

Quiché book. In the foreword to his principal work, the Dominican chronicler says that he translated the histories of the Indians into the Spanish language from the Quiché tongue in which he found them written "from the time of the Conquest, when (as they say there) they changed their way of writing their histories into our way of writing." And two paragraphs farther on, he repeats the same idea when he says that he determined "to set down and transcribe here all their histories, according to the way they have them written."[41]

Speaking of the accounts composed by the Indians after the Conquest, the Dominican chronicler who wrote the *Isagoge Histórica Apologética* says:

The Preaching Father Francisco Ximénez translated from the Quiché language into Spanish a very old manuscript, without giving the name of the author, and without [giving] the year in which it was written, and it is only known by the manuscript itself that it was written in the village of Santa Cruz of the Quiché, shortly after the conquest of this Kingdom.[42]

The Guatemalan historian, J. Antonio Villacorta, has advanced the hypothesis during recent years that the author of the Manuscript of Chichicastenango was Diego Reynoso,[43] a Quiché Indian who, according to Ximénez, was brought from the village of Utatlán to Guatemala City by Bishop Marroquín, who taught him to read and write Spanish. Unfortunately there is no proof or historical account of any kind which supports the theory that Reynoso might have been the author of the *Popol Vuh*. With regard to the discrepancy between Ximénez and Father Francisco Vázquez, author of the Chronicle of the Franciscan Province of Guatemala, about the date on which the battle of Quetzaltenango took place, previous to the conquest of the Quiché by Alvarado, the Dominican chronicler says that this battle was fought in March, and that this date agrees

with what Diego Reynoso says in his written accounts of those times

[41] *Historia de la Provincia de San Vicente de Chiapa y Guatemala*, I, Preface.
[42] Book L, Chap. VIII, p. 61 (1935 ed.).

(he was an Indian whom Bishop Marroquín took from the village of Utatlán and taught to read and write), that the conquest of the Quiché by Don Pedro de Alvarado took place at the beginning of April about Holy Week of this year of twenty-four, by the following Quiché words: "*Chupam ic abril caztahibal pascua xulic Donadiu ahlabal varal pa queche ta xporox tinamit, ta xcach ahauarem, ta xtane patan rumal ronohel amac xpatanih chiquivach ca mam ca cahau pa queche.*" Which mean: "During Lent, Donadiu, captain of the war, came here in the Quiché [country] and then the village, or town, was burned, and the Kingdom was ended and the tribes stopped paying tribute, the tribute which they had given to our fathers and grandfathers."

And Ximénez adds that this report is given by an "eyewitness who saw all of this."[44]

These words of Ximénez lead one to think that there was a chronicle or account of the Spanish Conquest composed by Reynoso in his mother tongue. Nevertheless, the author of the *Isagoge Histórica* quoting the words of the Quiché annalist, on the arrival of Alvarado, says:

This was at the end of Lent and the beginning of Eastertide of the year 1524, according to the ancient account of Diego Reinoso, principal Indian of said village of Utatlán, who, at the time of the destruction of the city of Guatemala [1541] was learning to read and to write by order of Sr. D. Francisco Marroquín. In a very devout book, on the passion of Our Lord, Jesus Christ, he [Reinoso] makes some very curious marginal notes worthy of attention about their antiquities, which the authors do not include, and in one of them he says in his language: "*Chupan Quaresma xul Donadi capitan ahlabal varal pa Quiché*, etc." [45]

It is possible that this book of devotion, with marginal notes by Reynoso, had been preserved in the Convent of Santo Domingo of Guatemala, and that the two chroniclers of the Order of the

[43] Villacorta and Rodas, *Manuscrito de Chichicastenango. El Popol Buj*, 157–60; Villacorta, *Prehistoria e Historia Antigua de Guatemala*, 170.

[44] *Historia de la Provincia de San Vicente de Chiapa y Guatemala*, Vol. I, Book I, Chap. XL, p. 119. The Quiché text is transcribed directly from the original manuscript.

[45] Book II, Chap. IV, p. 191 (1935 ed.).

Preaching Friars, Father Ximénez and the unknown author of the *Isagoge*, may have seen it there. But this same fact reveals that the Manuscript of Chichicastenango and Reynoso's marginal notes were not in the same handwriting, for had they been, there is little doubt but that Ximénez, who had studied, copied, and translated the Quiché Manuscript, would have identified it as the work of Reynoso, and would have made this fact known, as he did with the marginal notes about the arrival of Alvarado in Quiché, as well as with all the sources of information which he used in composing his well-documented *Historia de la Provincia de San Vicente de Chiapa y Guatemala*.

Reynoso collaborated in the writing of the *Título de los Señores de Totonicapán*, another indigenous document. Of this manuscript, written in Quiché in 1554, only a Spanish translation, made in 1834 by Father Dionisio José Chonay, curate of Sacapulas, is known. In it is found the well-known fourth chapter, which begins with these words:

Hear what I am going to relate, what I am going to declare, I, Diego Reynoso Popol Vinak, son of Lahuh Noh.[46]

He goes on to describe the voyage which the Quiché princes, Qocaib, Qocavib, Qoacul, Acutec, and, shortly afterward, Nim Chocoh Cavek, made to the East to receive the royal investiture from the hands of Emperor Nacxit. The *Popol Vuh* takes up the same matter in one of its final chapters;[47] but there are such marked differences between the two accounts that it is impossible to believe that they were written by the same person. Furthermore, although in general the account of the legendary deeds of the Quiché is somewhat similar in both documents, in the *Título de los Señores de Totonicapán* there are many variations which, although they sometimes supplement the more extensive information given in the *Popol Vuh*, themselves show that these two documents are the work of two or more different authors.

[46] Among the Quiché, the title *Popol Vinac* denoted a member of the council or public assembly which considered matters of interest to the community. It was also an honorary title.

[47] Part III, Chap. 6.

Finally, it does not seem likely that a man like Reynoso, who gives his name, his titles, and his origin in one of the chapters of the Totonicapán document, and identifies himself as the author of some marginal notes in a book of the Passion of Jesus Christ, should have preferred to remain unknown as the author of such an outstanding and important work as the Manuscript of Chichicastenango.

The well-known philologist Rudolf Schuller believes that there is basis for attributing the authorship of the *Popol Vuh* to Diego Reynoso; but he interprets the citations of Ximénez and of the *Título de los Señores de Totonicapán* differently, and, in my judgment, inaccurately. He believes that because this document contains expressions such as: "Hear what I am going to say," "I am going to tell," and the like, which, he says, are also to be found in the *Popol Vuh*, it is evident that Reynoso wrote both documents. This coincidence is of little importance, and, besides, similar expressions appear also in other documents of the American Indians.[48] And so far as the reference which Ximénez makes to the writings of Reynoso is concerned, "of reports of those times," and that Schuller repeats, it is clarified by the passage of the *Isagoge* which identifies such writings as notes placed in the margins of a book of devotion.

In his article on the author of the *Popol Vuh*, Schuller calls attention to the error into which Señor Villacorta falls, in confusing the Quiché Indian whom Bishop Marroquín taught to read and write in 1541 with the missionary, Fray Diego de Reynoso, author of the *Arte y Vocabulario en lengua Mame dirigido a nuestro Reverendísimo Padre Maestro F. Marcos Salmeron, Calificador del Supremo Consejo de la Inquisicion, General de todo el .Orden de Nuestra Señora de la Merced, Señor de la Varonía de Algar.* The dedication of this work is dated October 20, 1643, and it was printed in Mexico in 1644 by Francisco Robledo.

Beristain says of Reynoso only that he was "a native of North America, a religious missionary of the military order of Our Lady

[48] Schuller, "*Der Verfasser des Popol Vuh*," *Anthropos*, Vol. XXVI, Nos. 5–6 (September–December, 1931), 932.

of Mercy," and that he wrote the *Arte en lengua Mame*.[49] There is no account of his ever having visited Guatemala, and it is likely that he may have learned the Mame language in the district of Soconusco and in the province of Chiapas, Mexico, where to this day that language is still spoken, as well as in the departments of Huehuetenango and San Marcos in Guatemala.

Señor Villacorta has also declared that on March 17, 1538, in Guatemala "a very intelligent Indian of the Quiché race who a few years before, had been baptized as Diego Reynoso [became a friar], upon assuming the habit of the Order of Mercy, and took the name of Fray Diego de la Anunciación."[50] However, he has furnished no proof that Reynoso and the Mercedarian friar were the same man. The chronicler Remesal, whom he quotes in this connection, says only, in referring to the beginnings of the Order of Mercy in Guatemala, that "on the seventeenth of March in this year of 1538, the house of Our Lady of Mercy was already formed, and with the title of Comendador Father Fray Juan Zambrano gave the habit to Fray Diego de la Anunciación."[51] Remesal does not mention Reynoso, nor does he identify the new Brother of Mercy, nor, finally, does he state the fact, which in those times would have been very noteworthy, that this new brother was an Indian of the conquered race. Ximénez, as has been said before, makes it clear that Reynoso was not taken to the city of Guatemala until 1539, that is to say, the year in which Bishop Marroquín blessed Utatlán, baptized it, and gave it the name of Santa Cruz, and, according to the *Isagoge*, our Quiché Indian was learning to read and write in 1541 by order of the same illustrious prelate.

For many years ecclesiastical pursuits were denied to the Indians of America. Writing almost two hundred years after the Conquest, Ximénez observed that "if their ministers and priests were of their own nation, the results would have been more fruit-

---

[49] Beristain de Souza, *Biblioteca Hispano Americana*, III, 14.

[50] Villacorta and Rodas, *Manuscrito de Chichicastenango. El Popol Buj*, 157.

[51] Remesal, *Historia de la Provincia de San Vicente de Chiapa y Guatemala* (1932 ed.), Vol. I, Book III, Chap. XIX, p. 218.

[52] Ximénez, *Historia de la Provincia de San Vicente de Chiapa y Guatemala*, I, 59.

ful" with the Indians,[52] because they had great mistrust of the Spaniards; but, he added, because of their vices, they were "almost unfitted to be ministers of the Church." The same was true with respect to their entrance into the religious orders.[53] It is fitting to observe also that in the *Título de los Señores de Totonicapán*, dated 1554, the Quiché Indian, who speaks in the fourth chapter, continues to call himself Diego Reynoso and that he not only gives no indication whatsoever of having become a Christian missionary, but he continues, on the contrary, to use the title of Popol Vinak, dating from the time of his paganism.

It is well to clarify here these points about the person of Diego Reynoso, because they are concerned with one of the few known Indian authors who have left written accounts subsequent to, or contemporary with, the Conquest. Although educated by the Spanish priests, Reynoso never renounced his name and status as that of a noble Quiché Indian, and the fact that he never joined any of the Spanish religious orders gives greater validity to his accounts of the ancient times of his nation.

The problem relative to the author of the *Popol Vuh* must nevertheless remain unsolved; and so long as no new evidence is discovered which will throw light upon the matter, the famous manuscript must be considered as an anonymous account, written by one or more descendants of the Quiché race according to the traditions of their forefathers.

In his interesting study of the *Popol Vuh*, Lewis Spence expresses the opinion that this book is "a monument of very considerable antiquity";[54] but adds that it would be only mere con-

---

[53] Writing about the year 1612, Father Torquemada devotes a chapter of his *Monarquia Indiana* to explaining why the Indians were not received into the religious orders. He says that "in that period of Christianity the Indians did not have the ability to give orders nor to govern, but only to be commanded and governed . . . ; they are not good as teachers, but as pupils, nor for prelates, but for subjects, and for this, they are the best in the world. And the most important reason is that they are subject to drunkenness and addicted to wine, and for this reason they must not be members of the religious orders."—Book 17, Chap. XIII, p. 240.

[54] *The Popol Vuh. The Mythic and Heroic Sagas of the Kichés of Central America*, 31.

jecture to try to discover the approximate date of its original composition. He believes that the ancient Quiché book was not written in the native ideographic-phonetic hieroglyphic system, and
that more likely it was preserved by oral transmission, being thus
passed down from generation to generation, as was the custom
among other American peoples. This opinion, coupled with that
of the other authorities previously cited, confirms the belief that
the unknown author of the Manuscript of Chichicastenango was
more likely a compiler, endowed with undeniable talents of co-
ordination and literary expression, who gathered the stories of his
people, taking them from oral tradition and old, written or painted
accounts, hieroglyphic manuscripts, which told of the glorious
episodes in the lives of his ancestors. Possibly the compiler considered that he did not have the right to call himself the author of
a work which was only a transcription and compilation of other
people's accounts, and for this reason he did not let his name be
known. A similar condition is found in the *Books of Chilan Balam*,
written in Maya, but with Latin characters, in various villages of
Yucatán after the Conquest. The names of their respective authors
are not generally found in these books, and Brinton observes that
this is due to the fact that they are probably copies of older manuscripts, with merely the occasional addition of current items of
note by the copyist.[55]

IV. *The Writings of Father Ximénez*

From the first years of the colonization, the Spanish
missionaries were aware of the need to learn the languages of the
Indians in order to communicate with them directly and to instruct them in Christian doctrine. The first Bishop of Guatemala,
Señor Marroquín, recommended that the friars and secular clergy
study the native dialects and compose their preachings and ser-
mons in the mother tongues of the natives. The same prelate com-

[55] *The Maya Chronicles*, 68 ff.; *ibid., Essays of an Americanist*, 259.

posed some of the first works of this kind, and thus began the long series of grammars and vocabularies which were written during the Colonial Period. A distinguished Dominican friar, Father Domingo de Vico, who in 1555 sacrificed his life in the pacific conquest of the provinces to the north of Verapaz, wrote several works for teaching the languages of the country, many short works of a religious nature, and a voluminous treatise on the Christian doctrine entitled *Teología de Indios*. According to the historian Remesal, Father Vico also composed a book which contained "all the histories, fables, councils, fiction, and errors in which they [the Indians] lived, refuting them in order to dissuade the natives from them." An admirer of the works of Father Vico said, since those times, that what he wrote in the Indian languages might be compared, without exaggeration, to what Saint Thomas wrote in Latin.[56]

The *Teología de Indios*, written in several of the vernacular languages, and some of the linguistic works of Father Vico are still preserved. The bibliography of this type of writing is extensive, especially in regard to the Cakchiquel, Quiché, and Poconchi languages. Some of these works have been published; many have been lost; and others, like those of Anleo, Basseta, and Ximénez, about the Quiché language, may be consulted in the original manuscripts, and in photographic copies in the libraries and archives of America and Europe.

The name of Father Francisco Ximénez, however, stands out among the other writers of the Colonial Period for his notable work in the fields of philology, natural, religious, and political history. Ximénez was born in Ecija, province of Andalusia, Spain, in 1666, and came to Guatemala "in a boatload of clerics," as he himself says, in 1688. At the end of his novitiate he was ordained priest in Chiapas, and in Guatemala he took the habit of the Dominican Order. His superiors in 1694 sent him to work in communities predominantly Indian, which gave him the opportunity to learn the local dialects perfectly. This also provided the stimu-

[56] Remesal, *Historia de la Provincia de San Vicente de Chiapa y Guatemala* (1932 ed.), II, 380; Ximénez, *Historia de la Provincia de San Vicente de Chiapa y Guatemala*, I, 57.

lus which finally led to his making a deep study of the structure of those native languages and to organizing them into a didactic system for the use of beginners in such interesting material.

From 1701 to 1703 he was priest of Santo Tomás Chuilá, or Chichicastenango, and during this period he discovered the manuscript presented here which contains the history of the Quiché Indians. The next year found him in Rabinal, another community of Quiché Indians, where he remained for ten years. In 1715 he was in charge of the parish of Xenacoj, in the Valley of Sacatepéquez. There, in that year, he began to write his most extensive work, the *Historia de la Provincia de San Vicente de Chiapa y Guatemala*. From 1718 to 1720 he was parish priest of the Candelaria Church in Guatemala City. The year 1721 found him again in Quiché territory in charge of the parish of Sacapulas where he remained, in all probability, until 1725. In the chapter of the Dominican Order held in the latter year, he was named Superior of the Order's house at Sacapulas. In this quiet and peaceful place he must have written the rest of the *Historia de la Provincia*, and there, on August 30, 1722, he says he began his last work, the *Historia Natural del Reino de Guatemala*, only the first volume of which has come down to us. In Sacapulas, in 1721, he finished Book V of the *Historia de la Provincia*, and he probably completed this work in 1722. In 1729 he returned to the capital of the Colony and again took charge of the parish of Candelaria. In November of the same year at the request of the congregation of Santo Domingo, he was named *Presentado*, because of his preaching. He must have died at the end of that year or at the beginning of the following one, for, according to the record of the provincial chapter of the Order held in Guatemala on January 13, 1731, the Letters of Patent of his appointment which arrived in 1730 could not be executed, because he was already dead.[57]

A product of the active and industrious life of Father Ximénez is the series of works of inestimable value in the different branches of learning to which that illustrious friar had devoted his time and exceptional faculties. Fortunately for us, most of those works have

[57] Rodríguez Cabal, *Apuntes para la vida del M. R. Padre presentado y predicador general Fr. Francisco Ximénez*, 38.

been preserved, although some of them have weathered many perils and vicissitudes.

The long and well-spent days of Ximénez' life among the Indians of the interior of Guatemala proved to him how necessary it was for the clergy to have a thorough knowledge of the languages of those places. The Spanish government had ordered that the natives be taught in the Spanish language, but this would have required the establishment of hundreds of village and rural schools which were never founded in the Colonial Period. Therefore, the Indians had to be addressed in their own language and even in the dialect of each regional district. To further the priests' and friars' communications with the Indians for all their material and spiritual needs, Ximénez wrote an excellent grammar of the Quiché language and several religious treatises in the three principal dialects of Guatemala. He showed preference for the Quiché language, which he spoke for more than twenty years and for which he had a very high regard, as is evident in Chapter XXV of Book I of his *Historia de la Provincia*. Far from being a barbaric language, Quiché, says Ximénez, is so orderly, harmonious, and exact, and so consistent in character with the nature and properties of things, that he became convinced that "this language is the principal one of the world." Our linguistically-minded historian, casting aside all modesty, declares that through diligence and study he came to understand the Quiché language better than anyone else and that not wishing to hide the talent, which God gave to him, he wrote "three volumes in folio, entitled *Tesoro de las Lenguas Cacchiquel, Quiché, y Tzutuhil*, which are very similar."[58]

The first volume of this work carries the title *Primera Parte de el Tesoro de las Lenguas Cacchiquel, Quiché, y Tzutuhil*, and forms a volume of 204 double folios. In the bibliographical notes which precede his translation of the *Popol Vuh*, Brasseur de Bourbourg says that the first volume of the *Tesoro* written by Ximénez passed through many other hands until it came to Colonel Juan Galindo (an Irish soldier of fortune, who served in Guatemala under the administration of Don Mariano Gálvez, and who became interested in the antiquities of the country). The book

[58] *Historia de la Provincia de San Vicente de Chiapa y Guatemala*, I, 65.

33

finally reached Paris. Brasseur de Bourbourg included it in his collection of American documents, and after his death, this volume passed to the Bancroft Library of the University of California.

The second volume, entitled *Arte de las tres lenguas Cacchiquel, Quiché y Tzutuhil, escrito por el R. P. Francisco Ximénez, Cura Doctrinero por el Real Patronato del Pueblo de Santo Tomás Chuilá*, forms a manuscript of 92 double folios which make 184 pages. This second volume also fell into the hands of Abbé Brasseur de Bourbourg, who says in his *Bibliothéque Mexico-Guatémalienne* that he got it from one Ignacio Coloche, a noble Indian of the town of Rabinal. Edward E. Ayer acquired the manuscript in Europe and gave it with the rest of his valuable collection to the Newberry Library in Chicago.

The whereabouts of the third volume of the *Tesoro* is unknown. Ximénez says, in his *Historia*, that the formation of the words in the languages of Guatemala is so simple that one has only to combine the vowels and consonants into the resulting monosyllables, and then arrange them according to the alphabet in order to list all the original nouns and verbs; and that this is clearly seen in the tables which he put in the third part of the *Tesoro*.

In the *Tesoro de las Lenguas*, Ximénez made a profound study of the structure of the Quiché language, of which he gives an exposition according to the method followed in Latin grammars, accompanied by a vocabulary which contains the roots of the words of the three languages. Brasseur de Bourbourg made good use of this valuable material in writing his *Grammaire de la Langue Quichée* (Paris, 1862), which contains the chapters written by Ximénez and some explanations in French that the Abbé included to aid the readers who were not versed in the Spanish language to understand the text better.

Bound in the same volume with the *Arte de las tres lenguas* is a *Confesionario* and a *Catecismo de Indios*, also in the three languages, works of short length; and finally, in a volume consisting of 112 pages, written in two parallel columns with remarkable neatness and care, is the copy of the Manuscript of Chichicastenango written by Ximénez following the original text, accompanied by his first translation of it into Spanish. This valuable document has the following title: *Empiezan las historias del origen de los Indios de esta provincia de Guatemala, traduzido de la lengua quiché en la castellana para más comodidad de los Ministros del Sto. Evangelio, por el R.P.F. Franzisco Ximénez, Cura doctrinero por el Real Patronato del Pueblo de Sto. Thomás Chuilá*. In the opinion of Brasseur de Bourbourg, this manuscript may be considered the original of the *Popol Vuh*.[59]

This, in effect, is the only old copy, known to have survived, of the Quiché manuscript composed by an unknown author about the middle of the sixteenth century. This translation is the first one which Ximénez made, and it was also the first one to be published, when it was printed in Vienna, in 1857, under the auspices of the Imperial Academy of Sciences.

This document is followed by the *Escolios a las Historias de el Origen de los Indios, escoliadas por el R.P.F. Franzisco Ximénez, Cura Doctrinero por el Real Patronato del Pueblo de Sto. Thomás Chichicastenango, del Sagrado Orden de Predicadores, etc*. These scholia consist only of a foreword and a chapter, and it seems that the author did not write more in this place. The material which they contain was used, in part, in the first book of his *Historia de la Provincia*, where the author continues his commentaries and writes in detail of the origin of the Quiché kingdom and the customs and ancient beliefs of its inhabitants. .

Obeying a command of the Superior of the Dominican Order, and following his own inclinations, Ximénez composed the *Historia de la Provincia de San Vicente de Chiapa y Guatemala*, in four volumes, in folio, which includes an account of the conquest and the founding of Guatemala, the conversion of the Indians to the Roman Catholic faith, the work of his Dominican Order and the important events of the colony up to the year 1720. Although, according to the first chapter of the *Historia*, the purpose of this work was to describe the suffering which members of the Order had endured in the province of Guatemala and the great services its ministers of the Gospel had rendered in the conversion of the natives, Ximénez, who had lived among the Indians and felt a

[59] *Bibliothèque Mexico-Guatémalienne, 155.*

deep affection for them and compassion for their sufferings under the Colonial regime, believed that it was useful and fitting to begin his chronicle by making known the beliefs of the Quiché, their social and political organization, and the state in which they were found at the time of the Conquest. With this object, he begins his work with the histories of the origin of the Indians, that is to say, the revised translation of the Manuscript of Chichicastenango, and he continues with an account of the deeds of the Quiché kings down to Don Juan de Rojas, the last of the line, who lived miserably under Spanish domination in the middle of the sixteenth century. The first book ends with seven chapters on the religion, customs, and governmental systems of the Indians. The author says that these chapters are a transcription of those which Father Jerónimo Román of the Augustinian Order gives in his work entitled *Repúblicas de Indias*. Román, in his turn, had copied them almost literally from the *Apologética Historia* of Father Las Casas.

In the second book, Ximénez tells of the conquest of Guatemala by the Spaniards and begins the main part of his work, that is, the participation of the clergy in the pacification of the land and in the founding of the colony. Naturally he stresses the work done by his own Dominican Order and contradicts some observations made by the chronicler Vázquez, who was an apologist for the Franciscans. The third book has been lost. The four remaining books treat religious subjects and the development of Spanish administration in the Central American colonies.

The *Historia* by Father Ximénez consisted of three volumes which were jealously guarded in the Convent of Santo Domingo in Guatemala, and which for more than one hundred years remained unknown. The anonymous author of the *Isagoge Histórica*, written in the eighteenth century, mentions Ximénez as the discoverer and translator of the Manuscript of Chichicastenango, but the *Isagoge* itself was not published until 1892. The original manuscript of the *Historia* of Ximénez, which was lost for many years, is still preserved, although incomplete, in Guatemala. The first volume appeared in the library of Don José Cecilio del Valle, one of the fathers of the independence of Central America, and this first volume is today in the possession of his descendants in Guatemala City. This volume, as has been said, contains the first two books of the Chronicle of Ximénez and begins with the revised translation of the *Historias del origen de los indios*. The third volume, containing Books VI and VII of the *Historia*, is preserved at the Government Archives of Guatemala.

At the end of the eighteenth century, Don Ramón de Ordóñez y Aguiar, canon of Chiapas, and author of the *Historia de la Creación del Cielo y de la Tierra*, which remained unpublished until 1907, was living in Guatemala. In the foreword to this work, Ordóñez y Aguiar says that he had found a valuable book written by Father Francisco Ximénez, who, as a result of his teachings, had discovered it among the Indians of the Quiché nation, and translated it literally, including its contents "in the first of the four volumes which, under the title of *Historia de la Provincia de San Vicente de Chiapa y Guatemala* he composed and in manuscript form are preserved in the library of his convent of Preaching Fathers of this capital."[60] The text of the quotations from Ordóñez y Aguiar and the pages from which he says he has taken some sections which he included in his work show, however, that he did not consult the original of the *Historia*, but the copy which was kept in the Convent of Santo Domingo until 1830, when it was placed in the library of the University of Guatemala.

In his *Historia de la Creación*, Ordóñez y Aguiar reproduced the second version of the *Historias del Quiché*, taking it, as he himself says, from the first volume of the *Historia de la Provincia de San Vicente de Chiapa y Guatemala*. This transcription is sometimes literal, sometimes hardly more than an extract, and sometimes it seems to have been noticeably corrected and is different from the original. In the episode of Vucub-Caquix, Ordóñez y Aguiar departs from the simple language of Ximénez and writes a paraphrase in the style of Cervantes, which reveals his gifts of imagination and literary composition, but which is very far from the simplicity and ingenuity of the original Quiché, with which the Canon of Chiapas evidently was not familiar.[61]

[60] *Historia de la Creación del Cielo y de la Tierra*, in *Bibliografía Mexicana del Siglo XVIII*, Sec. 1, Part 4, p. 7.
[61] Through not knowing it, and because of having blindly followed the

The Italian Félix Cabrera, a contemporary of Ordóñez y
Aguiar, also lived in Guatemala at the end of the eighteenth century, and Ordóñez y Aguiar accused him of having appropriated
his work about Votán, the hero of the Tzeltal. Cabrera is author
of the *Teatro Crítico Americano*, an investigation into the history of the Americans, written in 1794, which was published in
English in 1822 in London, together with a translation of the
*Descripción de las Ruinas de Palenque*, by Captain Antonio del
Río. In the first of these works, Cabrera included the following
bibliographical reference:

Many valuable documents may be found in the archives of the
different bishoprics and in the libraries of convents; indeed in the
Dominican convent of this city [Guatemala] there are some learned
manuscripts in six folio volumes, that were written by Father Francisco Ximénez, relative to the conquest of this province, the progress
of religion, and the apostolic fathers who disseminated Christianity.
In the first volume he has given a history of the creation of the world
as believed by the Indians of Chiapas; to ascertain this from the natives cost him a great deal of labour, for so he expresses himself. Such
a document will add much to the fame of Don Ramón Ordóñez who,
I am told, has introduced it in his work *Del Cielo y de la Tierra*.[62]

---

text of the copy of the *Historia* by Ximénez which he had in his hands, Ordóñez
makes various errors, the most serious of which is in Chapter VI of his work,
where he says that "the mother of Hunahpú and Xbalanqué is called Hunbatz and
is at the same time the wife of Hunhunahpú, mother of herself and daughter and
mother of Hucub-Hunahpú, who never was married and remained single." From
this confusion, Ordóñez draws the most extreme conclusions, going so far as to
identify Hucub-Hunahpú with the Holy Ghost. The confusion into which
Ordóñez falls here results from his omission of a line of the original in the copy
which he consulted, an error which persists in the edition published by the
Sociedad de Geografía e Historia de Guatemala in 1929. Brasseur de Bourbourg
rightly says in the foreword to his *Histoire des Nations Civilisées du Mexique
et de l'Amérique Centrale* that Ordóñez drew the most absurd conclusions from
the Ximénez translation.

[62] *Teatro Crítico Americano*, in Del Río's *Description of the Ruins of an
Ancient City*, 110. The *Teatro Crítico Americana* contains some information concerning the beliefs of the Tzeltal Indians, about Votán, as well as extensive commentaries on the origin of the inhabitants of America, who the author believed
had come from the vicinity of the Orient, Palestine, Chaldea, Carthage, etc.
Ordóñez declares that these reports were in the *Probanza de Votán*, a document

Brasseur de Bourbourg says that around the middle of the nineteenth century the curator of the National Museum of Mexico, Don Rafael Isidoro Gondra, gave him a draft of the first volume of the work of Ordóñez y Aguiar, which contains the larger part of the translation made by Father Ximénez of the Manuscript of Chichicastenango, published in 1851.[63] Brasseur de Bourbourg claims the honor of having been the first to make known to the scientific world the existence of the work of Ximénez, in the first of his four *Cartas para servir de introducción a la Historia primitiva de las Naciones Civilizadas de la América Septentrional.* However, as has been seen, Cabrera was the author of the oldest published references about Father Ximénez, who Brasseur de Bourbourg said was the first to translate the Indian *Teogonía,* accompanying it with comments, etymological notes, and documents relating to the ancient history of the Quiché, Tzeltal, and so on, and who, with the help of this rich material, later wrote the *Historia de la Provincia de San Vicente de Chiapa y Guatemala,* his *opus magnum* "which has remained in manuscript and is completely unknown."[64]

The Viennese doctor, Carl Scherzer, visited Central America in 1853 and 1854. He was in Guatemala for six months and had occasion to visit the library of the University, where he found the volumes of the works of Ximénez kept there after the expulsion of the friars and the closing of the convents in 1829. In the *Memoria* which he sent to the Imperial Academy of Sciences at

which the Indians gave him and which he entrusted in an unfortunate moment to Cabrera when he had asked the Italian's opinion about the work which the latter had written on those matters. Cabrera denied the charge of plagiarism and instituted criminal action against Ordóñez for injuries and calumny. The dispute between the two writers was finally taken to the Royal Audience of Guatemala, before which Cabrera appeared in 1794 and asked that their works be compared in order to prove that he had not stolen from Ordóñez' work. Cabrera's petition may be seen in the *Anales de la Sociedad de Geografía e Historia de Guatemala,* March, 1931.

[63] *Histoire des Nations Civilisées du Mexique et de l'Amérique Centrale,* Vol. I, p. IX, n. I.

[64] Brasseur de Bourbourg, *Cartas para servir de introducción a la historia primitiva de las naciones civilizadas de la América septentrional,* 9.

Vienna in 1856,[65] Scherzer claims the honor of having been the first to have called the attention of the educated world to the writings of Ximénez and to have been, in part, responsible for their publication. This honor, as mentioned above, was disputed by Brasseur de Bourbourg. Perhaps for this reason, when the *Historia del origen de los indios* was published in Vienna the following year, Scherzer inserted in his introduction to the work the notice about Ximénez and his writings which the French Abbé gives in his letter from Mexico addressed to the Duke of Valmy in 1850.

Scherzer found only the third volume of the *Historia de la Provincia de San Vicente de Chiapa y Guatemala* in the University library in 1854, and although he searched elsewhere for the remaining three volumes of that work, all his efforts were in vain. On the other hand, he found in the library a vocabulary of the Quiché and Cakchiquel languages and the volume which contains the *Arte de las tres lenguas,* a *Confesionario,* a *Catecismo de Indios,* and the *Historias del origen de los indios de esta provincia de Guatemala, traducidas de la lengua Quiché a la Castellana.* This last treatise is the one which was first published by Scherzer in 1857. The text of the Vienna edition agrees, in general, with the Ximénez manuscript; but it contains many errors, due in part to the foreign printer and also in part to the inaccuracy of the copyist who made the transcription which Scherzer used, and who evidently was not familiar with the ancient writing. Only the first chapter of the *Escolios,* which formed the appendix of the book, appears in the manuscript of the *Historias.* Scherzer says that he completed them by means of a copy, "taken from the original," which was given to him by Don Juan Gavarrete. The original in this case is the *Historia de la Provincia,* the first book of which contains the chapters of the *Escolios* published as a supplement.

The same Señor Gavarrete who had collaborated in the preparation of the Vienna edition had the opportunity years later to make known the opinion he had formed of it, and said that "it is very incorrect because of the little ability of those who copied it and the printers in the Spanish language." Gavarrete added this

---

[65] *Mitteilungen über die Handschriftlichen Werke des Padre Francisco Ximénez in der Universitäts-Bibliothek zu Guatemala.*

comment, which since has been repeated by other historians: "We shall note, in passing, that the publication of this book has changed the whole course of the historical studies which are now being made about Central America."[66]

Scherzer's reports about the culture and traditions of the Quiché Indians gave rise to many discussions in European journals, which at that period were first concerning themselves with these matters. The German weekly *Das Ausland* in its edition of July 6, 1855, published an interesting article on "the pre-Columbian history of Guatemala," in which it gave an analysis of the content of the *Historias del origen de los Indios*, which Scherzer had found and proposed to publish. The Americanist editor, Nicolaus Trübner, reproduced, in part, the German writer's analysis, and discussed the question of priority in bibliographical data relative to Father Ximénez in an extensive article entitled "Central American Archaeology" published in the *London Athenaeum* of May 31, 1856.

Charles Etienne Brasseur de Bourbourg, the well-known French Americanist, arrived in Guatemala in 1855. Following the footsteps of Scherzer, he traveled through the Central American countries, and, like Scherzer, he also became interested in the ancient history of the country. Previously in Mexico he had made important historical and linguistic studies and had copied many old manuscripts. In Guatemala he found a fertile field for his investigations. Dr. Mariano Padilla and Don Juan Gavarrete, who had assisted Scherzer, extended their generosity to Abbé Brasseur de Bourbourg to the extent of giving him many documents from the collection of the former as well as from the public archives of which the latter was in charge. Others were given to him by Don Francisco García Peláez, the archbishop of Guatemala, who was likewise devoted to this kind of study. The Archbishop also entrusted him with the administration of the parish of Rabinal, where the French traveler learned the Quiché language, and, as he confesses, spent the most agreeable year of his stay in Central Ameri-

[66] *"Catalogo razonado de los objetos con que se inauguró el departamento etnográfico del Museo Nacional,"* published in *La Sociedad Economica de Guatemala,* May, 1866.

41

ca. In this important center of indigenous population, Brasseur de Bourbourg translated into French the Manuscript of Chichicastenango, which he had so easily obtained together with the Spanish translation of Ximénez. Speaking of his stay in Rabinal, Brasseur de Bourbourg says:

> This village contains around 7,000 Indians who speak the Quiché language, and with them I prepared myself not only to speak and write it, but even to translate the most difficult documents, among them the manuscript which Father Ximénez found at Santo Tomás Chichicastenango, and which is so important for [the study of] American origins and in particular for the history of Guatemala.[67]

Abbé Brasseur de Bourbourg also had charge, although for a short time only, of the parish of San Juan Sacatepéquez, where he perfected himself in the Cakchiquel language, in order to be able to translate the *Memorial Cakchiquel de Sololá*, which he called the *Memorial de Tecpán-Atitlán*, a valuable Indian document which had belonged to the convent of the Franciscans and which "a young and zealous Guatemalan archaeologist, Don Juan Gavarrete, one of the notaries of the ecclesiastical court" gave to him. On a second voyage to Guatemala, Brasseur de Bourbourg traveled through other parts of the country and added new and important acquisitions to his collection of historical documents, the richest and most valuable which had been assembled in the country by a single individual up to that time. These documents the French Abbé used in writing on the ancient history of Guatemala and Mexico, and on the Indian languages.

The best known of Brasseur de Bourbourg's works is that published in Paris in 1861 under the title of *Popol Vuh, Le Livre Sacré et les mythes de l'antiquité américaine*. This volume, which immediately attracted great attention in both Europe and America, contains the Quiché text of the Manuscript of Chichicastenango and the translation into French of this document, accompanied by philological notes and an extensive commentary. In the

[67] *Histoire des Nations Civilisées du Mexique et de l'Amérique Centrale*, Vol. I, pp. xxv–xxvi.

foreword, the author says that in 1855 he saw in the library of the University of Guatemala two copies of the *Historia de la Provincia de Predicadores de San Vicente de Chiapa y Guatemala* and that this work, which had remained in manuscript,

consisted of four volumes in folio and of it there were two copies, which were transferred from the archives of this monastery to the library of the University at the time that the religious houses were suppressed under Morazán, in 1830. Both copies were incomplete when we saw them in 1855, and only three volumes existed which did not even agree among themselves . . . the first volume which we had occasion to consult began with the text and the translation of the Quiché manuscript, which is the subject of this book. From there, we copied it for the first time, adding the original.

Scherzer had not been able to see the first volume of Ximénez' *Historia* in 1854, and for this reason he did not know the version of the *Popol Vuh* which appears at the beginning of that work. The text published by him was copied, as has already been explained, from the manuscript of the *Historias del origen de los indios,* which is bound together in the same volume with the *Arte de las tres lenguas.* Scherzer examined this volume in the University library, and in the foreword to the Vienna edition gives a thorough description of the documents which it contains. The same manuscript appeared a little later in the possession of the Abbé Brasseur de Bourbourg, who says in the foreword to *Le Livre Sacré* that he obtained it in Rabinal, and in *Bibliothèque Mexico-Guatémalienne* he says that in former times it belonged to Ignacio Coloche, a noble Indian of Rabinal, from whom he got it.[68] It is a little difficult to understand how, between 1854 and 1855, this manuscript could pass from the shelves of the Univer-

[68] Page 155. According to what Brasseur de Bourbourg says in this work, Ignacio Coloche was chief of one of the principal native families of Rabinal and secretary of the native municipality. He appears to have been a collector of ancient documents, and Brasseur de Bourbourg says that, in addition to the manuscript of Ximénez, he received from him various other documents, among them the *Coplas e himnos del P. Luis Cancer, an Arte de la lengua cacchi,* a *Vocabulario de la lengua cakchiquel y española,* and an *Art* of the same language.

sity library of Guatemala City into the hands of the noble Indian of Rabinal, and subsequently to those of Brasseur de Bourbourg.

The wording of the paragraph quoted above from Brasseur de Bourbourg is very confusing; but it is certain that the volume which he says he had occasion to consult in the University library, which begins with the text and the translation of the Quiché manuscript and which he copied, "adding the original," was not the first volume of the *Historia de la Provincia de San Vicente de Chiapa y Guatemala,* for that does not contain the Quiché text. Brasseur de Bourbourg copied the original text and the first translation by Ximénez from the treatise entitled *Empiezan las Historias del Origen de los Indios de esta Provincia de Guatemala,* inserted at the end of the *Arte de las tres lenguas.* The Quiché text and the Spanish version appear on alternate pages in Brasseur de Bourbourg's copy, made up of 124 folios, which is kept in the Bibliothèque Nationale of Paris and which is followed by a second copy of the *Arte de las tres lenguas.* This proves that the volumes of the *Arte* and of the *Historias de los Indios* were still in the library of the University in 1855. Probably the traveling investigator obtained them there with the same ease with which the other manuscripts of his celebrated collection of Americana came into his hands.

Brasseur de Bourbourg did not read the *Historia de la Provincia de San Vicente de Chiapa y Guatemala,* and he mentions only the few passages which Archbishop García Peláez gives in his work, *Memorias para la historia del antiguo reino de Guatemala.* The only part of the *Historia* that appears among the documents in the *Bibliothèque Mexico-Guatémalienne* (catalog of the Brasseur de Bourbourg collection) is the first thirty-six chapters of the first book copied by Don Juan Gavarrete "in Guatemala, October 23, 1847." This copy, containing fifty-four folios, includes the translation of the Quiché manuscript and the "history of the ancient Quiché Kingdom," which form Chapters 27 to 36 of Book I of the Ximénez *Historia.*[69]

In regard to the other works of Father Ximénez, Brasseur de Bourbourg, as has already been noted, used the *Tesoro* of the three

[69] Brasseur de Bourbourg, *Bibliothèque Mexico-Guatémalienne,* 156.

44

languages freely, not only to interpret the documents of the Quiché Indians, but also to compose his *Grammaire Quichée*, which was printed in Paris in 1862. He likewise used and commented extensively upon the Manuscript of Chichicastenango in his work entitled *Histoire des Nations Civilisées du Mexique et de l'Amérique Centrale* (1857) and in his *Quatre Lettres sur le Mexique* (1868).

The publication of the *Popol Vuh* (1861) and of the other works just mentioned aroused the interest of the scientific world and opened the way for additional works on the mythology and the pre-Columbian history of Guatemala, most important of which are those by Bancroft, Brinton, Charencey, Chavero, Müller, Raynaud, Seler, Spence, and Genêt.

After Brasseur de Bourbourg's death his collection of manuscripts and printed books was scattered. The largest part was acquired by Alphonse Pinart. Daniel G. Brinton bought the original manuscript of the *Memorial de Tecpán-Atitlán*, which he published in 1885 under the title *The Annals of the Cakchiquels*, and other documents relating to the languages of Guatemala, which after his death passed to the library of the museum of the University of Pennsylvania. Bancroft bought another part of the collection which is now in the library of manuscripts which bears his name at the University of California in Berkeley. When Pinart's collection was put on sale in 1884, the largest part of it remained in France at the Bibliothèque Nationale. Another part was acquired by Count H. de Charencey, and upon the death of this distinguished Americanist his widow presented his collection to the Bibliothèque Nationale in Paris.

The German translator of the *Popol Vuh*, Noah Elieser Pohorilles, says that Otto Stoll had told him that at various times Pinart had offered him "the original manuscript of the *Popol Vuh*" for the sum of ten thousand francs. This manuscript, as was said above, was acquired by Edward E. Ayer, together with other documents of Brasseur de Bourbourg's collection, and is now in the Newberry Library in Chicago. Finally, William Gates obtained some documents which had belonged to Brasseur de Bourbourg and included them in his valuable historical and philological collection, composed of original documents and photographic copies of almost all the known existing manuscripts in the libraries previously mentioned.

Don Juan Gavarrete, "the man most sincerely inspired by love for the ancient history of the country," according to the Abbé Brasseur de Bourbourg, undertook the arduous task of transcribing the old volumes of the *Historia de la Provincia de San Vicente de Chiapa y Guatemala* which were in the Convent of Santo Domingo and which, in 1830, were placed in the library of the University. According to Gavarrete's statement in the introduction of the version of the *Popol Vuh* published in the Guatemalan magazine *La Sociedad Económica* (1872–73), the first copy of this document, which was taken from Book I of the *Historia* by Ximénez, was the one which that paleographist "wrote in his hand in the library of the University in 1845." Another transcription "faithfully copied by Don Juan Gavarrete" in Guatemala, October 23, 1847, was, as has been noted, in the collection of Brasseur de Bourbourg, and in addition to the translation of the *Popol Vuh* also contained Chapters 27 to 36 of Book I of the *Historia de la Provincia* with the title *Historia del antiguo Reino de Quiché*, written by "Father Fray Francisco Ximénez." Brasseur de Bourbourg observes that "this document is a copy taken from the *Historia General de Guatemala* by Father Ximénez which was in manuscript in the library of the University of that city," and adds that this same copy is the original which Scherzer used for the Vienna edition. Nevertheless, this statement is correct only so far as it concerns Chapters 27 to 35 and the beginning of Chapter 36, which were included by Gavarrete in the *Escolios a las Historias de el origen de los indios*, printed at the end of the *Historias* in 1857. The text of the *Historias*, which forms the first part of the Vienna edition, was taken from the *Arte de las tres lenguas*.

The transcription of Father Ximénez' *Historia* which Gavarrete made contains six volumes totaling about 2,200 pages in folio, and is preserved in the National Library of Guatemala. In the beginning of this transcription, Gavarrete inserted some biographical notes about the author and about the copy of these chronicles,

46

which appears to have been dated in Guatemala on April 13, 1875. Gavarrete says:

The present copy was taken from the volumes which were in the convent of Santo Domingo of this capital and which in 1830 were placed in the library of the University. It is important to note that these volumes do not contain the original by Ximénez, but a careless and imperfect copy of that document. Consequently, the present copy, although carefully compared with [the old copy] and corrected in all those places in which now and then undoubtedly there were errors, it has defects which could only have been avoided had one had the original at hand.

Señor Gavarrete also says that he had to restore the spelling of the work in general; and as far as the Indian words and proper names are concerned, he was careful to compare them with the sources, whenever possible. Despite this care, Gavarrete's transcription contains many errors in his spelling of the words and Indian names, and there are important omissions, sometimes of several lines, which completely change the meaning of some parts of the Quiché book. Ximénez is not responsible for these errors, for they do not appear in the original manuscript and must, therefore, be attributed to the unknown author of the old copy. Gavarrete's transcription was published in three volumes by the Society of Geography and History of Guatemala between 1929 and 1931.

Brasseur de Bourbourg speaks of two and even three copies of the *Historia* by Ximénez.[70] An article about Francisco Jiménez in the *Diccionario Enciclopédico Hispano-Americano* states that "in the Provincial Library of Córdoba in Spain, there must be another incomplete copy" of this work. Ramón A. Salazar, who for several years was director of the National Library of Guatemala, says in a work published in 1897 that there are in the library two copies of the *Historia* by Ximénez; the modern one copied under the direction of Don Juan Gavarrete, and another "old and faded, although legible, with difficulty, which was the one taken from

---

[70] *Popol Vuh. Le Livre Sacré et les mythes de l'antiquité américaine, avec les livres heroïques et historiques des Quichés*, p. xiii; ibid., *Histoire des Nations Civilisées du Mexique et de l'Amérique Centrale*, Vol. I, p. lxxx.

the Convent of Santo Domingo and placed in the library of the University in 1830, at the time of the expulsion of the friars."[71] This copy has now disappeared from the National Library, and it is likely that it is the same one that Walter Lehmann obtained in Guatemala and took to Germany in 1909, and which the Duke of Loubat gave to the Royal Library of Berlin.[72] The Newberry Library has photographic copies of 183 pages of one part of the Berlin manuscript, which is entitled *Historia de la Provincia de Predicadores de Chiapa y Guatemala.*

In an article on the calendar of the Quiché Indians, published in the German magazine *Anthropos* in 1911, Lehmann says that among the numerous and valuable documents which it was his good fortune to obtain during his travels in Central America (1907–1909) is to be found the voluminous manuscript of Father Francisco Ximénez (three volumes) which contains the famous Book of Legends of the Quiché. He adds that unfortunately the style is very heavy and diffuse so that the reading of this thick document with its many thousands of pages, in folio, is not exactly a pleasure, but that the wealth of important information which it contains on the history of the ancient inhabitants of Chiapas and Guatemala well compensates for the labor of reading it.[73] In this article, Lehmann reproduces in the original Spanish, the part of Chapter 36 of Book I of the Ximénez *Historia* which deals with the calendar. Evidently the German Americanist believed that the manuscript which he acquired in Guatemala was the original of the *Historia* by the Dominican chronicler. Instead, however, it was the old copy which at one time belonged to the library of the University, and later to the National Library of Guatemala.

The *Historia de la Provincia de San Vicente de Chiapa y Guatemala* was not published until 1929, when the first volume of the edition prepared by the Society of Geography and History of Guatemala appeared. The second and the third volumes were

[71] Salazar, *Historia del desenvolvimiento intelectual de Guatemala. La Colonia,* 141.

[72] *Encyclopaedia Britannica* (Thirteenth Edition), XVIII, 333n. This copy is now at the Ibero-Amerikanischen Institut of Berlin.

[73] *Anthropos,* Vol. VI (1911), 403-10.

published in 1931. This edition contains the text of the work according to the copy of Gavarrete, and does not include Book III, that is, the second volume of the work in manuscript, which had already disappeared at the time Gavarrete made his copy, and Book VII, which was not copied at all. Likewise, the chapters of Book VI are not complete. The index of the work contains the following note by Gavarrete:

Not being of equal historical interest, the material of Book VI, volume 4 of the *Historia de la Provincia de San Vicente de Chiapa y Guatemala* by Father Fr. Francisco Ximénez, the undersigned in making this copy, which must be preserved in the National Museum, omitted those chapters which were not of interest to the general history of the country; but in order that at all times the contents of those chapters which had been omitted should be known, he will make reference to them in this index, quoting only the folios included in this copy.

In all, the copy and the printed book lack thirty chapters of Book VI and the thirty-four chapters which constituted Book VII.

I
v. *The Translations of the Popol Vuh*

In a convincing argument in favor of the authenticity of the *Popol Vuh*, Lewis Spence declares:

The very fact that it was composed in the Quiché tongue is almost sufficient proof of its genuine American character. The scholarship of the nineteenth century was unequal to the adequate translation of the *Popol Vuh;* the twentieth century has as yet shown no signs of being able to accomplish the task. It is therefore not difficult to credit that if modern scholarship is unable to properly translate the work, that of the eighteenth century was unable to create it.[74]

[74] *The Popol Vuh. The Mythic and Heroic Sagas of the Kichés of Central America*, 33.

Despite his undeniable and profound knowledge of the Quiché language, Father Francisco Ximénez by himself alone would not have been able to compose the Manuscript of Chichicastenango, the most notable literary expression of native American genius. On the other hand, this distinguished historian and linguist does not claim other than the title of discoverer of the Indian document. Defects, unfortunately, appear in his two versions of this work which have come down to us; these defects reveal that sometimes Ximénez was not able to perceive the meaning of the text, showing that the thought and phraseology of the ancient Quiché frequently escape comprehension even by those Europeans best qualified to interpret it.

The two principal translations which have been made, both in Spanish and in French, of the Quiché document are well known. The first, as has been said, is the work of Father Ximénez, who translated, verbatim, the histories of the Indians into the Spanish language from the Quiché, in which they had been written from the time of the Conquest. This first is a literal translation, closely following the phraseology of the original text. In it the translator not only wanted to give the meaning of the words, but many times tried to preserve the Quiché syntax, dropping the Spanish syntax and thus confusing the very meaning which he was trying to interpret. From the beginning of Ximénez' translation, one finds the passive form of the verbs preceding the possessive, which imitates the morphology of the original Quiché language, but which lacks meaning in Spanish. When Ximénez translates "his being declared and manifested," "his being related," and "his being said," or "his being formed," he reveals the peculiar forms of the Quiché construction, but he makes it impossible to understand the document, until the reader familiarizes himself with those forms and converts them into the corresponding substantives; "the declaration," "the manifestation," "the relation." "the formation," and so on.[75]

[75] The English language has similar forms, and in it, Quiché passive forms may be translated as "its being declared," "its being told," "its being formed," etc., which are equivalent expressions. Nevertheless, the English reader, like the Spanish, would probably prefer the substantive forms which correspond.

It must be noted here that these passive forms gradually disappear in the course of the translation and the style becomes easier and more natural.

In other places the translator, in an exaggerated effort to be faithful to the original, retains the metaphorical expressions of the Quiché text without giving the Spanish equivalents. For example when Hun-Ahpú and Xbalanqué decide to get rid of their envious brothers, Hun Batz and Hun Chouén, the translator has them say, "We will only change their stomachs into other things," using a metaphor which could be interpreted by saying that they would change only their figure, as in effect they did, transforming them into monkeys. In this same passage the sense is very obscure, because Ximénez limits himself to translating, word for word, the extremely abbreviated sentences of the original Quiché without developing them more extensively, as they require in Spanish. These examples are cited in order to give an idea of the difficulties which, in general, the reader of the first version of the *Popol Vuh* will find.

Ximénez' translation with all its defects represents a work of infinite patience, which must have taken a long time, years perhaps, of the life of the translator. The first version may be read in the right column of the manuscript of the *Historias de los Indios*, and is the same which Carl Scherzer published in Vienna in 1857, with numerous errata. The copyist who made the transcript which the editor used did not know how to interpret some of the abbreviations which Ximénez employed; he read parts of the manuscript wrong, omitted words and even whole sentences, and confused many of the proper names and common Quiché words. Some of these errors are undoubtedly those of the Guatemalan copyist; but he is not altogether to blame, and it must be supposed that the Vienna printer made some of the errors which are found in that edition, which, however, in general is a very good one.

The first translation appears to have been made during the time in which Ximénez administered the parish of Santo Tomás. On the title page of the *Historias de los Indios* one reads that the translator was the priest who taught the Christian doctrine by royal appointment in the town of Santo Tomás Chuilá, today

Santo Tomás Chichicastenango. Years later, on undertaking his longer work, the *Historia de la Provincia de San Vicente de Chiapa y Guatemala*, Ximénez revised his first translation of the Indian document, deleting many repetitions which are peculiar to the Quiché language, divided the account into chapters, and made it in general easier to read, although less true to the original text. In this condensed translation some of the redundancies of the first draft have disappeared, but some of the concepts and words and, at times, even entire paragraphs have been omitted. It must be taken into account, however, that this second version is known only through the transcription made by Señor Gavarrete, a transcription which served for the edition of the work printed in Guatemala in 1929. It is to be hoped that the authentic text of this second version of Ximénez will be published as it is found in the original manuscript which is preserved in Guatemala. The numerous errors and omissions, the defective spelling, and other faults which, unfortunately, fill the 1929 edition, must be attributed to its successive transcriptions, since Gavarrete himself said, as early as 1872, that his was not a direct copy of the original, but of another copy made carelessly and with many imperfections. This copy must have been very old, because the errors and omissions which it contains are also observed in the chapters which Ordóñez y Aguiar inserted at the end of the eighteenth century in his *Historia de la Creación del Cielo y de la Tierra*.

Luckily, the manuscript of the first version having been preserved together with the original copy of the Quiché, it is still possible to appreciate the translation in its primitive form, without the errors which mar the two printings of 1857 and 1929 respectively.

Despite its defects, this translation is a work of great merit and inestimable value. Our linguistically-minded friar knew the Quiché language of the sixteenth century better than any other of the modern translators and commentators, and at the same time he knew the mentality of the Indians of that race. For this reason the Spanish translator almost always kept his text at the same intellectual level as that of the Quiché narrator, without elevating himself to spheres foreign to pre-Columbian American culture, and without letting himself be carried away by fantasy, as has occurred in the case of the first French translator.

The Abbé Brasseur de Bourbourg says that Father Ximénez lacked a critical sense and previous knowledge of the general history of the Indians, and that for this reason, he could not make more than a rough translation into Spanish, in which he almost always gives a literal word for word version, which at times does not make sense; and he sometimes omits four or five sentences of the original.[76] Brasseur de Bourbourg goes on to criticize the Ximénez translation, accusing Ximénez of not having been sufficiently informed about American antiquities or in the writings of Sahagún and Torquemada; and he adds that the Spanish translator did not know how to get the real essence of the material which he had in his hands, and that in translating it he let himself be dominated by the prejudices of the Church at that time. In supporting these charges, Brasseur de Bourbourg cites the interpretation which Ximénez gives to the passages relating to the empire of Xibalba, "which is changed under his pen to the mansion of the damned, the inferno, and their princes, into demons."[77]

The charge that Ximénez did not know American antiquities is notoriously unjust, and confirms the opinion that I have already expressed concerning the lack of knowledge that Brasseur de Bourbourg himself had of the *Historia de la·Provincia de San Vicente de Chiapa y Guatemala*, of which he makes mention in various places in his works, but which he evidently had never read. He had in his possession the copy which Gavarrette made of the first thirty-six chapters of Book I of the *Historia de la Provincia*, but he appears to have paid no attention to it. In this part of his work, Father Ximénez mentions and comments on the opinions of Torquemada and reproduces, at length, the principal chapters of the *Repúblicas de Indias* by Father Jerónimo Román, which latter work contains ample information about the customs, laws, and beliefs of the Indians of Guatemala and Mexico. As has already been said, the chapters of Román which deal with these

[76] *Histoire des Nations Civilisées du Mexique et de l'Amérique Centrale,* Vol. I, pp. xxv, xxvi.
[77] *Ibid.,* Vol. I, p. lxxx.

matters are copied almost word by word from the *Apologética Historia* of Fray Bartolomé de las Casas, who claims to have written all these reports in accordance with the testimony of the Franciscan and Dominican friars who learned the languages, and who had a thorough knowledge of the good and bad customs of those people.[78]

At the same time, Ximénez refers to the prophecies of the Maya Indians of Yucatán and mentions those places in the history of Father Cogolludo where he deals with them; he speaks of the chronicles of Herrera and Remesal and shows that he was well versed in what a cultivated man of his time might have known about Americana.

As to the prejudices which the Abbé Brasseur de Bourbourg attributes to Father Ximénez, there may be cited the example which he gives about the empire of Xibalba, which Ximénez identifies with the inferno. This is a very debatable matter, and, as will be shown later, it cannot be denied that the legend of Xibalba refers to the lower regions, inhabited by evil spirits who are tormentors of men. The Quiché conception of the underworld of Xibalba is similar to that of Mictlan of the Mexican Indians and to the Hades of the Greeks. Ximénez does not stray entirely afield in recognizing it as a place of punishment, the *infierno* of the Spaniards.

One might also attribute to prejudice the fact that Ximénez translates the word *Cabauil* (god) by *idol*, in the passages of the *Popol Vuh* relating to the gods which the tribes worshiped on their migration into the mountains in the interior of Guatemala. But apart from these minutiae of interpretation, it must be recognized that Ximénez translated the Quiché manuscript with impartiality and with care designed to give his readers a faithful version of the traditions and beliefs of these people, although according to his judgment they held great errors and superstitions,

[78] *Apologética Historia de las Indias*, Vol. I, Chap. CCXIX, p. 574. Sr. Serrano y Sanz justly compares the work of the first translator of the *Popol Vuh* with the work of Father Sahagún when he writes: "Father Jiménez brought to the common heritage his very precious Indian traditions (the *Historias del origen de los indios*, etc.), doing what P. Sahagún had done earlier in Mexico."— *Relaciones Históricas y Geográficas de América Central*, Introduction.

as he says in his notes and comments. With all its imperfections, the translation of the *Popol Vuh* by Ximénez is the basis for our interpretation of the most notable manuscript of ancient American literature. It was already so when Brasseur de Bourbourg began his interpretation of this document; and in spite of his objections to it, he declared that the translation by Father Ximénez had been very useful to him and that he had "preserved it entirely in almost all of its parts, not having done more than clarify its obscurities and fill in the gaps."[79]

In 1855 the Abbé Brasseur de Bourbourg found in Guatemala the manuscript of the *Historias de los Indios* which contained the original transcription of the Quiché text and the first Spanish translation of it made by Father Ximénez. Sent to the parish of Rabinal by Archbishop García Peláez, who, according to Brasseur de Bourbourg, wanted to further his archaelogical investigations and his studies of the Indian languages, the famous French traveler moved to that Quiché center, learned how to read and write the language of the people, and prepared himself sufficiently to undertake the translation of the Quiché book, according to what he says in the foreword to his *Histoire des Nations Civilisées du Mexique et de l'Amérique Centrale*.

In this way Brasseur de Bourbourg had the opportunity to learn the dialect spoken at Rabinal and to consult the Indians of that town on the difficult passages of the *Popol Vuh*. Furthermore, during his trips to Central America, he acquired a valuable collection of grammars and old vocabularies of the Indian languages which were most useful to him in his interpretation of the Guatemalan documents. The Quiché *Vocabulario* of Fray Domingo Basseta which is in the Bibliothèque Nationale at Paris is full of Brasseur de Bourbourg's annotations, which show the constant use which he made of it in his work of translation.

In 1861 the *Popol Vuh, Le Livre Sacré*, which contains the Quiché text of the Manuscript of Chichicastenango was published in Paris, divided into chapters and phoneticized according to Brasseur de Bourbourg's ideas, in order to facilitate its reading by

[79] *Histoire des Nations Civilisées du Mexique et de l'Amérique Centrale*, Vol. I, p. xxvi.

the people of his country. According to these ideas, the Abbé introduced the letter "k" which does not exist in the original, and substituted it for the "c" and the 'q' which Ximénez used in transcribing the Quiché manuscript. On the other hand, he kept the "v" which was used in the Colonial Period to represent the sound of "u" as in the words *varal, vinac*, etc.

The Abbé Brasseur de Bourbourg's version of the *Popol Vuh* is a notable work in which he tried to interpret, with the precision and elegance of the French language, the ancient and simple thought of the Quiché race. As he himself says, this translation is based on the Spanish of Ximénez and supplemented with the parts which the Dominican friar omitted.[80] In general, the Abbé interpreted the Quiché manuscript correctly, although there are many errors which he committed in his translation, despite the evident care that he took. His version, however, shows one major defect. Despite having lived some time among the American Indians, the Abbé never succeeded in understanding their primitive mentality, and he attributed to them ideas and thoughts as elevated as those of the peoples of the Old World, the heirs of a classical culture of many centuries.

The German writer Noah Elieser Pohorilles published a version of the *Popol Vuh* in Leipzig in 1913 under the title of *Das Popol Wuh. Die mytische Geschichte des Kicé-Volkes von Guatemala nach dem Original-Texte übersetz und bearbeitet.* In general, the German translator follows Brasseur de Bourbourg in interpreting the Quiché document, despite the fact that in the title of his work he says that it is a translation from the original text. In a study on the "Significance of the Myths of the Popol Vuh," Eduard Seler indicates that he does not consider that the

[80] "Brasseur de Bourbourg's unfavorable criticism [of the translation of Father Ximénez] is entirely unjust. Furthermore, the French Abbé has used the Spanish text by Ximénez much more than he confesses. Not only did he translate [the latter] literally, but he accepted without any discussion many of Ximénez' errors. Besides, in his translation [the Abbé] has obviously misinterpreted the Ximénez text. Finally, it is certain that Father Ximénez, despite all the defects of his translation, better understood the way in which the Indians told their 'stories' than did Brasseur."—Schuller, "*Das Popol Vuh und das Ballspiel der K'icé Indianer von Guatemala, Mittelamerika*," *Intern. Achiv für Ethnogr.*, Vol. 33, p. 107, n. 5.

Pohorilles translation had improved that of Brasseur de Bourbourg, rather the contrary.[81]

Professor Georges Raynaud of the Sorbonne spent many years studying the Indian manuscripts of the Americas, and in Paris in 1925, he published a new version of the *Popol Vuh*, under the title of *Les dieux, les héros et les hommes de l'ancien Guatémala d'après le Livre du Conseil.* A Spanish translation of this work was published in 1927.

Professor Raynaud's translation is, according to my judgment, the best and most accurate of the modern interpretations of the Quiché document. This translator had the advantage of being able to consult the vocabularies of the languages of Guatemala which the Bibliothèque Nationale of Paris possesses, in order to clarify many expressions contained in the versions of Ximénez and Brasseur de Bourbourg, upon which, generally speaking, all modern translations of this work are based. Raynaud's translation is more precise than those made before it and as a whole is the most acceptable.

The defects of Raynaud's translation are due principally to the fact that the Sorbonne professor did not have the original manuscript before him and had to follow the transcription of Brasseur de Bourbourg, which, as has been noted, was not always faithful. Furthermore Raynaud did not know Guatemala, and it was not possible for him to understand the mentality of the Indians of that country or to inform himself accurately about their character and customs.

Finally there should be mentioned the version of Licenciado J. Antonio Villacorta and Don Flavio Rodas N. contained in a volume entitled *Manuscrito de Chichicastenango (Popol Buj). Estudio sobre las antiguas tradiciones del Pueblo Quiché. Texto indígena fonetizado y traducido al Castellano. Notas etimológicas, etc.* (Guatemala, 1927). This is the first modern translation to be published in Guatemala. In the preface of the work one reads that the authors undertook the translation because a faithful version of the Manuscript had not yet been made. Señor Rodas, well

[81] *"Der Bedeutungswandel in den Mythen des Popol Vuh. Eine Kritik,"* *Anthropos,* Vol. VIII (1913), 388.

versed in the modern Quiché language, took the text transcribed
by Brasseur de Bourbourg and phoneticized it according to Spanish spelling "in order that the Indians and other people who speak
the language could read it." The Quiché text appears in this form
accompanied by a Spanish translation. Studies on the Quiché, the
Maya, and the Tolteca, the calendar, and the pre-Columbian
manuscripts precede the translation, and at the end there are
several pages of notes and etymology.

The work of phonetization is useful for the reader who speaks
Spanish, for whom it was evidently made. It is noticeable, however, that certain Quiché names have been changed, such as
Hunahpú to Junajup, and that Vucub Hunahpú, who was only
one person and brother of the former, is presented as a group of
seven Ajups in various passages of this translation.

The work of Villacorta and Rodas suffers from a number of
defects, some of which have been pointed out by foreign critics.[82]
Many careless errors and inaccuracies are noted in the translation,
even in passages which do not offer great difficulty. Furthermore,
the authors appear to have lacked the aid of the old vocabularies,
which must be consulted in order to understand the significance
of many terms no longer used by the modern Quiché Indians.

In his introduction to *Märchen der Azteken und Inkaperuaner,
Maya and Muisca* (in which he also included the legends of the
Quiché book), Walter Krickeberg mentions the linguistic course
which Eduard Seler gave in the University of Berlin, in which
this Americanist explained some chapters of the *Popol Vuh* and
the *Annals of the Cakchiquels* of Sololá. Lewis Spence studies
the *Popol Vuh* extensively in his work *The Magic and Mysteries
of Mexico* and declares that Seler, a short time before his death,
was working upon a translation of the Quiché book, directly
from the original, but that he did not get to publish it. His vast
knowledge of the mentality, history, and languages of the Ameri-

[82] Schuller, *"Der Verfasser des Popol Vuh," Anthropos*, Vol. XXVI, Nos.
5–6 (September-December, 1931); *ibid., "Das Popol Vuh und das Ballspiel der
K'icé Indianer von Guatemala, Mittelamerika," Intern. Achiv für Ethnogr.*,
Vol. 33, pp. 105–16; Imbelloni, *"El Génesis de los pueblos proto-históricos de
América," Boletín de la Academia Argentina de Letras*, Vol. VIII, No. 32 (Octo-
ber-December, 1940,), 539–628.

can Indians gave Seler complete authority to interpret these documents, as he has demonstrated in the criticism he made of the
works of Pohorilles and other studies on the myths of the Quiché
and Cakchiquel of Guatemala, which he published in scientific
magazines in his own country. In the foreword to Volume V of
his *Gesammelte Abhandlungen zur amerikanischen Sprach-und
Altertumskunde,* his widow, Caecilie Seler, said in 1923 that she
had not entirely given up the hope of publishing Volume VI of
his assembled works, which would contain his translations of
Sahagún and the *Popol Vuh,* whose value for the understanding
of ancient America appear to be so important that they must not
be left in obscurity. Seler's translation of Sahagún appeared in
1927, but that of the *Popol Vuh* still remains unpublished.

A well-known Austrian investigator, Rudolph Schuller, left
an English translation of the Quiché book, according to Dr.
Samuel K. Lothrop's report in his archaelogical study on the
region of Lake Atitlán (Carnegie Institution of Washington, September, 1933). Lothrop adds that he himself also has prepared a
translation of the same document.

In his book *An introduction to Mythology,* Lewis Spence says:

> There is an abridgment in English by the present writer. An
> English translation of the whole appeared in an American magazine
> entitled *The Word* during 1906 and 1907, from the pen of Dr. Ken-
> neth Sylvan Guthrie, but whether from the Spanish, or original Kiche,
> I do not know. It is, moreover, couched in Scriptural language, and
> such treatment assists the vulgar error that the *Popol Vuh* is merely
> a native travesty of portions of the Old Testament.[83]

Dr. Guthrie states that his translation was made independently,
"but some felicitous terms have been added" from another translation from the first book of the *Popol Vuh* by James Pryse, which
appeared in *Lucifer* in 1894–95.

A new German translation by Leonhard Schultze Jena was
published in Stuttgart in 1944, together with the original text as
transcribed by Ximénez, under the title of *Popol Vuh. Das heiliges
Buch der Quiché Indianer von Guatemala.*

[83] Page 270.

The Ayer Collection in the Newberry Library of Chicago has an unpublished English translation of the *Popol Vuh* made by Colonel Beebe. It is a manuscript of 264 pages, apparently based on the French translation of Brasseur de Bourbourg.

The legends of the *Popol Vuh* have been used by some modern writers in the composition of stories and narratives for children, as one can see in the collection of Krickeberg and in the *Tales from Silver Lands* by Charles Finger. Isolated passages of the *Popol Vuh* have been dramatized many times. And the German writer, Oswald Claassen, using the same episodes, composed a long poem, entitled *Die Ahnen des Mondes*, and *Das Gefass des Schicksals*, inspired by the translation of Pohorilles.

In this way modern authors have justified the opinion, somewhat ironical, that Ximénez expressed when he wrote, "I well know that all these histories are children's stories," although this opinion certainly did not deter the austere friar from dedicating much of the time which his ecclesiastical duties left free, to transcribing and translating them into Spanish and commenting upon them.

In his study on the Indian authors and their works (*Aboriginal American Authors and Their Productions*), Brinton comments on the narrative of the mythology and traditional history of the Quiché, and the translations of Ximénez and Brasseur de Bourbourg, and declares that neither of these translations is satisfactory. According to Brinton, Ximénez wrote with all the prejudices of a Spanish monk, and Brasseur de Bourbourg was an euhemerist of the most advanced type, who saw in every myth the expression of a historical fact. And adds "there is need for a re-translation of all the work, with critical linguistic notes attached." Other critics have seconded this eminent Americanist in his observation. Since the time he wrote, new translations have been published which have clarified some of the obscure parts of the Quiché book, but the field is very wide and the subject is always new and attractive. The present translation and the philological and historical study which accompanies it have been born of this attraction which the old Indian document exerts; and although it does not pretend to answer the particular need indicated by Brinton, it is hoped that it will at least contribute to reawakening interest in these ancient American things.

T
VI. *Summary of the Ancient History of the Quiché*

he *Popol Vuh* presents the complete picture of the popular traditions, religious beliefs, migrations, and development of the Indian tribes which populated the territory of the present Republic of Guatemala after the fall of the Maya Old Empire. It is a substitute, according to notices of its compiler, for the old book in which the kings used to read, which was no longer to be seen at the time of the Spanish Conquest and colonization, and, apart from complying with its declared aim, this document corroborates other documents of Guatemala and of Mexico, which deal with the historical evolution of the peoples of this part of the New World.

In 1524, when the Spaniards invaded the territories immediately to the south of Mexico, they found the country inhabited by a flourishing population which possessed a civilization not inferior to that of their neighbors to the north. The Quiché kingdom extended from the Pacific Coast to the borders of Petén occupied by the Itzá; to the west were the Indians called Mam, who occupied the territory now known as the departments of Huehuetenango and San Marcos in Guatemala and the district of Soconusco in southeastern Chiapas, Mexico. To the east lived the Cakchiquel, rivals of the Quiché; the Zutuhil who lived around Lake Atitlán; and the Pocomam who lived around Lake Amatitlán and in the mountains that surround the valley in which Guatemala City is now located. At the north were the Quekchi and Poconchi in the district which, later, the Dominicans subdued, by peaceful means, and which for that reason was called Vera Paz.

It is not possible to estimate exactly the population of the different Indian kingdoms of Guatemala at the time of the Conquest. The country was densely populated. The Quiché raised an army of many thousands of men to fight against the Spaniards, and the Mam of Huehuetenango, the Zutuhil of Atitlán, the Pocomam of Mixco, and the Pipil of the Pacific Coast did not surrender until they saw their large hosts annihilated. The Cakchiquel opened their arms to the invaders, but shortly afterwards they also were forced to fight, when Alvarado and his officers with their acts of cruelty and avarice provoked the people to rise against them. The Cakchiquel insurrection which endangered the new Spanish colony was also the cause for the killing of thousands of that tribe, who, although tardily, fought with desperation to regain their independence.

The Indian people of present-day Guatemala descend from the common stock of the Maya which developed their marvelous civilization in the northern part of the country, in the Petén, and in the territory of present-day Yucatán, Mexico. The physical characteristics of this people and the similarity which exists among their several languages give sufficient proof of the relationship which united them among themselves and with a common mother. And as a complement, the documents of the Quiché and Cakchiquel, which fortunately have come down to us, coincide with the documents of Yucatán and Mexico in giving the same story of the origin of the inhabitants of the vast territory included between the central Mexican plateau and the northern half of Central America.

In the third part of this book of the history of the Indians, one reads that the four first men, the leaders, Balam-Quitzé, Balam-Acab, Mahucutah, and Iqui-Balam, were created out of a paste made of corn, the plant most venerated by the ancient Maya Indians, and that these four first men were the forefathers of the Quiché race. The Yaqui, Tolteca, or Mexican nation, "the people of the sacrificers," united with the Quiché and the other tribes and, together with them, waited anxiously for the rising of the sun. "They had notice of a city and they went to it," says the text, and adds that the city was called Tulán-Zuiva, Vucub-Pec (Seven Caves), Vucub-Ziván (Seven Ravines). The Mexican legend puts the cradle of the people, who established themselves in Anahuac at a place called Chicomoztoc, which word has the same

62

significance in Nahuatl, i.e., Seven Caves or Ravines. The *Book of Chilan Balam of Maní* says that the four Tutul Xius left the land and the home of Nonoual to the west of Zuiva, and that the country from which they came was called Tulapan. And the *Book of Chilam Balam of Chumayel* says that of the four branches of the people, one came from the east, another from the north, another came from Holtun Zuyva (the cave of Zuyva) in the west, and the last one came from the south, the Hill of Canek, the land called the Nine Hills (*Bolonpel uitz*).

A Cakchiquel manuscript (*the Memorial de Sololá o Tecpán-Atitlán*) states that the forefathers of that people came from Tulán; that originally the tribes came from the west to that legendary place: "From the west we came to Tulán"—says the Cakchiquel document—"from the other side of the sea, and it was in Tulán where we were engendered and given birth by our mothers and our fathers."

The prehistoric migration of the tribes has been described by the majority of the writers on this subject. Sahagún tells of it thus:

It has been countless years since the first settlers of this part of New Spain arrived [and] . . . they landed in Panutla [Panuco] and from that port they began to travel by the seacoast, looking at the snow-covered mountains and the volcanoes until they came to the Province of Guatemala, being guided by their priest, who brought with him their God, with whom he always consulted about which he must do, and they went to populate Tamoanchán where they remained for a long time.[84]

There is no indication of the time when the Guatemalan tribes left Tulán, but supposing they emigrated about the same time as the future founders of Uxmal and Chichén Itzá in the peninsula of Yucatán, one may calculate that their exodus began in the seventh century of our era. The *Popol Vuh*, as well as the *Memorial Cakchiquel*, tells the way that the tribes crossed the sea on stones and sand, when they came from Tulán. The second of these documents gives more definite information on the inter-

[84] *Historia general de las cosas de Nueva España* (1938 ed.), Vol. III, Book X, Chap. XXIX, p. 136.

mediate places through which they passed before establishing themselves in the interior of Guatemala. They were, says the *Memorial*, at a place called Teozacuán and at Meahauh; there they all reunited, and then left for the place called Valval Xucxuc, where they rested. From there they went on to a place called Tapcu Olomán, and continuing their journey toward the east, they encountered armed people, the Nonoualcat and the Xulpit, who were at the edge of the sea and whom they attacked and defeated; they followed them, in their canoes, and crossed the sea always in the direction of the east, until they entered the city and homes of the Zuyva, to the terror of the inhabitants. Nevertheless, they could not resist the attack of the men, the dogs, and the wasps, nor the magic and the witchcraft of their enemies who ascended to the sky and also disappeared into the earth. Battered and bruised, the Cakchiquel and Quiché finally withdrew to Tapcu Olomán, where they mourned their losses; and seeing that the country was hostile to them, they decided to abandon the seacoast and go toward the interior in search of more suitable land.

The words "Tapcu Olomán," which in the *Popol Vuh* in one place appear as "Tepeu Olomán," and in another as "Tepeu and Olimán" naturally refer to the Olmeca who lived in the region of Vera Cruz and who established an advance post to the southeast, in what is now the state of Tabasco, at a place called Xicalanco. In the *Historia Chichimeca* of Ixtlilxóchitl, one reads that Quetzalcoatl "preached" to the Olmeca-Xicalanca during the stay of this Toltec civilizer in Yucatán. Mendieta says that the Xicalanca extended their power along the coast beyond Coatzacualco. Gómara in his *Crónica de la Nueva España* says that Xicalanco, being a great commercial center, all the coast of the Atlantic was called Anahuac Xicalanco. Sahagún says that the land of the Olmecas was a true Garden of Eden, abounding in all the products of the earth, and that their inhabitants had come from Tulán, following the Tolteca who were also called Chichimeca, but adds that those who were there after the rising of the sun were called Olmeca, Uixtotin, and Nonoualca, and were not called Chichimeca.[85]

[85] *Ibid.*, Book X, Chap. XXIX.

The *Anales de Chimalpahin* state that these places are called
Nonoualco or Nontiaco, which means "land of the dumb," that
is, the land of the foreign tongue, because the merchants who
came from the south did not understand the local idiom. This
was the intermediate zone between the people of the north and
the Maya to the south, who spoke a language different from theirs.
The *Anales de Chimalpahin* identify Nonoualco, with Tlapallan, the legendary region to which, it is said, Quetzalcoatl went
to live and to die after his departure from Tulán. Ixtlilxóchitl
gives in his *Relaciones* these interesting facts about the expedition
of Quetzalcoatl:

> He left for Tlapallan, traveling over the deserts by night, until
> he arrived at that place, where he lived for almost thirty years, served
> and showered with gifts by the Tlapaltecas, and he died at the age of
> 104 years.

And in another place:

> In the same way, those Tultecas who escaped, went by the south
> and north coasts of the sea, namely, Huatimala, Cuauhtzacualco, Cam-
> peche, Tacolotlan, and the islands and coasts from one sea to another.

The group which went to Guatemala and to Tacolotlan (or
Tecolotlan, the ancient name of Vera Paz) was the Yaqui or Toltec nation of which the *Popol Vuh* frequently speaks. The region
of Xicalanco, Nonoualco, and Tlapallan was that drained by the
large rivers called Tabasco and Usumacinta, toward the lower
ends of their courses, and the region of the Laguna de Términos
and southwest of Yucatán. Torquemada says that Quetzalcoatl
went to "the lands of Onohualco which are near the sea and are
those which today we call Yucatán, Tabasco, and Campeche."[86]
In the *Anales de Chimalpahin*, Quetzalcoatl is called god of the
East (*Teotl Ixca*) of the Nonoualca, which means of the inhabitants of the coast of Tabasco.

These reports of Mexican origin aid us in interpreting the
references in the *Popol Vuh* and in the Cakchiquel manuscript,

[86] *Monarquia Indiana*, Book III, Chap. 7.

and help us to locate the places where the Guatemalan tribes were, probably for many years, before their migration to the interior of the country. Teozacuancu is probably the place of Coatzacualco; the name is written in the form in which Hernández Arana remembered it when, six hundred years later, he related the legends of his forefathers.

Tapcu Olomán or Tepeu Olimán is the Cakchiquel and Quiché version of Olmeca Xicalanca who were the men of Olimán, of Olmecatl Uixtotli, the leader who, according to Sahagún, "had a pact with the devil." The Nonoualca, according to the reference cited from Sahagún, were the same people as these Olmeca and the same as the people of Zuiva, who, according to the Cakchiquel book, probably lived on the island which today is called Carmen in the Laguna de Términos. A glance at the map of this interesting region shows that the Laguna de Términos was the only large body of water in the path of the tribes which came from the northwest. The *Título de los Señores de Totonicapán* says that when they were already on this side of the sea, "they came to the shore of a lake in which there was a multitude of animals: There they built huts, but becoming disgusted with the place, they left it."

The Mexicans gave this region the name of Acallan, from the Náhuatl *a calli*, boat, and their inhabitants, as Seler observes, maintained commercial intercourse with Tabasco and Xicalanco, and to the south with Golfo Dulce and other places in the interior of Guatemala, using the many waterways and the courses of the large rivers. In his expedition to Honduras in 1524–25, Cortés was received and aided by the inhabitants of the town of Acallan, the center of this great intermediate zone. Lehmann records that in the *Historia de los Reyes de Colhua y Mexico* the country of Acallan is mentioned among the lands conquered by Quetzalcoatl, and refers to the passage from Hymn XVIII of the Nahuas (inserted in the book *Ancient Náhuatl Poetry* by Brinton) in which it is said that the noble companions of Quetzalcoatl left Cholula and, weeping, went by water toward Acallan.

In this same region, at the place called Chakanputún (probably the Champotón of modern times in the present state of Campeche, Mexico) there lived for the space of 250 years a tribe called the Itzá, which had originally come from the south, from the mountains of Lacandón, according to Herrera, bringing with them the civilization of the ancient Maya Old Empire. This tribe was probably the division which, according to the *Book of Chilan Balam of Chumayel* came from the south from the hill Canek, named after the ruling house of the Petén Itzá, and they came from the land of the Nine Hills (*bolonpel uitz*), a place important for its salt springs, located along the edge of the Chixoy or Salinas River, a principal tributary of the Usumacinta.

In a Katun 8 Ahau of the Maya Short Count, probably A. D. 928–948, a group of Maya-speaking people began moving slowly northeastward across the peninsula. Part of these at least were Itzá, although others, under a leader named Kukulcán, certainly were of central Mexican (highlands) origin, but they had been living in what is now southwestern Campeche for some two to two and one-half centuries. After forty years of wandering, they finally reached Chichén Itzá, where they established their capital in a Katun 4 Ahau, A. D. 968–987. With these invaders, or rather before or after them, a great lord arrived, who, according to the Maya traditions, was called Kukulcán, who founded the rich city of Mayapán, taught the people the arts and the sciences, and, after a time, disappeared, announcing that he was returning to Mexico. This person was no other than the king of the Tolteca, Quetzalcoatl. On his part, Tutul Xiu and his companions, who had left Tulapan at the west of Zuyva, established themselves at Uxmal and constructed the splendid city of that name at the same time that Kukulcán was reconstructing Chichén Itzá and founding Mayapán.[87] The *Memorial Cakchiquel*, as has been seen, says that the Guatemalan tribes fought with the Ah Nonoualcat and the Ah Xulpiti in the region of the Laguna de Términos and entered the city and the houses of the Ah Zuyva. It is not too much to believe that those from Ah Xulpiti were the people of the Tutul Xiu, who still, many years after, used the "language of Zuyva" according to the *Book of Chilan Balam of Chumayel*.

It is possible that the Guatemalan tribes, after a long stay in

[87] Morley, *The Ancient Maya*, 84–87.

the region of the Laguna de Términos and Chakanputún, had been obliged to leave these places, not only because the many peoples coming from the north and the south and centering here had made food scarce, but also because of the tyranny of the Itzá, a race of "tricksters and rascals," as the old Maya chronicles called them. A passage from the *Popol Vuh*, speaking of the Lords of Xibalba, who, according to the legend, cruelly suppressed the Quiché, says that these lords, tormentors of humanity, caused fright; they were vicious, *Ah-Tza*, and that they promoted evil and war.

In their pilgrimage toward the interior, the Guatemalan tribes probably followed up the course of the Usumacinta River and its tributaries, the Chixoy, which carried them to the west, and the Pasión to the east of the present territory of Guatemala, and others penetrated to the Valley of the Motagua and its tributaries, by which they also proceeded to the central part of the country. As is well known, these rivers in pre-Columbian times were great arteries of commerce among the Maya Indians of Yucatán and Tabasco and their brothers of Guatemala. The emigrants established themselves in the highlands of the interior of the country which gave them means of subsistence and defense against their enemies. Nevertheless, the first places in the interior which the *Memorial Cakchiquel* mentions are the mountains of Meme and Tacna, undoubtedly the land of the Mam tribe and the Volcano of Tacaná, in the present department of San Marcos, Guatemala, and the district of Soconusco in Chiapas, Mexico, on the Pacific Coast, which would make it appear that the Cakchiquel came directly to this region, going up the great Chiapas or Tabasco River, which empties into the Gulf of Mexico in the region of Xicalanco. However, this document, as well as the Quiché book, places the principal establishments of the tribes in the center of the country.

The thought of their Mexican brothers was not erased from the memory of the Guatemalan tribes, and we shall see how, even in the hour of their greatest happiness, at the rising of the sun of their civilization, they wept for the absence of those who had remained behind in the lands to the north, that is, "in the East," which was the name they gave to the country whence they had come and of which they still had, at the end of many years, very indefinite and vague ideas.

The Quiché tribes, nevertheless, remained loyal to the great leader of their people, Quetzalcoatl, or Kukulcán, who had established himself "in the East," by the sea near Xicalanco, and later at Chichén Itzá. In fact, one of the first acts of the Quiché princes, when they had already fixed their residence in Guatemala, was to go to the East, obeying the command that their parents had given them before the latter's death, in order that they should receive from Lord Nacxit, the royal investiture, honors, and dignity of which all the native documents of Guatemala speak. The Lord Nacxit, in whom one easily recognizes Topiltzin Acxitl Quetzalcoatl, or one of his immediate successors who continued using the same name, received the Quiché princes with affection and showered them with honors and gifts, among which figured in a significant manner "the paintings of Tulán in which they put their histories."

The Guatemalan documents enumerate the tribes which arrived together in the interior of the country. The *Popol Vuh* mentions the three branches of the Quiché family, the Cavec, the Nimhaib, and the Ahau-Quiché; the tribe of Tamub and Ilocab, the thirteen tribes of Tecpán, those of Rabinal, the Cakchiquel, those of Tziquinahá, of Sacahá, of Lamac, of Cumatz, of Tuhalhá, of Uchabahá, of Chumilahá, of Quibahá, of Batenab, of Acul Vinac, of Balamihá, of Canchahel, and of Balam-Colob. These were only the principal tribes, according to the Quiché book; after leaving Tulán, the language of the different tribes had been altered, and from then on, the supremacy of the Quiché had been established after they had received the insignia and title of sovereignty. The *Memorial Cakchiquel* contains a long list of the places and tribes, with which we need not concern ourselves at this time. The geographical names which this document gives guide the reader who desires to follow the Cakchiquel in their wanderings to the east and north of the present territory of the Quiché.

It is a common characteristic, both in the Guatemalan and

Mexican documents, to find constant communication going on between mankind and the gods, who advised men and stimulated them to go farther on in their wandering. The Quiché, as well as the Tolteca, chose their priests as chiefs "who were the sages and soothsayers, who knew incantations," as Sahagún says. The close relation between the Quiché and the Tolteca goes much further, because, according to the *Popol Vuh*, the sacrificers who accompanied the tribes were Yaqui, or Mexicans.

Their wanderings through the woods, rivers, and mountains were not easy in that remote time, and the problem of feeding so many people must have been of continuous concern to the chiefs. The people suffered terrible hunger and at times, according to the documents, they were even forced to smell the points of their staffs in order to deceive their empty stomachs. A Quiché document says that the misery and the frightful hardships suffered by the pilgrims were principally due to the fact that they had lost the precious corn-seed which they had brought from Tulán, and that they only recovered it when they found three plants of this grain in a place called Pambilil, the kernels of which served them in planting their next harvest, "multiplying it from planting to planting, until the present century."[88]

Finally they arrived at the mountain called Chi-Pixab, or The Command or The Council. In Chi-Pixab all the tribes reunited and organized themselves under the different names which they chose. First there were the three branches of the Quiché; the Quiché proper, those of Tamub, and those of Ilocab. There they gave to the Cakchiquel their name (*Cakchequeleb*), which means "those from the red tree"; and in the same way names were given to those from Rabinal, another Quiché people, and to those from Tziquinahá, of the Zutuhil race. These were the most important groups of the tribes, who came to occupy the region.

After remaining for some time in Chi-Pixab, the Quiché received from their gods the order to take them to a secret place, in order to avoid their being exposed to attack from their enemies when day broke. The Quiché obeyed the order and moved their

[88] *MS Quiché de D. Francisco Calel Yzumpam*, 1561, extracted by Fuentes y Guzmán, *Recordación Florida* (1933 ed.), II, 391–92.

gods to the mountains, Avilix, Hacavitz, and Patohil, which lie to the north of the Quiché country, and on the second of these mountains, Hacavitz, they were reunited with the people of Rabinal, the Cakchiquel and the Zutuhil or Ah-Tziquinahá, in order to await the rising of the sun. Not far from Hacavitz were the tribes of Tamub, in a place called Amag-Tan, and the Ilocab in Uquincat. The Quiché priests, Balam-Quitzé, Balam-Acab, Mahucutah and Iqui-Balam, were found on Hacavitz, anxiously awaiting the rising of the sun; they did not sleep nor eat and their hearts were filled with sorrow. "If we lived in harmony in our country, why did we leave it?" they said to each other, in the midst of their sadness and affliction, and with mournful voices. "The gods are seated in the ravines, in the forests, they are among the air-plants, among the mosses; not even a seat of boards were they given."

But soon they were filled with joy again when they saw the Morning Star appear on the horizon, the brilliant Icoquih, the herald of the sun. Immediately they burned incense which they brought from the East and they danced, looking toward the place where the sun should appear. Finally, the sun arose "like a man" and lighted the world and dried the moisture from the earth. The men and the animals were filled with joy and the bird called Queletzú burst into song, its hymn of the glory of god which lights, heats, and fructifies the face of the earth. All the tribes, including the Yaqui-Tepeu, prostrated themselves and worshiped the sun. Nevertheless, in the midst of their joy the Quiché did not forget their brothers, those whom they had left behind in the country to the north. "We at last have seen the sun; but they, where are they, now that it has dawned?" So they spoke, remembering their brothers, the Yaqui, those of Tepeu and Olimán, to whom the dawn must have come there in the land of Mexico, "as now we call it," adds the book of the Quiché.

Located on the mountain Hacavitz, the Quiché dominated all the tribes and begat daughters and sons until they became very numerous. Balam-Quitzé, Balam-Acab, Mahucutah and Iqui-Balam were pleased with their work; but the time had come when they had to withdraw from this world, and they announced their

71

departure to their children. They gave them their last advice, gave them the symbol of the royal power, and disappeared from sight. A short time later, the heirs of the three royal families undertook a journey to the East, whence their parents had originally come, and there in the East, they received the investiture and insignia of royalty from the hands of Lord Nacxit.

Some time having passed, the princes returned to Hacavitz, where they were received with demonstrations of joy by their people, by those of Rabinal, the Cakchiquel and the Zutuhil. The population had increased and the lands which they occupied were not sufficient to support and feed them. For this reason they left their old lands and began anew to wander to other places, the names of which are given in the *Título de los Señores de Totonicapán*, until they finally came to Chi-Quix (among the thorns), where they remained for some time, extending their occupation of the country to the neighboring places of Chichac, Humetahá, and Culba-Cavinal. From there, the *Popol Vuh* adds, they watched the mountains, looking for uninhabited mountains, because they were now very numerous. This information is most interesting, because it shows that at least part of the territory had been occupied before the arrival of the Quiché. The inhabitants of the mountains were doubtless the descendants of the Maya of the Old Empire who had located in the highlands, after the ruin of the large cities of the valleys of the Motagua River and of the Petén.

The fourth generation of kings governed when the Quiché founded the city at Izmachí. There they erected houses of stone and built a magnificent city, says the text. However, the aggrandizement of the three royal houses of Cavec, Nihaib, and Ahau Quiché provoked the jealousy of the Tamub and the Ilocab, who decided to kill their three kings and annihilate the Quiché nation; but having failed in their attempt, those of these tribes were sacrificed in great numbers, or reduced to slavery. Their failure, on the contrary, resulted in consolidating the power of the Quiché. The place of Izmachí, not being sufficient to support the increasing population, the Quiché decided to move their capital again, and established it at Gumarcaah, which the Mexicans called Utatlán (place of reeds), and which was the last capital of the

Quiché kings. This happened under Kings Cotuhá and Gucumatz, princes of the fifth generation, who began the expansion of the kingdom, extending its frontiers to the sea and occupying the distant lands which they seized from their lords and owners. But now we are already on solid historical ground.

The new capital developed rapidly and became the metropolis of a great empire. Under the government of Quicab, the Quiché kingdom carried its conquests as far as the mountains of the Mam, on the Pacific Coast as far southwest as Soconusco, the lands of the Cakchiquel and the Zutuhil, and north to the borders of Petén. In the capital, beautified by works of art, they raised the temples of their gods and the twenty-four palaces of their nobility, and the teeming population overflowed the wide plains and ravines which surrounded the city. All the other nations which had been conquered and subdued by Quicab had to pay tribute. The Quiché for many years received a tremendous tribute from the neighboring peoples, who, without question, recognized the political hegemony of the Quiché. The Quiché star, however, had declined by the end of the fifteenth century, after disastrous wars which weakened, equally, all the people of Guatemala; but when the Spanish hosts appeared on the frontiers of the empires bent upon conquest, the Quiché did not hesitate to throw themselves into the struggle, and marched out courageously to fulfill their destiny.

In the last chapter of this work the author lists the generations and successions of the Quiché kings and lords, beginning with the founders of the dynasties, Balam-Quitzé, Balam-Acab, Mahucutah, and Iqui-Balam, who came together and governed jointly. The generations of kings, from these founders down to those who, with a mere shadow of their ancient power, held the title of such under the Spaniards, numbered fourteen. Ximénez calculates that the succession of the kings in Quiché history occupied a period of 480 years, and in this way he fixes the beginning of the kingdom as in the year 1054.[89] To arrive at this result, Ximénez counted the duration of each generation of kings as forty years. This calculation, at first glance, seems somewhat high, but there are at least

[89] *Historia de la Provincia de San Vicente de Chiapa y Guatemala*, I, 71.

two factors, which certainly our priest-historian seems not to have noticed, that must be taken into account: first, with the exception of what he says about the three first kings, the *Popol Vuh* presents as a single generation not only the ruling monarch or Ahau-Ahpop, but also his assistant the Ahpop Camhá, who was destined to succeed him and who exercised the command until he died; the Ahpop Camhá was usually the oldest son of the monarch and for that reason much younger than the Ahpop himself, so that the period of government of forty years mentioned— twenty years for each one—does not appear excessive; and second, according to the explanation given in the *Título de los Señores de Totonicapán*, the succession of Balam-Quitzé by Qocavib, or from the first to the second generation which the *Popol Vuh* describes, was not direct, but Balam-Quitzé begat Qotzahá, Qotzahá begat Tziquín, and the latter begat Ahcán, and finally Ahcán begat Qocaib and Qocavib. The first of these two brothers made the journey to the East in order to receive his investiture from the hands of Lord Nacxit; nevertheless, his name does not appear in the list of the reigning princes. His younger brother, Qocavib, figures as the immediate successor of Balam-Quitzé, and, as has been previously pointed out, between him and his distant ancestor much time must have elapsed, more than a century if the information contained in the *Título* is correct, or forty years according to the data of the *Popol Vuh* and the count of Ximénez.

The calculation of the Spanish chronicler, which fixes the beginning of the Quiché dynasty at 1054, is near enough to the calculations which I have made in respect to the coming of the tribes from the Laguna de Términos, in the time of the foundation of the cities of the Maya New Empire of Yucatán (end of the tenth century), leaving a reasonable margin for the long wanderings of the tribes and their continuous stops before their arrival at their final destination. It must be noticed, furthermore, that it is not necessary to suppose that the leaders of the peoples from their arrival at Tulán were the same as those who began the historical period, but that their names and titles may well have been adopted and continued by other chiefs, who succeeded them and assumed the leadership of the vital mission of guiding the wanderers through the dangers and hazards of the way. "The sons of Balam-Quitzé ... took the names of their fathers," says the *Título de Totonicapán*.

This, in short, is the history which the pages of this book contain, written with ingenuity and simplicity by a representative of the Quiché race. To our great good fortune, that intelligent and warlike people have left us, in this valuable manuscript, a true picture of their high culture. This manuscript is, without doubt, the most vigorous, literary, and significant effort achieved by the American Indian in the fields of mythology and history.

It is fair to devote a final word to the Quiché language in which this book is written. Father Ximénez, who translated it for the first time into Spanish at the beginning of the eighteenth century, maintains that the Quiché language is the principal one in all the world. Without entirely sharing the enthusiastic opinion of the venerable historian and eminent linguist, I must observe that only a highly developed language, possessed of a rich vocabulary and a highly flexible syntax which lends itself to clarity and elegance of style and fluency in narration, could serve as an instrument for composing this work, which has the interest and beauty of a novel and the austerity of history, and which paints in brightest colors the life and thoughts of a great people.

*Courtesy Newberry Library*

First page of the original Ximénez manuscript of the *Popol Vuh*

# PREAMBLE

T his is the beginning of the old traditions of this place called Quiché.[1] Here we shall write and we shall begin the old stories,[2] the beginning and the origin of all that was done in the town of the Quiché, by the tribes of the Quiché nation.

[1] *Aré u xe oher tzih varal Quiché u bi.* At the very beginning of the ancient chronicles of the Quiché race and in the following words, the unknown author of this manuscript gives the name *Quiché* to the country: *varal Quiché u bi;* to the city, *Quiché tinamit;* and to the tribes of the nation, *r'amag Quiché vinac.* The word *quiché, queché,* or *quechelah* means "forest" in many of the Indian dialects of Guatemala, and comes from *qui, quiy,* "many," and *che,* "tree," an original Maya word. Quiché, "land of many trees," "covered with forests," was the name of the most powerful nation of the interior of Guatemala in the sixteenth century. The Náhuatl word *Quauhtlemallan* has the same meaning, which is probably a direct translation of the Quiché name and aptly describes the mountainous, fertile country which lies south of Mexico. Without doubt the Aztec name *Quauhtlemallan,* from which the modern name of Guatemala is derived, was applied to the entire country and not only to the capital of the Cakchiquel, Iximché (the tree now called breadnut in English), which the Tlaxcalteca, who arrived with Alvarado, called Tecpán-Quauhtlemallan. All this territory situated to the south of Yucatán and the Petén-Itzá region was known since before the Spanish Conquest as Quauhtlemallan and Tecolotlán (the Verapaz of today). Sahagún is very explicit when he says (*Historia general de las cosas de Nueva España* [1938 ed.] Book X, Chap. XXIX) that the first inhabitants of New Spain landed in Panutla (Pánuco) and traveled along the seacoast looking toward the snow-covered mountains and volcanoes until they came to the province of Guatemala.

[2] *Varal x-chi ca tzibah vi, x-chi ca tiquiba-vi oher tzih,* in the original. In order to write the ancient chronicles about the origin and development of the Quiché nation, the author probably made use not only of oral traditions, but also of the ancient paintings or picture-writings. Sahagún says that the Toltec

77

And here we shall set forth the revelation, the declaration, and the narration of all that was hidden, the revelation by Tzacol, Bitol, Alom, Qaholom, who are called Hunahpú-Vuch, Hunahpú-Utiú, Zaqui-Nimá-Tziís, Tepeu, Gucumatz, u Qux cho, u Qux Paló, Ah Raxá Lac, Ah Raxá Tzel, as they were called.[3] And [at

priests as they journeyed toward the East (Yucatán) took with them "all their paintings in which they had all the things of ancient times and of the arts and crafts." In Chapter 5 of Part IV of this book one reads that Lord Nacxit (Quetzalcoatl) gave to the Quiché princes, among other things, "the paintings of Tulán [*u tzibal Tulán*], the paintings as those were called in which they put their chronicles."

[3] These are the names of the divinity, arranged in pairs of creators in accord with the dual conception of the Quiché: Tzacol and Bitol, Creator and Maker. *Alom,* the mother god, she who conceived the sons, from *al,* "son," *alán,* "to give birth." *Qaholom,* the father god who begat the sons, from *qahol,* "son of the father," *qaholah,* "to beget." Ximénez calls them Mother and Father; they are the Great Father and the Great Mother, so called by the Indians, according to Las Casas; and they were in heaven.

*Hunahpú-Vuch,* a hunting-fox bitch, or *tacuazín* (opossum), god of the dawn; *vuch* is the moment which precedes dawn, *Hunahpú-Vuch* is the divinity in the feminine capacity, according to Seler. *Hunahpú-Utiú,* a hunting coyote, a variety of wolf (*canis latrans*), god of the night, is the name in the masculine capacity.

*Zaqui-Nimá-Tziís,* great white *coati mundi* (*Nasua nasica*), gray with age, mother of god; and her consort, *Nim-Ac,* great wild pig, or wild boar, wanting in this passage through unintentional omission, but given in the following chapter.

*Tepeu,* "king" or "sovereign," from the Náhuatl *Tepeuh, tepeuani,* which Molina translates as "conqueror" or "vanquisher in battle"; the Maya form is *ah tepehual,* and was probably taken from the Mexicans. Gucumatz, a serpent covered with green feathers, from the Quiché word *guc* (*kuk* in Maya), "green feathers," particularly those of the quetzal, and *cumatz,* serpent; it is the Quiché version of Kukulcán, the Maya name for Quetzalcoatl, the Toltec king, conqueror, culture hero, and god of Yucatán during the period of the Maya New Empire. The profound Mexican influence in the religion of the Quiché is reflected in this Creator-couple who continue to be invoked throughout the book until the divinity took the bodily form of Tohil, who in Part III is specifically identified with Quetzalcoatl.

*U Qux Cho,* the heart, or the spirit of the lake. *U Qux Paló,* the heart or spirit of the sea. As will be seen, the divinity was also called the Heart of Heaven, *u Qux Cah;*

*Ah Raxá Lac,* the Lord of the Green Plate, or the earth; *Ah Raxá Tzel,* the Lord of the Green Gourd or of the blue bowl, as Ximénez says, meaning the sky.

The name Hunahpú has been the subject of many interpretations. Literally it means a "hunter with a blowgun," a "shooter"; etymologically it is the same,

the same time] the declaration, the combined narration of the Grandmother and the Grandfather, whose names are Xpiyacoc, and Xmucané,[4] helpers and protectors, twice grandmother, twice grandfather, so called in the Quiché chronicles. Then we shall tell all that they did in the light of existence, in the light of history.[5]

This we shall write now under the Law of God and Christianity; we shall bring it to light because now the *Popol Vuh*, as it is called,[6] cannot be seen any more, in which was clearly seen the

and is a word of the Maya tongue, *ahpú* in Maya meaning "hunter," and *ah ppuh ob*, the plural form, the "hunters," who go forth to the chase, according to the *Diccionario de Motul*. It is evident, nevertheless, that the Quiché had to have some more plausible reason than this particular etymology for giving the name to their principal divinity. The hunter in primitive times was a very important personage; the people lived by the products of the chase and the wild fruits of the earth before the beginning of agriculture. Hunahpú would be, consequently, the universal hunter who provided man with food; *hun* in Maya also has the meaning of "general" and "universal." But possibly the Quiché who descended directly from the Maya, wished to reproduce, in the name Hunahpú, the sound of the Maya words *Hunab Ku*, "the only god," which they used to designate the principal god of the Maya pantheon, and which could not be represented materially since he was incorporeal. The painting of a hunter might have served in ancient times to represent the sound of Hunab Ku, which contained the abstract idea of a spiritual and divine being. The procedure is common in pre-Columbian pictographic writing. Hunahpú is also the name of the twentieth day of the Quiché calendar, the day most venerated by the ancients; it is equivalent to the Maya *Ahau*, "lord" or "chief," and to the Náhuatl *Xóchitl*, "flower" and "sun," symbol of the sun god or Tonatiuh.

[4] Xpiyacoc and Xmucané, the old man and the old woman (in Maya, *xnuc* is "old woman"), equivalents of the Mexican gods Cipactonal and Oxomoco, the sages who, according to the Toltec legend, invented their astrology and arranged the counting of time, that is, the calendar. Although in the Quiché legend there was also the other abstract pair previously mentioned, Xpiyacoc and, above all, his consort Xmucané, this pair had a more direct contact with the things of this world; together they were what the Mexican archaeologist Enrique Juan Palacios calls "the active Creator-couple who are directly concerned with the making of material things."

[5] *Ta x-qui tzihoh ronohel ruq x-qui ban chic chi zaquil qolem, zaquil tzih.*

[6] *Popo Vuh*, or *Popol Vuh*, literally the "Book of the Community." The word *popol* is Maya and means "together," "reunion," or "common house." *Popol na* is the "house of the community where they assemble to discuss things of the republic," says the *Diccionario de Motul*. *Pop* is a Quiché verb which means "to gather," "to join," "to crowd," according to Ximénez; and *popol* is a thing belonging to the municipal council, "communal," or "national." For this reason Ximénez interprets *Popol Vuh* as Book of the Community or of the

coming from the other side of the sea and the narration of our obscurity, and our life was clearly seen.[7] The original book, written long ago, existed, but its sight is hidden to the searcher and to the thinker. Great were the descriptions and the account of how all the sky and earth were formed, how it was formed and divided into four parts; how it was partitioned, and how the sky was divided; and the measuring-cord was brought, and it was stretched in the sky and over the earth, on the four angles, on the four corners,[8] as was told by the Creator and the Maker, the Mother and the Father of Life,[9] of all created things, he who gives breath and thought, she who gives birth to the children, he who watches over the happiness of the people, the happiness of the human race, the wise man, he who meditates on the goodness of all that exists in the sky, on the earth, in the lakes and in the sea.

---

Council. *Vuh* or *uúh* is "book," "paper," or "rag" and is derived from the Maya *húun* or *úun*, which means at the same time both paper and book, and finally the tree, the bark of which was used in making paper in ancient times, and which the Nahua call *amatl*, commonly known in Guatemala as *amatle* (*Ficus cotinifolia*). Note that in many words the *n* from the Maya is changed to *j* or *h* in Quiché. *Na*, "house" in Maya, is changed to *ha*, or *ja*; *húun* or *úun*, "book" in Maya, becomes *vuh* or *úuh* in Quiché.

[7] *Ilbal zac petenac chacá paló, u tzihoxic ca muhibal, ilbal zac qazlem.* Brasseur de Bourbourg enclosed the last seven words in quotation marks, but in the original these marks do not appear.

[8] *Cah tzuc, cah xucut*, in the original. The four cardinal points, according to Brasseur de Bourbourg. It is the same idea of the four *Bacabs* which in Maya mythology support the sky.

[9] When the *Popol Vuh* enumerates persons of the two sexes, it will be observed that it gallantly mentions the woman first.

# PART I

This is the account of how all was in suspense, all calm, in silence; all motionless, still, and the expanse of the sky was empty.

This is the first account, the first narrative. There was neither man, nor animal, birds, fishes, crabs, trees, stones, caves, ravines, grasses, nor forests; there was only the sky.

The surface of the earth had not appeared. There was only the calm sea and the great expanse of the sky.

There was nothing brought together, nothing which could make a noise, nor anything which might move, or tremble, or could make noise in the sky.

There was nothing standing; only the calm water, the placid sea, alone and tranquil. Nothing existed.

There was only immobility and silence in the darkness, in the night. Only the Creator, the Maker, Tepeu, Gucumatz, the Fore-fathers,[1] were in the water surrounded with light.[2] They were hidden under green and blue feathers, and were therefore called

---

[1] *E Alom*, literally, those who conceive and give birth, *e Qaholom*, those who beget the children. In order to follow the conciseness of the text here I translate the two terms as the "Forefathers."

[2] They were in the water because the Quiché associated the name Gucumatz with the liquid element. Bishop Núñez de la Vega says that Gucumatz is a serpent with feathers, which moves in the water. The Cakchiquel Manuscript says that one of the primitive peoples which migrated to Guatemala was called Gucumatz because their salvation was in the water.

Gucumatz.[3] By nature they were great sages and great thinkers.[4] In this manner the sky existed and also the Heart of Heaven, which is the name of God and thus He is called.

Then came the word. Tepeu and Gucumatz came together in the darkness, in the night, and Tepeu and Gucumatz talked together.[5] They talked then, discussing and deliberating; they agreed, they united their words and their thoughts.

Then while they meditated, it became clear to them that when dawn would break, man must appear.[6] Then they planned the creation, and the growth of the trees and the thickets and the birth of life and the creation of man. Thus it was arranged in the darkness and in the night by the Heart of Heaven who is called Huracán.

The first is called Caculhá Huracán. The second is Chipi-Caculhá. The third is Raxa-Caculhá. And these three are the Heart of Heaven.[7]

[3] *E qo vi e mucutal pa guc pa raxón. Guc* or *q'uc, kuk* in Maya, is the bird now called quetzal (*Pharomacrus mocinno*); the same name is given to the beautiful green feathers which cover this bird's tail; in Náhuatl they are called *quetzalli. Raxón*, or *raxom*, is another bird with sky-blue plumage, according to Basseta; it is a bird with "chestnut-colored breast and blue wings," according to the *Vocabulario de los Padres Franciscanos*. In the common native language of Guatemala it is called *ranchón*, the *Cotinga amabilis*, a turquoise blue bird with purple breast and throat, which the Mexicans call *Xiuhtototl*. The feathers of these tropical birds, which abound especially in the region of Verapaz, were worn as decorations in the ceremonials by the kings and noblemen from the most ancient Maya times.

[4] *E nimac etamanel, e nimac ahnaoh*, in the original.

[5] *X chau ruq ri Tepeu, Gucumatz*. Here the word *ruq* indicates the reciprocal form of the verb.

[6] *Ta x-calah puch vinac*. With the conciseness of the Quiché language, the author says how the idea was clearly born in the minds of the Makers, how the necessity for creating man, the ultimate and supreme being of the creation, was revealed to them, according to the philosophy of the Quiché. Brasseur de Bourbourg interprets this phrase as follows: "*et au moment de l'aurore, l'homme se manifesta.*" This interpretation is erroneous; the idea of creating man was conceived then, but as will be seen farther on in the account, it was not actually carried out until a much later time.

[7] *Huracán*, a leg; *Caculhá Huracán*, flash of a leg or the lightning; *Chipi-Caculhá*, small flash. This is Ximénez' interpretation. The third, *Raxa-Caculhá*, is the green flash, according to the same author; and, according to Brasseur de Bourbourg, it is the lightning or thunder. The adjective *rax* has, among other

Then Tepeu and Gucumatz came together; then they conferred about life and light, what they would do so that there would be light and dawn,[8] who it would be who would provide food and sustenance.

Thus let it be done! Let the emptiness be filled![9] Let the water recede and make a void, let the earth appear and become solid; let it be done. Thus they spoke. Let there be light, let there be dawn in the sky and on the earth! There shall be neither glory nor grandeur in our creation and formation until the human being is made, man is formed. So they spoke.

Then the earth was created by them. So it was, in truth, that they created the earth. Earth! they said, and instantly it was made.

Like the mist, like a cloud, and like a cloud of dust was the creation, when the mountains appeared from the water;[10] and instantly the mountains grew.

Only by a miracle, only by magic art were the mountains and

meanings, that of "sudden" or "instantly." In Cakchiquel *Raxhaná-hih* is lightning. Nevertheless, despite all this, in both Quiché and Cakchiquel, *racan* means "large" or "long." According to Father Coto, it means a long thing, rope, etc. And also giant (*hu racán*), "a name which applies to every animal which is larger than others of its species," Father Coto adds. These ideas agree with the form of the flash and the lightning as it is drawn in the sky. The Caribs of the West Indies adopted the name *huracán* to designate other natural phenomena equally destructive, and the word was later incorporated into modern languages. See Brinton, *Essays of an Americanist.*

[8] *Hupachá ta ch'auax-oc, ta zaquiró puch.* Here and in other places in this book, Ximénez and Brasseur de Bourbourg confuse the form of the Quiché verb *auax, auaxic,* which corresponds to the verb and substantive "dawn," with *auan,* "plant," and *auix,* the "cornfield." The Maya language has the word *ahalcab* which means "dawn," "break of day," and *ahan cab,* "it has already dawned," from *ahal,* "awaken." In olden times the two verbs "to sow" and "to dawn" were also very similar in Maya. According to the *Diccionario de la lengua maya* by José Pío Pérez, *oc cah* is to sow grain or seed, and *ah cah cab,* to dawn, to make light. It is curious to observe that the Maya cognate was preserved in the ancient Quiché; and it seems probable that these analogous forms in the Maya and the Quiché had a common root.

[9] *Qu'yx nohin-tah.*

[10] *X-ta pe pa ha ri huyub,* the mountains came, or emerged from the water. The similarity of the words *x-ta pe* with *tap,* "crab," suggested to Ximénez the comparison of the mountains with the crab. Brasseur de Bourbourg followed him in this. Nevertheless, the sentence could not be clearer.

valleys formed; and instantly the groves of cypresses and pines put forth shoots together on the surface of the earth.[11]

And thus Gucumatz was filled with joy, and exclaimed: "Your coming has been fruitful, Heart of Heaven; and you, Huracán, and you, Chipi-Caculhá, Raxa-Caculhá!"

"Our work, our creation shall be finished," they answered.

First the earth was formed, the mountains and the valleys; the currents of water were divided, the rivulets were running freely between the hills, and the water was separated when the high mountains appeared.

Thus was the earth created, when it was formed by the Heart of Heaven, the Heart of Earth, as they are called who first made it fruitful, when the sky was in suspense, and the earth was submerged in the water.

So it was that they made perfect the work, when they did it after thinking and meditating upon it.

CHAPTER 2

Then they made the small wild animals, the guardians of the woods, the spirits of the mountains,[1] the deer, the birds, pumas, jaguars, serpents, snakes, vipers, guardians of the thickets.

And the Forefathers asked: "Shall there be only silence and calm under the trees, under the vines? It is well that hereafter there be someone to guard them."

[11] *Xaqui naual, xaqui puz x-banatah vi*. The expression *puz naual* is used to indicate the magic power to create or transform one thing into another. *Puz naual haleb*, says Father Barela, was the sorcery used by the Indians to transform themselves into balls of fire, eagles, and animals.

[1] *U vinaquil huyub*, literally, "the little man of the forest." The Indians in ancient times believed that the forests were peopled with these little beings, guardians, spirits of the forests, a species of hobgoblin similar to the *alux* of the Maya. The *Memorial Cakchiquel* calls them *ru vinakil chee*, from *che*, "tree," which Father Coto translates as "the hobgoblin which walks in the mountains," and by another name, the Zakikoxol. According to the *Memorial*, the ancient Cakchiquel used to speak with these little men who were the spirits of the volcano of Fuego, *ru cux huyu chi Gag*, called Zakikoxol.

So they said when they meditated and talked. Promptly the deer and the birds were created. Immediately they gave homes to the deer and the birds. "You, deer, shall sleep in the fields by the river bank and in the ravines. Here you shall be amongst the thicket, amongst the pasture; in the woods you shall multiply, you shall walk on four feet and they will support you. Thus be it done!" So it was they spoke.

Then they also assigned homes to the birds big and small. "You shall live in the trees and in the vines. There you shall make your nests; there you shall multiply; there you shall increase in the branches of the trees and in the vines." Thus the deer and the birds were told; they did their duty at once, and all sought their homes and their nests.

And the creation of all the four-footed animals and the birds being finished, they were told by the Creator and the Maker and the Forefathers: "Speak, cry, warble, call, speak each one according to your variety, each, according to your kind." So was it said to the deer, the birds, pumas, jaguars, and serpents.

"Speak, then, our names, praise us, your mother, your father. Invoke then, Huracán, Chipi-Caculhá, Raxa-Caculhá, the Heart of Heaven, the Heart of Earth, the Creator, the Maker, the Forefathers; speak, invoke us, adore us," they were told.

But they could not make them speak like men; they only hissed and screamed and cackled; they were unable to make words, and each screamed in a different way.

When the Creator and the Maker saw that it was impossible for them to talk to each other, they said: "It is impossible for them to say our names, the names of us, their Creators and Makers. This is not well," said the Forefathers to each other.

Then they said to them: "Because it has not been possible for you to talk, you shall be changed. We have changed our minds: Your food, your pasture, your homes, and your nests you shall have; they shall be the ravines and the woods, because it has not been possible for you to adore us or invoke us. There shall be those who adore us, we shall make other [beings] who shall be obedient. Accept your destiny: your flesh shall be torn to pieces. So shall it be. This shall be your lot." So they said, when they made known their will to the large and small animals which are on the face of the earth.

They wished to give them another trial;[2] they wished to make another attempt; they wished to make [all living things] adore them.

But they could not understand each other's speech; they could succeed in nothing, and could do nothing. For this reason they were sacrificed, and the animals which were on earth were condemned to be killed and eaten.

For this reason another attempt had to be made to create and make men by the Creator, the Maker, and the Forefathers.

"Let us try again! Already dawn draws near:[3] Let us make him who shall nourish and sustain us! What shall we do to be invoked, in order to be remembered on earth? We have already tried with our first creations, our first creatures; but we could not make them praise and venerate us.[4] So, then, let us try to make obedient, respectful beings who will nourish and sustain us." Thus they spoke.

Then was the creation and the formation. Of earth, of mud, they made [man's] flesh. But they saw that it was not good. It melted away, it was soft, did not move, had no strength, it fell down, it was limp, it could not move its head, its face fell to one side, its sight was blurred,[5] it could not look behind. At first it spoke, but had no mind. Quickly it soaked in the water and could not stand.

And the Creator and the Maker said:[6] "Let us try again because our creatures will not be able to walk nor multiply. Let us consider this," they said.

Then they broke up and destroyed their work and their crea-

---

[2] *Ta x-r'ah cu qui tih chic qui quih* in the original.

[3] *Mi x-yopih r'auaxic u zaquiric.* "Already the time of planting nears" is the meaning which Brasseur de Bourbourg incorrectly gives to this sentence, getting ahead of events, because man had not yet been created, nor had agriculture yet been practiced.

[4] *Mavi mi x-utzinic ca quihiloxic, ca calaixic puch cumal,* in the original text.

[5] *Xa cul u vach.*

[6] *Ahtzac, Ahbit,* variants of *Tzacol* and *Bitol.*

tion. And they said: "What shall we do to perfect it, in order that our worshipers, our invokers, will be successful?"

Thus they spoke when they conferred again: "Let us say again to Xpiyacoc, Xmucané, Hunahpú-Vuch, Hunahpú-Utiú: 'Cast your lot again. Try to create again.'" In this manner the Creator and the Maker spoke to Xpiyacoc and Xmucané.

Then they spoke to those soothsayers, the Grandmother of the day, the Grandmother of the Dawn,[7] as they were called by the Creator and the Maker, and whose names were Xpiyacoc and Xmucané.

And said Huracán, Tepeu, and Gucumatz when they spoke to the soothsayer, to the Maker, who are the diviners: "You must work together and find the means so that man, whom we shall make, man, whom we are going to make, will nourish and sustain us, invoke and remember us."

"Enter, then, into council, grandmother, grandfather, our grandmother, our grandfather, Xpiyacoc, Xmucané, make light, make dawn, have us invoked, have us adored, have us remembered by created man, by made man, by mortal man.[8] Thus be it done.

"Let your nature be known, Hunahpú-Vuch, Hunahpú-Utiú, twice mother, twice father,[9] Nim-Ac,[10] Nima-Tziís,[11] the master of emeralds, the worker in jewels, the sculptor, the carver, the maker of beautiful plates, the maker of green gourds, the master

[7] *R' atit quih, R'atit zac.* The word *atit* may be taken here in the collective sense, including the two grandparents Xpiyacoc and Xmucané, who are later called by their names in the text. The same expression is found farther on.

[8] *Vinac poy, vinac anom. Poy anom,* in Cakchiquel, has the meaning of "the mortal."

[9] *Camul Alom, camul Qaholom.* The author calls Hunahpú-Vuch, "two times mother," and Hunahpú-Utiú, "two times father," thus giving the sex of each of the two members of the Creator-couple.

[10] Large wild boar, or wild pig. *Nim-Ac* is the father.

[11] *Nimá-Tziís,* the mother, large *pisote* or *coati mundi (Nasua nasica).* It might also be interpreted as large tapir *(Tix* in Poconchí, *tzimín* in Jacalteca). The tapir was the sacred animal of the Tzeltal Indians of Chiapas, and Bishop Núñez de la Vega says that, according to legend, Votán took a tapir to Huehuetlán, and that it multiplied in the waters of the river which runs through Soconusco, a district in the present state of Chiapas, Mexico.

of resin, the master Toltecat,[12] grandmother of the sun, grand-mother of dawn, as you will be called by our works and our creatures.

"Cast the lot with your grains of corn and the *tzité*[13] Do it thus,[14] and we shall know if we are to make, or carve his mouth and eyes out of wood." Thus the diviners were told.

They went down at once to make their divination, and cast their lots with the corn and the *tzité*. "Fate! Creature!"[15] said an old woman and an old man. And this old man was the one who cast the lots with Tzité, the one called Xpiyacoc.[16] And the old woman was the diviner, the maker, called Chiracán Xmucané.[17]

Beginning the divination, they said: "Get together, grasp each other! Speak, that we may hear." They said, "Say if it is well that the wood be got together and that it be carved by the Creator and the Maker, and if this [man of wood] is he who must nourish

---

[12] Here the text seems to enumerate the usual occupations of the men of that time. The author calls upon *ahqual*, who is evidently the one who carves emeralds or green stones; *ahyamanic*, the jeweler or silversmith; *ahchut*, engraver or sculptor; *ahtzalam*, carver or cabinetmaker; *ahraxalac*, he who fashions green or beautiful plates; *ahraxazel*, he who makes the beautiful green vases or gourds (called *Xicalli* in Náhuatl,)—the word *raxá* has both meanings; *ahgol*, he who makes the resin or copal; and, finally, *ahtoltecat*, he who, without doubt, was the silversmith. The Tolteca were in fact, skilled silversmiths who, according to the legend, were taught the art by Quetzalcoatl himself.

[13] *Erythrina corallodendron. Tzité, arbol de pito* in Guatemala; *Tzompan-quahuitl* in the Mexican language. It is used in both countries to make fences. Its fruit is a pod which contains red grains resembling a bean which the Indians used, as they still do, together with grains of corn, in their fortunetelling and witchcraft. In his *Informe contra Idolorum Cultores*, Sánchez de Aguilar says that the Maya Indians "cast lots with a large handful of corn." As is seen, the practice which is still observed by the Maya-Quiché is of respectable antiquity.

[14] *Chi banatahic xa pu ch'el apon-oc*, literally: "Do it so and it will be done."

[15] *Quih!, Bit!* The first word is "sun," and Brasseur de Bourbourg translates it as such, but it also means "fate," and this is evidently its meaning in this invocation.

[16] *Ah tzité*, he who tells the fortune by the grains of *tzité;* Basseta interprets the word as "sorcerer," who in this case, is Xpiyacoc.

[17] *Are curi atit ahquih, ahbit, Chiracan Xmucané u bi.* The *ahquih* was the priest and sorcerer, and these very respected officers are still so called in Quiché. *Ahbit* is the creator and maker. *Chiracán Xmucané* is the same as the Great Xmucané.

88

and sustain us when there is light when it is day!

"Thou, corn; thou, *tzité;* thou, fate; thou, creature; get together, take each other," they said to the corn, to the *tzité,* to fate, to the creature. "Come to sacrifice here, Heart of Heaven; do not punish Tepeu and Gucumatz!"[18]

Then they talked and spoke the truth: "Your figures of wood shall come out well; they shall speak and talk on earth."

"So may it be," they answered when they spoke.

And instantly the figures were made of wood. They looked like men, talked like men, and populated the surface of the earth.

They existed and multiplied; they had daughters, they had sons, these wooden figures; but they did not have souls, nor minds, they did not remember their Creator, their Maker; they walked on all fours, aimlessly.

They no longer remembered the Heart of Heaven and therefore they fell out of favor. It was merely a trial, an attempt at man. At first they spoke, but their face was without expression; their feet and hands had no strength; they had no blood, nor substance,[19] nor moisture, nor flesh; their cheeks were dry, their feet and hands were dry, and their flesh was yellow.

Therefore, they no longer thought of their Creator nor their Maker, nor of those who made them and cared for them.[20]

These were the first men who existed in great numbers on the face of the earth.

[18] *C'at quix la uloc, at u Qux cah, m'a cahizah u chi, u vach Tepeu, Gucumatz.* Here other translators have rendered the verb *quix* as "to shame." Brasseur de Bourbourg observes that it may also signify "to sting" or "take out blood" with a thorn. This was a common form of sacrifice among the Indians, and seems to indicate the real meaning of the sentence as used by the author. *Qahizan vach* is "to punish," according to the *Vocabulario de los Padres Franciscanos.* The entire passage is an invitation to the Heart of Heaven to come and take part in casting lots and not let the diviners fail.

[19] *Comahil,* "blood," substance of the person. Father Coto, *Vocabulario Cakchiquel.*

[20] *Alay quech, quxlaay quech.*

# I

mmediately the wooden figures were annihilated, destroyed, broken up, and killed.

A flood was brought about by the Heart of Heaven; a great flood was formed which fell on the heads of the wooden creatures.

Of *tzité*, the flesh of man was made, but when woman was fashioned by the Creator and the Maker, her flesh was made of rushes.[1] These were the materials the Creator and the Maker wanted to use in making them.

But those that they had made, that they had created, did not think, did not speak with their Creator, their Maker. And for this reason they were killed, they were deluged. A heavy resin fell from the sky. The one called Xecotcovach came and gouged out their eyes; Camalotz came and cut off their heads; Cotzbalam came and devoured their flesh. Tucumbalam[2] came, too, and broke and mangled their bones and their nerves, and ground and crumbled their bones.[3]

This was to punish them because they had not thought of their mother, nor their father, the Heart of Heaven, called Huracán. And for this reason the face of the earth was darkened and a black rain began to fall, by day and by night.

Then came the small animals and the large animals, and sticks

[1] The Quiché name *zibaque* is commonly used in Guatemala to designate this plant of the Typhaceae family, which is much used in making the mats called *petates tules* in that country. Basseta says it is the part of a reed with which mats are made.

[2] It is difficult to interpret the names of these enemies of man. Ximénez says that *Xecotcovach* was a bird, probably an eagle (*cot*) or sparrow hawk. The *Camalotz* which cut off men's heads was evidently the large vampire (*nimá chicop*) *Camazotz*, bat of death, which decapitated the young hero Hunahpú in Part II of the manuscript. *Cotzbalam* may be interpreted as the jaguar who lies in wait for his prey. *Tucumbalam* is another name for the danta or tapir. Seler (*Der Fledermausgott der Maya-Stämme*, Vol. II of *Gesammelte Abhand-lungen*) argues that these "wild animal demons of the *Popol Vuh*" are equivalent to the four monstrous figures which are seen in folio 44 of the *Codex Borgiano*. According to Seler, Tucumbalam is represented in that *Códice* as a species of shark or crocodile. The bat of the East had torn off the head of his neighbor in front of him, and the shark or crocodile of the West had torn off his foot.

[3] *X-cahixic, x-muchulixic qui baquil*, in the original.

and stones struck their faces. And all began to speak: their earthen jars,[4] their griddles,[5] their plates, their pots, their grinding stones,[6] all rose up and struck their faces.

"You have done us much harm; you ate us, and now we shall kill you," said their dogs and birds of the barnyard.[7]

And the grinding stones said: "We were tormented by you; every day, every day, at night, at dawn, all the time our faces went *holi, holi, huqui, huqui,* because of you.[8] This was the tribute we paid you. But now that you are no longer men, you shall feel our strength. We shall grind and tear your flesh to pieces," said their grinding stones.

And then their dogs spoke and said: "Why did you give us nothing to eat? You scarcely looked at us, but you chased us and threw us out. You always had a stick[9] ready to strike us while you were eating.

"Thus it was that you treated us. You did not speak to us. Perhaps we shall not kill you now; but why did you not look ahead, why did you not think about yourselves? Now we shall destroy you, now you shall feel the teeth of our mouths; we shall devour you," said the dogs, and then, they destroyed their faces.[10]

[4] *Quebal,* which Ximénez translates "grinding stones," is a water jug or pitcher here. Brasseur de Bourbourg translates it incorrectly as *tout ce qui leur avait servi.*

[5] *Comalli* in the Mexican language, *xot* in Quiché, a large plate or the disk of clay upon which the corn *tortillas* are baked.

[6] *Qui caa,* in the original, grinding stone, *metate* in Mexico. Brasseur de Bourbourg read it incorrectly as *qui aq y* and translated the passage "their hens."

[7] The dogs which the wooden men ate were not like those which are now in America, but a species which the Spanish chroniclers called "silent dogs," because they did not bark. The barnyard fowls were the turkey, the pheasant, and the wild hen.

[8] These words are merely an imitation of the noise made when the corn is being ground by the grinding stone.

[9] *Yacal u bi,* "leaning against the wall," or "lying on the ground," according to the *Diccionario Cakchiquel.*

[10] To understand this paragraph better, it is necessary to re-establish the original punctuation which Brasseur de Bourbourg has altered in his transcription, so that it will read as follows: *Xere c'oh yv-u chaah vi; mavi c'oh chauic. Ma ta cu mi-x-oh camic chyve. Hupacha mavi mi-x-yx nauic, x-yx nau ta cut-chyvih? Ta cut x-oh zach vi, vacamic cut x-ch'y tih ca bac qo pa ca chi; x-qu'yx ca tio, x-e cha ri tzi chique, ta x-cut qui vach.*

91

And at the same time, their griddles and pots spoke: "Pain and suffering you have caused us. Our mouths and our faces were blackened with soot; we were always put on the fire and you burned us as though we felt no pain. Now you shall feel it, we shall burn you," said their pots, and they all destroyed their [the wooden men's] faces. The stones of the hearth,[11] which were heaped together, hurled themselves straight from the fire against their heads causing them pain.[12]

The desperate ones [the men of wood] ran as quickly as they could; they wanted to climb to the tops of the houses, and the houses fell down and threw them to the ground; they wanted to climb to the treetops, and the trees cast them far away; they wanted to enter the caverns, and the caverns repelled them.[13]

So was the ruin of the men who had been created and formed, the men made to be destroyed and annihilated; the mouths and faces of all of them were mangled.

And it is said that their descendants are the monkeys which now live in the forests;[14] these are all that remain of them because their flesh was made only of wood by the Creator and the Maker.

And therefore the monkey looks like man, and is an example

[11] They are the three hearthstones of the Indians on which the *comal*, or the cooking pots, rested.

[12] The idea of a flood in olden times and the belief in another which would be the end of the world, and would have had characters similar to those described here in the *Popol Vuh*, still existed among the Indians of Guatemala in the years following the Spanish conquest, according to the *Apologética Historia* (Chap. CCXXXV, p. 620). Bishop Las Casas says in this work that "They had, among them, information of the flood and of the end of the world, and called it *Butic*, which is the word which means flood of many waters and means [the final] judgment, and so they believe that another *Butic* is about to come, which is another flood and judgment, not of water, but of fire, which they say would be the end of the world, in which all the creatures would have to quarrel, especially those which serve man, like the stones on which they grind their corn and wheat, the pots, the pitchers, giving to understand that they will turn against man."

[13] *Xa chi yuch hul chi qui vach*, literally, the caverns covered their faces, scorned them.

[14] According to the *Anales de Cuauhtitlán*, in the fourth age of the earth, "many people were drowned and others hurled into the mountains and were changed into monkeys."

of a generation of men which were created and made but were only wooden figures.

# CHAPTER 4

It was cloudy and twilight then on the face of the earth. There was no sun yet. Nevertheless, there was a being called Vucub-Caquix[1] who was very proud of himself.

The sky and the earth existed, but the faces of the sun and the moon were covered.

And he [Vucub-Caquix] said: "Truly, they are clear examples of those people who were drowned, and their nature is that of supernatural beings.[2]

"I shall now be great above all the beings created and formed. I am the sun, the light, the moon," he exclaimed. "Great is my splendor. Because of me men shall walk and conquer. For my eyes are of silver, bright, resplendent as precious stones, as emeralds; my teeth shine like perfect stones, like the face of the sky. My nose shines afar like the moon, my throne is of silver, and the face of the earth is lighted when I pass before my throne.

"So, then, I am the sun, I am the moon, for all mankind.[3] So shall it be, because I can see very far."

[1] *Vucub-Caquix*, that is to say, Seven Macaws. Ximénez believed he saw in this personage a kind of Lucifer. To Brasseur de Bourbourg he was a prince, perhaps the chief of a large part of Central America. It is hardly necessary to point out that this entire episode of Vucub-Caquix and his sons is wholly imaginary and has no relation to historical fact. The Quiché frequently used the number seven (*vucub*) in their own names, as is seen throughout this book.

[2] This seems to be an allusion to the flood which destroyed the wooden men. Farther on the narrator says that Vucub-Caquix existed at the time of the flood. The general idea among the Indians was that not all the primitive men perished during the flood. In the place cited in Chap. 3, n. 12, Bishop Las Casas says: "They believed that certain persons who escaped the flood populated their lands, and that they were called the great father and the great mother."

[3] *Quehecut in quih vi, in pu ic rumal zaquil al, zaquil qahol*. This passage presents much difficulty for the translator. The *Vocabulario de las lenguas Quiché y Kakchiquel* defines the words *zaquil al, zaquil qahol*, as it "shall be the human family." The meaning generally accepted is that of vassals or descendants.

So Vucub-Caquix spoke. But he was not really the sun; he was only vainglorious of his feathers and his riches. And he could see only as far as the horizon, and he could not see over all the world.

The face of the sun had not yet appeared, nor that of the moon, nor the stars, and it had not dawned. Therefore, Vucub-Caquix became as vain as though he were the sun and the moon, because the light of the sun and the moon had not yet shown itself. His only ambition was to exalt himself and to dominate. And all this happened when the flood came because of the wooden people.

Now we shall tell how Vucub-Caquix was overthrown and died, and how man was made by the Creator and the Maker.

CHAPTER 5

This is the beginning of the defeat and the ruin of the glory of Vucub-Caquix brought about by two youths, the first of whom was called Hunahpú and the second, Xbalanqué. They were really gods.[1] When they saw the harm which the arrogant one had done, and wished to do, in the presence of the Heart of Heaven, the youths said:

"It is not good that it be so, when man does not yet live here

[1] Hunahpú, a hunter; Xbalanqué, small jaguar, the prefix *ix* is the sign of the feminine and also of the diminutive. It may also be "little sorcerer," because *balam* has two meanings, "jaguar" and "sorcerer." *Xavi e qabauil*, "these were also gods," according to Ximénez' translation. The Spanish missionaries found among the Quiché the word *Qabauil*, or *cabauil*, with which they designated their gods, and they usually translated it as "idol" or "demon"; the missionaries tried to compel the Indians to forget it, together with all their ancient religion, and to use only the new Spanish word, God, to refer to the Christian divinity. The Franciscan friars in Yucatán used the same method with respect to the word *ku*, God, and *kauil*, a Maya adjective meaning "venerable," and one which almost always accompanies the name *Itzamná*, the sun, the principal god of the ancient Maya pantheon. In the early texts the name appears as Itzamná Kauil (*Chronicle of Chumayel*, Landa's *Relación*, etc.), In the *Relación* describing his two entrances into the Petén in 1695 and 1696, Father Avendaño says that he knew that among the gods which the Itzás had was "one, Itzamná Kauil, which means the Devil's horse." The similarity between the Maya term *kauil* and the Quiché *qabauil* suggests a very close relationship between them.

on earth. Therefore, we shall try to shoot him with our blowgun when he is eating. We shall shoot him and make him sicken, and then that will be the end of his riches, his green stones, his precious metals, his emeralds, his jewels of which he is so proud.[2] And this shall be the lot of all men, for they must not become vain, because of power and riches.

"Thus shall it be," said the youths, each one putting his blowgun to his shoulder.

Well, now Vucub-Caquix had two sons: the first was called Zipacná, the second was Cabracán; and the mother of the two was called Chimalmat,[3] the wife of Vucub-Caquix.

Well, Zipacná played ball with the large mountains: with Chigag,[4] Hunahpú,[5] Pecul,[6] Yaxcanul,[7] Macamob,[8] and Huliznab. These are the names of the mountains which existed when it dawned and which were created in a single night by Zipacná.

In this way, then, Cabracán moved the mountains and made the large and small mountains tremble.

And in this way the sons of Vucub-Caquix proclaimed their

[2] *Chi ca coh vi u yab, ta quiz-oc u quinomal, u xit, u puvac, u cual, u yamanic ri cu gagabeh*, in the original text.

[3] Zipacná, a giant who carried mountains on his back. His food consisted of fish and crabs. Cabracán, "double giant," "earthquake" in Quiché. The similarity between the names Chimalmat, the wife of Vucub-Caquix, and Chimalman, the mother of Quetzalcoatl, has been noted. It may be merely a coincidence, but it may also be due to the influence of the Mexican legend.

[4] Mouth of fire, *Chi Gag*, in the Cakchiquel Manuscript; the volcano of Fuego.

[5] Volcano of Agua. The *Vocabulario Cakchiquel* (No. 41, at the Bibliothéque Nationale of Paris) translates Hunahpú as "fragrant flower," *fleur odoriférante*, according to Raynaud. Father Vázquez, the Franciscan chronicler, calls it a small spray or bouquet of flowers. This interpretation is interesting because Hunahpú is the twentieth day of the Quiché and Cakchiquel calendars and corresponds to Xochitl, the twentieth day of the Mexican calendar, which also means flower.

[6] Volcano of Acatenango. The three volcanoes known under the names of Fuego, Agua, and Acatenango dominate the landscape of central Guatemala, and the valley in which the Spanish Colonial capital was located.

[7] Volcano of Santa María in the western part of the country. *Gagxanul* in Cakchiquel.

[8] Volcano of Cerro Quemado in Quezaltenango, according to Herman Prowe; volcano of Zunil in the same zone, according to Villacorta and Rodas.

pride. "Listen! I am the sun!," said Vucub-Caquix. "I am he who made the earth!" said Zipacná. "I am he who shook the sky and made the earth tremble!" said Cabracán. In this way the sons of Vucub-Caquix followed the example of their father's assumed greatness. And this seemed very evil to the youths. Neither our first mother nor our first father had yet been created.

Therefore, the deaths of Vucub-Caquix and his sons and their destruction was decided upon by the youths.

CHAPTER 6

Now we shall tell how the two youths shot their blowguns at Vucub-Caquix and how each one of those, who had become arrogant, was destroyed.

Vucub-Caquix had a large nantze tree[1] and he ate the fruit of it. Each day he went to the tree and climbed to the top. Hunahpú and Xbalanqué had seen that this fruit was his food. And they lay in ambush at the foot of the tree, hidden among the leaves. Vucub-Caquix came straight to his meal of nantzes.

Instantly he was injured by a discharge from Hun-Hunahpú's[2] blowgun which struck him squarely in the jaw, and screaming, he fell straight to earth from the treetop.

Hun-Hunahpú ran quickly to overpower him, but Vucub-Caquix seized his arm and wrenching it from him, bent it back to the shoulder. In this way Vucub-Caquix tore out Hun-Hunahpú's arm. Surely the two youths did well in not letting themselves be defeated first by Vucub-Caquix.

Carrying Hun-Hunahpú's arm, Vucub-Caquix went home, and arrived there nursing his jaw.

"What has happened to you, my lord?" said Chimalmat, his wife.

---

[1] *Byrsonima Cotinifolia, B. crassifolia,* a beautiful tropical tree which produces a very aromatic fruit similar to the white cherry.

[2] Hun-Hunahpú appears in this passage instead of the usual Hun-Ahpú, an error which is corrected in the course of the narration.

"What could it be, but those two demons who shot me with blowguns and dislocated my jaw? For that reason my teeth are loose and pain me very much. But I have brought it [his arm], to put it on the fire. Let it hang there over the fire, for surely these demons will come looking for it." So said Vucub-Caquix as he hung up the arm of Hun-Hunahpú.

Having thought it over, Hun-Hunahpú and Xbalanqué went to talk with an old man who had snow-white hair and with an old woman, really very old and humble, both already bent, like very old people. The old man was called Zaqui-Nim-Ac and the old woman, Zaqui-Nima-Tziis.[3] The youths said to the old woman and the old man:

"Come with us to Vucub-Caquix's house to get our arm. We will follow you, and you shall tell them: 'These with us are our grandchildren; their mother and father are dead; so they follow us everywhere we are given alms, for the only thing that we know how to do is take the worm from the teeth.'[4]

"So Vucub-Caquix shall think we are boys and we shall also be there to advise you," said the two youths.

"Very well," answered the old man and woman.

Then they started out for the place where they found Vucub-Caquix reclining on his throne. The old woman and man walked along followed by the two boys, who stayed behind them. In this way they arrived at the house of the lord who was screaming because his tooth pained him.

When Vucub-Caquix saw the old man and the old woman and those who accompanied them, he asked, "Where do you come from, grandparents?"

"We come looking for something to eat, honorable sir," they answered.

"And what do you eat? Are those not your sons who are with you?"

---

[3] Zaqui-Nim-Ac, the Great White Wild Boar; Zaqui-Nimá-Tziís, the Great White *Coati*. The old man and the old woman represent the Creator-couple who, under different names, appear throughout the first part of these chronicles.

[4] It is a common belief among the Indians of Guatemala that toothache is caused by a worm which gets inside the tooth and produces pain and discomfort.

"Oh, no, sir! They are our grandsons; but we are sorry for
them and what is given to us, we share with them, sir," answered
the old woman and the old man.

Meanwhile, the lord was suffering terrible pain from his
tooth, and it was only with great difficulty that he could speak.

"I earnestly beseech you to have pity on me. What can you
do? What do you know how to cure?" the lord asked them.

And the old ones answered, "Oh, sir! we only take the worm
from the teeth, cure the eyes, and set bones."

"Very well. Cure my teeth, which are really making me
suffer day and night, and because of them and of my eyes I cannot
be calm and cannot sleep. All of this is because two demons shot
me with a pellet [from their blowgun] and for that reason I cannot eat. Have pity on me, then, tighten my teeth with your hands."

"Very well, sir. It is a worm which makes you suffer. It will
end when these teeth are pulled and others put in their place."

"It is not well that you pull my teeth, because it is only with
them that I am a lord and all my ornaments are my teeth and my
eyes."

"We will put others of ground bone in their place." But the
ground bone was nothing but grains of white corn.

"Very well, pull them out, come and relieve me," he replied.

Then they pulled Vucub-Caquix's teeth; but in their place
they put only grains of white corn, and these grains of corn
shone in his mouth. Instantly his features sagged and he no longer
looked like a lord. They removed the rest of his teeth which shone
like pearls in his mouth. And finally they cured Vucub-Caquix's
eyes, piercing the pupils of his eyes, and they took all his riches.

But he felt nothing any more. He only watched, because at
the advice of Hunahpú and Xbalanqué, they took from him all of
the things of which he had been so proud.

Then Vucub-Caquix died. Hun-Hunahpú recovered his arm.
Chimalmat, the wife of Vucub-Caquix, also perished.

In this way Vucub-Caquix lost his riches. The healer took all
the emeralds and precious stones which had been his pride here
on earth.

The old woman and the old man who did this were miraculous

beings; and having recovered the arm of Hun-Hunahpú, they put it in place, and it was all right again.

It was only to bring about the death of Vucub-Caquix that they did this, because it seemed wicked to them that he should become so arrogant.

And then the two youths went on, having in this way carried out the order of the Heart of Heaven.

CHAPTER 7

Here now are the deeds of Zipacná, the elder son of Vucub-Caquix.

"I am the creator of the mountains," said Zipacná.

Zipacná was bathing at the edge of a river when four hundred youths passed[1] dragging a log to support their house. The four hundred were walking, after having cut down a large tree to make the ridge-pole of their house.

Then Zipacná came up, and going toward the four hundred youths, said to them: "What are you doing, boys?"

"It is only this log," they answered, "which we cannot lift and carry on our shoulders."

"I will carry it. Where does it have to go? What do you want it for?"

"For a ridge-pole for our house."

"All right," he answered, and lifting it up, he put it on his shoulders and carried it to the entrance of the house of the four hundred boys.

"Now stay with us, boy," they said. "Have you a mother or father?"

"I have neither," he answered.

"Then we shall hire you tomorrow to prepare another log to support our house."

[1] *Omuch Qaholab*, "four hundred young men." The collective noun is used to indicate a great number, a crowd.

99

"Good," he answered.

The four hundred boys talked together then, and said:

"How shall we kill this boy? Because it is not good what he has done lifting the log alone. Let us make a big hole and push him so that he will fall into it. 'Go down and take out the earth and carry it from the pit,' we shall tell him, and when he stoops down, to go down into the pit, we shall let the large log fall on him and he will die there in the pit."

So said the four hundred boys, and then they dug a large, very deep pit. Then they called Zipacná.

"We like you very much. Go, go and dig dirt, for we cannot reach [the bottom of the pit]," they said.

"All right," he answered. He went at once into the pit. And calling to him as he was digging the dirt, they said: "Have you gone down very deep yet?"

"Yes," he answered, beginning to dig the pit. But the pit which he was making was to save him from danger. He knew that they wanted to kill him; so when he dug the pit, he made a second hole at one side in order to free himself.

"How far [have you gone]?" the four hundred boys called down.

"I am still digging; I will call up to you when I have finished the digging," said Zipacná from the bottom of the pit. But he was not digging his grave; instead he was opening another pit in order to save himself.

At last Zipacná called to them. But when he called, he was already safe in the second pit.

"Come and take out and carry away the dirt which I have dug and which is in the bottom of the pit," he said, "because in truth I have made it very deep. Do you not hear my call? Nevertheless, your calls, your words repeat themselves like an echo once, twice, and so I hear well where you are." So Zipacná called from the pit where he was hidden, shouting from the depths.

Then the boys hurled the great log violently, and it fell quickly with a thud to the bottom of the pit.

"Let no one speak! Let us wait until we hear his dying screams," they said to each other, whispering, and each one covered his face as the log fell noisily. He [Zipacná] spoke then, crying out, but he called only once when the log fell to the bottom.

"How well we have succeeded in this! Now he is dead," said the boys. "If, unfortunately, he had continued what he had begun to do, we would have been lost, because he already had interfered with us, the four hundred boys."

And filled with joy they said: "Now we must make our *chicha*² within the next three days. When the three days are passed, we shall drink to the construction of our new house, we, the four hundred boys." Then they said: "Tomorrow we shall look, and day after tomorrow, we shall also look to see if the ants do not come out of the earth when the body smells and begins to rot. Presently we shall become calm and drink our *chicha*," they said.

But from his pit Zipacná listened to everything the boys said. And later, on the second day, multitudes of ants came, going and coming and gathering under the log. Some carried Zipacná's hair in their mouths, and others carried his fingernails.

When the boys saw this, they said, "That devil has now perished. Look how the ants have gathered, how they have come by hordes, some bringing his hair and others his fingernails. Look what we have done!" So they spoke to each other.

Nevertheless, Zipacná was very much alive. He had cut his hair and gnawed off his fingernails to give them to the ants.

And so the four hundred boys believed that he was dead, and on the third day they began the orgy and all of the boys got drunk. And the four hundred being drunk knew nothing any more. And then Zipacná let the house fall on their heads and killed all of them.

Not even one or two among the four hundred were saved; they were killed by Zipacná, son of Vucub-Caquix.

In this way the four hundred boys died, and it is said that they became the group of stars which because of them are called Motz,³ but it may not be true.

² A drink of the Guatemalan Indians, made of fermented corn.

³ A mass, the Seven Little Sisters, the Pleiades. Brasseur de Bourbourg notes

CHAPTER 8

Now we shall tell how Zipacná was defeated by the two boys, Hunahpú and Xbalanqué.

Now follows the defeat and death of Zipacná, when he was overcome by the two boys, Hunahpú and Xbalanqué.

The boys' hearts were full of rancor because the four hundred young men had been killed by Zipacná. And he only hunted fish and crabs at the bank of the river, which were his daily food. During the day he went about looking for food, and at night he carried mountains on his back.

With a leaf of the *ec* plant[1] which is found in the forest, Hunahpú and Xbalanqué quickly made a figure to look like a very large crab.

With this they made the stomach of the crab; the claws, they made of *pahac*,[2] and for the shell, which covers the back, they used a stone. Then they put the crab at the bottom of a cave at the foot of a large mountain called *Meaguán*,[3] where he was overcome.

Then the boys went to find Zipacná on the river bank.

"Where are you going, young man?" they asked him.

"I am not going anywhere," Zipacná answered, "only looking for food, boys."

"And what is your food?"

"Fish and crabs, but there are none here and I have not found any; I have not eaten since day before yesterday, and I am dying of hunger," said Zipacná to Hunahpú and Xbalanqué.

---

that *Omuch qaholab*, the four hundred young men who perished in an orgy, are the same as those who were worshiped in Mexico under the name *Centzon-Totochtin*, the four hundred rabbits who were implored as gods to protect the *pulque* and the drunkards.

[1] *Ec*, a bromeliaceous plant of large, brilliant leaves which grows on the trees. "A large-leafed grass with which the rafters are covered during the feasts," says Basseta.

[2] Other smaller leaves called *pahac*, says Ximénez.

[3] The mountain Meaguán rises at the west of the village of Rabinal, in the region of the Chixoy River.

"Over there in the bottom of the ravine there is a crab, a really large crab, and it would be well if you would eat it! Only it bit us when we tried to catch it and so we were afraid. We wouldn't try to catch it for anything," said Hunahpú and Xbalanqué.

"Have pity on me! Come and show it to me, boys," begged Zipacná.

"We do not want to. You go alone, you will not get lost. Follow the bank of the river and you will come out at the foot of a large hill; there it is making a noise at the bottom of the ravine. You have only to go there," said Hunahpú and Xbalanqué.

"Oh, unfortunate me! Won't you accompany me, boys? Come and show it to me. There are many birds which you can shoot with your blowguns and I know where to find them," said Zipacná.

His meekness convinced the boys. And they asked him: "But, can you really catch him? Because it is only for you that we are returning; we are not going to try to get it again because it bit us when we were crawling into the cave. After that we were afraid to crawl in, but we almost caught it. So, then, it is best that you crawl in," they said.

"Very well," said Zipacná, and then they went with him. They arrived at the bottom of the ravine and there, stretched on his back, was the crab, showing his red shell. And there also in the bottom of the ravine was the boys' hoax.[4]

"Good! Good!" said Zipacná happily. "I should like to have it in my mouth already!" And he was really dying of hunger. He wanted to try to crawl in, he wanted to enter, but the crab was climbing. He came out at once and the boys asked, "Did you not get it?"

"No," he answered, "because he was going up and I almost caught him. But perhaps it would be good if I go in from above," he added. And then he entered again from above, but as he was almost inside, with only the soles of his feet showing, the great hill slid and fell slowly down on his chest.

[4] *Qui cumatzih*, "their enchantment," according to Brasseur de Bourbourg; "their secret," according to Ximénez, *Mactzil* in Maya is "miracle," "marvel."

Zipacná never returned and he was changed into stone.

In this way Zipacná was defeated by the two boys, Hunahpú and Xbalanqué; he was the elder son of Vucub-Caquix, and he, according to the ancient legend, was the one who made the mountains.

At the foot of the hill called Meaguán he was vanquished. Only by a miracle was he vanquished, the second of the arrogant ones. One was left, whose history we shall tell now.

CHAPTER 9

The third of the arrogant ones was the second son of Vucub-Caquix who was called Cabracán.

"I demolish the mountains," he said.

But Hunahpú and Xbalanqué also defeated Cabracán. Huracán Chipi-Caculhá, and Raxa-Caculhá talked and said to Hunahpú and Xbalanqué:

"Let the second son of Vucub-Caquix also be defeated. This is our will, for it is not well what they do on earth, exalting their glory, their grandeur, and their power, and it must not be so. Lure him to where the sun rises," said Huracán to the two youths.

"Very well, honored sir," they answered, "because what we see is not right. Do you not exist, you who are the peace, you, Heart of Heaven?" said the boys as they listened to the command of Huracán.

Meanwhile, Cabracán was busy shaking the mountains. At the gentlest tap of his feet on the earth, the large and small mountains opened. Thus the boys found him and asked Cabracán:

"Where are you going, young man?"

"Nowhere," he answered, "here I am moving the mountains, and I am leveling them to the ground forever,"[1] he answered.

Then Cabracán asked Hunahpú and Xbalanqué, "What did you come to do here? I do not recognize you. What are your names?" said Cabracán.

"We have no names," they answered, "we are nothing more

[1] *Chi be quih, chi be zac* literally means "as long as there is sun and light."

104

than shooters of blowguns and hunters with bird-traps on the mountains. We are poor and we have nothing, young man. We only walk over the large and small mountains, young man, and we have just seen a large mountain, over there where you see the pink sky.[2] It really rises up very high and overlooks the tops of all the hills. So it is that we have not been able to catch even one or two of the birds on it, boy. But, is it true that you can level all the mountains?" Hunahpú and Xbalanqué asked Cabracán.

"Have you really seen the mountain of which you speak? Where is it? If I see it, I shall demolish it. Where did you see it?"

"Over there it is, where the sun rises," said Hunahpú and Xbalanqué.

"Very well, show me the road," he said to the two boys.

"Oh no!" they answered. "We must take you between us. One shall go at your left and the other at your right, because we have our blowguns, and if there should be birds we can shoot them." And so they set out happily, trying out their blowguns. But when they shot with them, they did not use the clay pellets in the tube of the blowgun; instead they felled the birds only with the puff of air when they shot them, which surprised Cabracán very much.

Then the boys built a fire and put the birds on it to roast, but they rubbed one of the birds with chalk,[3] covering it with a white earth soil.

"We shall give him this," they said, "to whet his appetite with the odor which it gives off. This bird of ours shall be his ruin, as we cover this bird with earth so we shall bring him down to the earth and bury him in the earth.

"Great shall be the wisdom of a created being, of a being fashioned, when it dawns, when there is light," said the boys.[4]

[2] *Xa qo qu'il caquiyc.* Brasseur de Bourbourg and Raynaud translate it "there where large precipices are seen." The neuter verb *caquer, caquic*, means the sky is suffused or is aflame with the red light of dawn.

[3] *Tahcab*, in Maya and Quiché, chalk or natural lime cement.

[4] *Ve nima etamanel hun tzac, hun bit ta ch'auax oc, ta zaquir oc, x-e cha ri qaholab.* This sentence, says Brasseur de Bourbourg, is extremely confusing and appears to have little relation with the history. The sentence is certainly incongruous, but Brasseur de Bourbourg did not translate it well either.

"As it is natural for man to wish to eat, so Cabracán desires food," said Hunahpú and Xbalanqué to each other.

Meanwhile the birds were roasting, they were beginning to turn golden brown, and the fat and juice which dripped from them made an appetizing odor. Cabracán wanted very much to eat them; they made his mouth water, he yawned, and the saliva and spittle drooled because of the smell which the birds gave off.

Then he asked them: "What is that you eat? The smell is really savoury. Give me a little piece," he said to them.

Then they gave a bird to Cabracán, the one which would be his ruin; and when he had finished eating it, they set out toward the east where the great mountain was. But already Cabracán's legs and hands were weakening and he had no strength because of the earth with which the bird he had eaten was rubbed, and he could do nothing to the mountains. Neither was it possible to level them.

Then the boys tied him, they tied his hands behind him and also tied his neck and his feet together. Then they threw him to the ground and there they buried him.

In this way Cabracán was overcome by Hunahpú and Xbalanqué. It would be impossible to tell of all the things they did here on earth.

Now we shall tell of the birth of Hunahpú and Xbalanqué, having first told of the destruction of Vucub-Caquix and that of Zipacná and of Cabracán, here on earth.

# PART II

Now we shall also tell the name of the father of Hunahpú and Xbalanqué. We shall not tell his origin and we shall not tell the history of the birth of Hunahpú and Xbalanqué. We shall tell only half of it, only a part of the history of his father.

Here is the story. Here are the names of Hun-Hunahpú [and Vucub-Hunahpú], as they are called. Their parents were Xpiyacoc and Xmucané. During the night[1] Hun-Hunahpú and Vucub-Hunahpú were born of Xpiyacoc and Xmucané.[2]

[1] *Chi agabal,* that is to say, before there was sun, or moon, or before man had been created.

[2] Hun-Hunahpú, 1 Hunahpú; Vucub-Hunahpú, 7 Hunahpú, are two days of the Quiché calendar. As is known, the ancient Indians of the Maya area designated the days by putting a number before each day, thus forming a series of thirteen days which are repeated without interruption until a cycle of 260 days is formed, which the Maya called *tzolkín,* the Quiché, *cholquih,* and the Mexicans, *tonalpohualli.* It was the custom to give an individual the name of the day upon which he was born.

The Quiché calendar is made up of twenty days. Each day is preceded by a number, a coefficient of from 1 to 13, and this is repeated indefinitely so that a name of a day and the number which accompanies it may not be repeated until 260 is reached, or 13 times 20. This period of 260 days constitutes the ritual year, or *cholquih.* The names of the days and their meaning in English are as follows:

1. *Imox,* name of a fish
2. *Ic,* moon, wind, spirit
3. *Acbal,* night
4. *Cat,* net with which to carry corn, or a lizard
5. *Can,* serpent
6. *Camey,* death
7. *Queh,* deer
8. *Canel,* wealth, ear of yellow corn
9. *Toh,* rain, storm
10. *Tzi,* dog
11. *Batz,* monkey
12. *E, ei,* teeth, brush

107

Well now, Hun-Hunahpú had begotten two sons; the first was called Hunbatz and the second Hunchouén.[3]

The mother of the two sons was called Xbaquiyalo.[4] Thus was the wife of Hun-Hunahpú called. As for the other son, Vucub-Hunahpú, he had no wife; he was single.

---

13. *Ah*, cane, or tender corn
14. *Balam*, jaguar
15. *Tziquin*, bird
16. *Ahmac*, owl

17. *Noh*, strong, resin
18. *Tihax*, edge, obsidian
19. *Caoc*, lightning and thunder
20. *Hunahpú*, hunter, chief, or lord

With these twenty days the Quiché formed the following eighteen months:

1. *Tequexepual*, time to plant the cornfields
2. *Tziba pop*, painted mat
3. *Zac*, white like certain flowers
4. *Ch'ab*, muddy ground
5. *Nabey mam*, first old man
6. *Ucab mam*, second old man (Both this and the preceding are months of ill-omen.)
7. *Nabey liquin ca*, soft and slippery soil
8. *Ucab liquin ca*, second month of soft and slippery soil
9. *Nabey pach*, first time of hatching
10. *Ucab pach*, second time of hatching
11. *Tzizil lakam*, the sprouts show
12. *Tziquin kih*, season of birds
13. *Cakam*, red clouds
14. *Botam*, tangled mats
15. *Nabey zih*, first month of white flowers
16. *Ucab zih*, second month of white flowers
17. *Rox zih*, third month of white flowers
18. *Chee*, trees, *Pariché*, in the Cakchiquel calendar

Brinton (*The Native Calendar of Central America and Mexico*) took these and other facts from various Indian calendars which date back to the seventeenth century and from the *Geografía* by Francisco Gavarrete.

[3] Brasseur de Bourbourg incorrectly translates this passage as follows: *Or, ces Hunhun-Ahpu étaient deux; ils avaient engendré deux fils légitimes, et le nom du premier né [était] Hunbatz and Hunchouén le nom du second.* As is seen farther on, Hunbatz and Hunchouen were only the sons of Hun-Hunahpú and Xbaquiyalo, his wife. Hun-Batz, 1 monkey, is the eleventh day of the Quiché calendar; Hun-Chouén, also, 1 Chuén, 1 monkey, is the eleventh day of the Maya calendar. Note that, with the exception of the indication that the names of the parents of Hunahpú and Xbalanqué will be given, these heroes are not mentioned again until their birth is announced in Chapter 5 of Part II. There the other half of the history is told, but in this part the reader is left intentionally in the dark.

[4] *Xbaquiyalo*, "of the fastened bones," according to Ximénez. It might also be "of the uneven bones."

By nature these two sons were very wise, and great was their wisdom; on earth they were soothsayers of good disposition and good habits. All the arts were taught to Hunbatz and Hunchouén, the sons of Hun-Hunahpú. They were flautists, singers, shooters with blowguns, painters, sculptors, jewelers, silversmiths; these were Hunbatz and Hunchouén.[5]

Well, Hun-Hunahpú and Vucub-Hunahpú did nothing but play dice and ball all day long; and when the four got together to play ball, one pair played against the other pair.

And Voc,[6] the messenger of Huracán, of Chipi-Caculhá, of Raxa-Caculhá came there to watch them, but Voc did not stay far from the earth nor far from Xibalba,[7] and in an instant he went up to heaven to the side of Huracán.

They were still here on earth when the mother of Hunbatz and Hunchouén died.

And having gone to play ball on the road to Xibalba, they were overheard by Hun-Camé and Vucub-Camé, the lords of Xibalba.[8]

"What are they doing on earth? Who are they who are making the earth shake, and making so much noise? Go and call them! Let them come here to play ball. Here we will overpower them! We are no longer respected by them. They no longer have consideration, or fear of our rank, and they even fight above our heads," said all the lords of Xibalba.

All of them held a council. Those called Hun-Camé and

[5] *Ah chuen*, in Maya, means "artisan." *Diccionario de Motul.*

[6] To the place where they played ball, *pa hom* in the original, *Voc* or *Vac*, the hawk, came to watch them. In speaking of the Maya of Yucatán, Bishop Landa says that "they played ball, and also with beans they played a game like dice."

[7] *Chi-Xibalba.* In ancient times, says Father Coto, this name *Xibalbay* meant the devil, or the dead, or visions which appeared to the Indians. It has the same meanings in Yucatán. Xibalba was the devil, and *xibil* is to disappear like a vision or a phantom, according to the *Diccionario de Motul.* The Maya performed a dance which they called *Xibalba ocot*, or "dance of the demon." The Quiché believed that Xibalba was the underground region inhabited by the enemies of man.

[8] Hun-Camé, 1 dead; Vucub-Camé, 7 dead; are days of the calendar. The Quiché hierarchy had frequently the numbers one to seven.

Vucub-Camé were the supreme judges. All the lords had been assigned their duties. Each one was given his own authority by Hun-Camé and Vucub-Camé.

They were, then, Xiquiripat and Cuchumaquic[9] lords of these names. They were the two who caused the shedding of blood of the men.

Others were called Ahalpuh and Ahalganá,[10] also lords. And their work was to make men swell and make pus gush forth from their legs[11] and stain their faces yellow, what is called Chuganal.[12] Such was the work of Ahalpuh and Ahalganá.

Others were Lord Chamiabac and Lord Chamiaholom,[13] constables of Xibalba, whose staffs were of bone. Their work was to make men waste away until they were nothing but skin and bone and they died, and they carried them with their stomach and bones stretched out. This was the work of Chamiabac and Chamiaholom, as they were called.

Others were called Lord Ahalmez and Lord Ahaltocob;[14] their work was to bring disaster upon men, as they were going home, or in front of it, and they would be found wounded, stretched out, face up, on the ground, dead. This was the work of Ahalmez and Ahaltocob, as they were called.

Immediately after them were other lords named Xic and Patán[15] whose work it was to cause men to die on the road, which is called sudden death, making blood to rush to their mouths until

[9] *Xiquiripat*, "flying pannier," according to Ximénez. *Cuchumaquic*, "gathered blood," according to the same translator.

[10] *Ahalpuh*, "he who makes pus." Name of a disease among the Cakchiquel. *Ahalganá*, "he who causes dropsy," according to Ximénez.

[11] *Chi pe puh chiri r'acan.*

[12] Literally, "in the yellow color of his body" (Ximénez); a kind of ictericia.

[13] *Chamiabac*, he who carries a staff of bone. *Chamiaholom*, he who carries a staff with a skull. Both are symbols of emaciation and death. *Ahchamí*, the man of the staff, symbol of authority, or of the big stick which the guardians of public order were accustomed to carry.

[14] *Ahalmez*, "he who makes filth" (Ximénez); "he who works in filth" (Brasseur de Bourbourg). *Ahaltocob*, "he who causes misery" (Ximénez); "he who works or produces misery" (Brasseur de Bourbourg). It might be he who causes wounds, the assassin. The verb *toc* means "to punch or stab," to wound, to behead. *Tocopé* has the same meaning.

they died vomiting blood. The work of each one of these lords was to seize upon them, squeeze their throats and chests, so that the men died on the road, making the blood rush to their throats when they were walking. This was the work of Xic and Patán.

And having gathered in council, they discussed how to torment and wound Hun-Hunahpú and Vucub-Hunahpú. What the Lords of Xibalba coveted were the playing implements of Hun-Hunahpú and Vucub-Hunahpú—their leather pads[16] and rings[17] and gloves[18] and crown[19] and masks[20] which were the playing gear of Hun-Hunahpú and Vucub-Hunahpú.

Now we shall tell of their journey to Xibalba and how they left behind them the sons of Hun-Hunahpú, Hunbatz, and [Hun] Chouén,[21] whose mother had died.

Then we shall tell how Hunbatz and Hunchouén were overcome by Hunahpú and Xbalanqué.

[15] *Xic*, hawk; *Patán*, leather band which the Indians wear around their foreheads and from which the load they carry on their backs hangs. It is known today by the Mexican name *mecapal*. Many of these names are found in the *Vocabulario de las lenguas Quiché and Kakchiquel* which classifies them as "names of demons," explaining that they are derived from *Ahau*, "lord"; Ahalpuh, Calel Ahau, Ahal Tocol, Ahal Xic, Ahal Canyá. The last is evidently the Ahalganá of the *Popol Vuh*. Father Pantaleón de Guzmán says that, among other deities, the Cakchiquel worshiped Ahal Puh, Ahal Tecob, Ahal Xic and Ahal Canyá— all of these in reality are also names of diseases; and in addition they worshiped Tatan bak and Tatan holom, father of bones and father of skulls, gods of death. These last names, as will be seen later, are not very different from Chamiabac and Chamiaholom. Ahal Puh seems to be the same god of death as that of the Maya of Yucatán, who knew him under the name of Ah Puch or Hunhau, and who had his kingdom in Mitnal or the Maya inferno.

[16] *Tzuun*, leather leggings, according to Ximénez. They were the leathers with which they covered their legs and thus protected them against blows by the ball.

[17] *Baté*, rings, collar for the neck (*Vocabulario Quiché-Cakchiquel*).

[18] *Pachgab*, gloves.

[19] *Yachvach*, crown, or adornment which they wore on the head.

[20] *Vachzot*, rim of the face, according to Ximénez, "mask." All of these objects were necessities for their strenuous ball game, and as decorations for the ball players.

[21] Like this in the original, by Hun-Chouén.

## CHAPTER 2

T he messengers of Hun-Camé and Vucub-Camé
arrived immediately.

"Go, Ahpop Achih!"[1] they were told. "Go and call Hun-
Hunahpú and Vucub-Hunahpú. Say to them, 'Come with us.
The lords say that you must come.' They must come here to play
ball with us so that they shall make us happy, for really they amaze
us. So, then, they must come," said the lords. "And have them
bring their playing gear, their rings, their gloves, and have them
bring their rubber balls, too," said the lords. "Tell them to come
quickly," they told the messengers.

And these messengers were owls: Chabi-Tucur, Huracán-
Tucur, Caquix-Tucur and Holom-Tucur.[2] These were the names
of the messengers of Xibalba.

Chabi-Tucur was swift as an arrow; Huracán-Tucur had only
one leg; Caquix-Tucur had a red back, and Holom-Tucur had
only a head, no legs, but he had wings.

The four messengers had the rank of Ahpop-Achih. Leaving
Xibalba, they arrived quickly, bringing their message to the court
where Hun-Hunahpú and Vucub-Hunahpú were playing ball,
at the ball-court which was called *Nim-Xob Carchah*.[3] The owl

[1] Title of some of the Quiché lords and chiefs.

[2] *Chabi-Tucur*, swift owl; *Huracán-Tucur*, owl with one leg, or gigantic
owl; *Caquix-Tucur*, macaw owl; *Holom-Tucur*, head of an owl, or owl distinguished by the head. *Tucur* is the Quiché name for owl. A town of Verapaz,
San Miguel Tucurú, is also so named. This night bird is known in Guatemala
by the name of *tucurú* and also as *tecolote*, from the Náhuatl *tecolotl*. Dr. Otto
Stoll (*Die Maya Sprachen der Pokom-Gruppe*) suggests that the name which
the Mexicans gave to Verapaz was Tecolotlán, or place of owls or *tecolotes*, i.e.,
the land of the *tucur*, and that the Spanish missionaries, through an error, wrote
it Teçolotlán, which later was changed to Tezulutlán. The name Verapaz was
given to that province after its peaceful conquest by the Dominican friars. In
fact, Ixtlilxóchitl says that the Tolteca emigrated to the south to Guatemala and
Tecolotlán, and Sahagún (*Historia general de las cosas de Nueva España*, Vol.
III, Book XI, Chap. II, p. 163) notes that the quetzal lives "in the province called
Tecolotlán, which is toward Honduras, or near."

[3] The great Carchah, an important center of population in Verapaz, the
region in which the Quiché seem to have placed the mythological deeds of the

messengers went directly to the ball-court and delivered their message exactly as it was given to them by Hun-Camé, Vucub-Camé, Ahalpuh, Ahalganá, Chamiabac, Chamiaholom, Xiquiripat, Cuchumaquic, Ahalmez, Ahaltocob, Xic, and Patan, as the lords were called who sent the message by the owls.

"Did the Lords Hun-Camé and Vucub-Camé really say that we must go with you?"

"They certainly said so, and 'Let them bring all their playing gear,' the lords said."

"Very well," said the youths. Wait for us, we are only going to say good-bye to our mother."

And having gone straight home, they said to their mother, for their father was dead: "We are going, our mother, but our going is only for a while.[4] The messengers of the lord have come to take us. 'They must come,' they said, according to the messengers.

"We shall leave our ball here in pledge,"[5] they added. They went immediately to hang it in the space under the rooftree. "We will return to play," they said.

And going to Hunbatz and Hunchouén they said to them: "Keep on playing the flute and singing, painting, and carving; warm our house and warm the heart of your grandmother."

When they took leave of their mother, Xmucané was moved and burst into tears. "Do not worry, we are going, but we have not died yet," said Hun-Hunahpú and Vucub-Hunahpú as they left.

Hun-Hunahpú and Vucub-Hunahpú went immediately and the messengers took them on the road. Thus they were descending the road to Xibalba, by some very steep stairs. They went down until they came to the bank of a river which flowed rapid-

---

*Popol Vuh*. The Cakchiquel Manuscript says that they and the Quiché went to populate Subinal, in the middle of Chacachil, to the middle of Nimxor, to the middle of Moinal, to the middle of Carchah (*nicah Carchah*). Some of these places still retain their ancient names today and may easily be identified in the Verapaz region. According to the Cakchiquel document, Nim Xor and Carchah were two different places.

[4] Which is to say, "that they go, but they will return."

[5] X-*chi canah cu caná va ca quic*. Here is a play on words; *canah* is to "stay," and *caná*, "pledge," "hostage," or "captive."

ly between the ravines called *Nuziván cul* and *Cuziván*,[6] and crossed it. Then they crossed the river which flows among thorny calabash trees.[7] There were very many calabash trees, but they passed through them without hurting themselves.

Then they came to the bank of a river of blood and crossed it without drinking its waters; they only went to the river bank and so they were not overcome. They went on until they came to where four roads joined, and there at the crossroads they were overcome.

One of the four roads was red, another black, another white,

[6] *Nu zivan cul*, "my ravine," or "the narrow ravine." *Cu zivan*, "narrow, close ravine." *Zivan* is "ravine," but the underground caves in Verapaz and the Petén are also called *Zivan*. The topographical data included in this chapter as well as similar indications found in other passages in Part II show that the ancient Quiché had very definite ideas about the location of the kingdom of Xibalba, where lived some cruel, despotic chiefs to whom they were subject in mythological time. In the present chapter, the large town of Carchah, which still stands a few miles from Cobán, capital of the department of Alta Verapaz, is named as the crossroads of the way to Xibalba. Leaving Carchah, the road leads down "by some very steep steps" until it comes to the ravines or caves, between which a swift river flows; which is to say, descending the mountains of the interior to the lowlands of the Petén, to the territory of the Itzá. At the end of Part II it is said that the people of Xibalba were the Ah-Tza, the Ah-Tucur, the evil ones, the owls. Nevertheless, these words may also be read as "those of Itzá [Petén]" and "those of Tucur," or Tecolotlán, the land of the owls (Verapaz). They are the two regions of northern Guatemala, very well known in the ancient Middle American world, over which the Quiché could not extend their conquests. These names confirm the topographical references in the text. Some of the tribes, which in relatively recent times came to establish themselves in the mountains of the interior of Guatemala, without doubt believed that the northern territory was inhabited by their old enemies, the same who, in former times, had taken the lives of their forefathers. These inhabitants of the north were the Maya of the Old Empire, one branch of which, the Itzá, was the last to surrender to the Spaniards in the later years of the seventeenth century. Other scattered data in the *Popol Vuh* reveal that Xibalba was a very deep, underground place, an abyss from which one had to *climb* up in order to come to the earth; but the same Quiché document explains that the Lords of Xibalba were not gods, nor were they immortals, that they were false of heart, hypocrites, envious, and tyrants. That they were not invincible is shown in the course of the narrative.

[7] *Chupan halhal ha zimah*. The Quiché word *Zimah* corresponds to the tree and fruit which the Mexican Indians call *Xicalli*, and in Guatemala is called *jícaro*. It is a tree of the Bignonia family, *Crescentia cujete*. The round or oval shaped fruit of this tree has a hard rind from which the Indians make vases called *jícaras* and *guacales*.

and another yellow. And the black road said to them: "I am the one you must take because I am the way of the Lord." So said the road.

And from here on they were already overcome. They were taken over the road to Xibalba and when they arrived at the council room of the Lords of Xibalba, they had already lost the match.

Well, the first ones who were seated there were only figures of wood, arranged by the men of Xibalba. These they greeted first:

"How are you, Hun-Camé?" they said to the wooden man. "How are you, Vucub-Camé?" they said to the other wooden man. But they did not answer. Instantly the Lords of Xibalba burst into laughter and all the other lords began to laugh loudly, because they already took for granted the downfall and defeat of Hun-Hunahpú and Vucub-Hunahpú. And they continued to laugh.

Then Hun-Camé and Vucub-Camé spoke: "Very well," they said. "You have come. Tomorrow you shall prepare the mask,[8] your rings, and your gloves," they said.

"Come and sit down on our bench," they said. But the bench which they offered them was of hot stone, and when they sat down they were burned. They began to squirm around on the bench, and if they had not stood up they would have burned their seats.

The Lords of Xibalba burst out laughing again; they were dying of laughter; they writhed from pain in their stomach, in their blood, and in their bones, caused by their laughter, all the Lords of Xibalba laughed.

"Go now to that house," they said. "There you will get your sticks of fat pine[9] and your cigar[10] and there you shall sleep."

---

[8] *Chuvec ch'y qaza u vach*, in the original. In the text transcribed by Brasseur de Bourbourg it is *ch' y qaza a vach*. The change of a single vowel makes the sentence incomprehensible. Schuller (*"Das Popol Vuh und das Ballspiel der K'icé Indianer von Guatemala"*) believed that it had been garbled by the French translator.

[9] *Chah* in Quiché, *ocotl* in the Mexican language. A resinous pine which the Indians use for lighting.

[10] *Ziq*, tobacco; *zikar*, to smoke.

Immediately they arrived at the House of Gloom.[11] There was only darkness within the house. Meanwhile the Lords of Xibalba discussed what they should do.

"Let us sacrifice them tomorrow, let them die quickly, quickly, so that we can have their playing gear to use in play," said the Lords of Xibalba to each other.

Well, their fat-pine sticks were round and were called *zaquitoc*, which is the pine of Xibalba.[12] Their fat-pine sticks were pointed and filed and were as bright as bone; the pine of Xibalba was very hard.

Hun-Hunahpú and Vucub-Hunahpú entered the House of Gloom. There they were given their fat-pine sticks, a single lighted stick which Hun-Camé and Vucub-Camé sent them, together with a lighted cigar for each of them which the lords had sent. They went to give them to Hun-Hunahpú and Vucub-Hunahpú.

They found them crouching in the darkness when the porters arrived with the fat-pine sticks and the cigars. As they entered, the pine sticks lighted the place brightly.

"Each of you light your pine sticks and your cigars; come and bring them back at dawn, you must not burn them up, but you must return them whole; this is what the lords told us to say." So they said. And so they were defeated. They burned up the pine sticks, and they also finished the cigars which had been given to them.

---

[11] *Qequma-ha.* Brasseur de Bourbourg compares this House of Gloom with the dark house which Votán constructed in Huehuetlán, in the province of Soconusco, according to Bishop Núñez de la Vega.

[12] *Are curi qui chah xa coloquic cha zaquitoc u bi ri chah u chah Xibalba.* Zaquitoc, literally, is "white knife." Brasseur de Bourbourg translates it *blanc silex.* Seler is of the opinion that *zaquitoc* was the knife used in human sacrifice to open the breasts of the victims. The description in the text clearly identifies the hard, bright flint point which both the ancient Maya and Quiché used, as a short, sharp weapon, as knives, lance points, and so on. The author plays here with the words *cha*, flint and obsidian, and *chah*, fat-pine sticks, etc. The purpose of this confusion and the true explanation of this entire paragraph is evidently to remember that the guests of Xibalba were threatened with the sacrificial knife.

There were many punishments in Xibalba; the punishments were of many kinds.

The first was the House of Gloom, Quequma-ha, in which there was only darkness.

The second was Xuxulim-ha, the house where everybody shivered, in which it was very cold. A cold, unbearable wind blew within.

The third was the House of Jaguars, Balami-ha, it was called, in which there were nothing but jaguars which stalked about, jumped around, roared, and made fun. The jaguars were shut up in the house.

Zotzi-há, the House of Bats, the fourth place of punishment was called. Within this house there were nothing but bats which squeaked and cried and flew around and around. The bats were shut in and could not get out.

The fifth was called Chayim-há, the House of Knives,[13] in which there were only sharp, pointed knives, silent or grating against each other in the house.

There were many places of torture in Xibalba,[14] but Hun-Hunahpú and Vucub-Hunahpú did not enter them. We only mention the names of these houses of punishment.

When Hun-Hunahpú and Vucub-Hunahpú came before Hun-Camé and Vucub-Camé, they said: "Where are my cigars? Where are my sticks of fat pine which I gave you last night?"

"They are all gone, Sir."

"Well. Today shall be the end of your days. Now you shall die. You shall be destroyed, we will break you into pieces and here your faces will stay hidden. You shall be sacrificed," said Hun-Camé and Vucub-Camé.

They sacrificed them immediately and buried them in the

[13] *Chay*, obsidian, glassy substance, black volcanic stone, the "stone of lightning" of the peasants; from it the Indians selected small sharp pieces which they used as knives, razors, and arrow points.

[14] *Quii nabec u tihobal Xibalba*. Ximénez thus interprets this sentence, and this is its logical meaning.

Pucbal-Chah, as it was called.[15] Before burying them,[16] they cut off the head of Hun-Hunahpú and buried the older brother together with the younger brother.

"Take the head and put it in that tree which is planted on the road," said Hun-Camé and Vucub-Camé. And having put the head in the tree, instantly the tree, which had never borne fruit before the head of Hun-Hunahpú was placed among its branches, was covered with fruit. And this calabash tree, it is said, is the one which we now call the head of Hun-Hunahpú.

Hun-Camé and Vucub-Camé looked in amazement at the fruit on the tree. The round fruit was every where; but they did not recognize the head of Hun-Hunahpú; it was exactly like the other fruit of the calabash tree. So it seemed to all of the people of Xibalba when they came to look at it.

According to their judgment, the tree was miraculous, because of what had instantly occurred when they put Hun-Hunahpú's head among its branches. And the Lords of Xibalba said:

"Let no one come to pick this fruit.[17] Let no one come and sit under this tree!" they said, and so the Lords of Xibalba resolved to keep everybody away.

The head of Hun-Hunahpú did not appear again,[18] because it had become one and the same as the fruit of the gourd tree. Nevertheless, a girl heard the wonderful story. Now we shall tell about her arrival.

---

[15] *Ta x-e puz cut, x-e muc cut chi Pucbal-Chah u bi.* Ximénez (*Historia de la Provincia de San Vicente de Chiapa y Guatemala*) translates this name as "the place where the ashes are dumped." Brasseur de Bourbourg translates it "the ash-pan." It seems evident that there is an error in transcription here and that the name of this place must have been Puzbal-Chah, that is, the place of sacrifice of the ball game. *Puzbal* is "place of sacrifice," according to Basseta, and *chah* is the game of ball. Raynaud also gives this last interpretation.

[16] *X-e muc vi,* a phrase in the original, which is missing in the text which Brasseur de Bourbourg publishes.

[17] *Ma qo ma chupuvic ri u vach.* Brasseur de Bourbourg does not translate this sentence, although it is present in the original, as well as in the text which he publishes.

[18] *Ma cu calah chiri u holom Hunhún-Ahpú.*

## CHAPTER 3

This is the story of a maiden, the daughter of a lord named Cuchumaquic.

A maiden, then, daughter of a lord heard this story. The name of the father was Cuchumaquic and that of the maiden was Xquic.[1] When she heard the story of the fruit of the tree which her father told, she was amazed to hear it.

"Why can I not go to see this tree which they tell about?" the girl exclaimed. "Surely the fruit of which I hear tell must be very good." Finally she went alone and arrived at the foot of the tree which was planted in Pucbal-Chah.

"Ah!" she exclaimed. "What fruit is this which this tree bears? Is it not wonderful to see how it is covered with fruit? Must I die, shall I be lost, if I pick one of this fruit?" said the maiden.

Then the skull which was among the branches of the tree spoke up and said: "What is it you wish? Those round objects which cover the branches of the trees are nothing but skulls." So spoke the head of Hun-Hunahpú turning to the maiden. "Do you, perchance, want them?" it added.

"Yes, I want them," the maiden answered.

"Very well," said the skull. "Stretch your right hand up here."

"Very well," said the maiden, and with her right hand reached toward the skull.

In that instant the skull let a few drops of spittle fall directly into the maiden's palm. She looked quickly and intently at the palm of her hand, but the spittle of the skull was not there.

"In my saliva and spittle I have given you my descendants," said the voice in the tree. "Now my head has nothing on it any more, it is nothing but a skull without flesh. So are the heads of the great princes, the flesh is all which gives them a handsome appearance. And when they die, men are frightened by their bones. So, too, is the nature of the sons, which are like saliva and spittle,

[1] *Cuchumaquic,* gathered blood; *Xquic,* little blood, or blood of a woman.

they may be sons of a lord, of a wise man, or of an orator.[2] They do not lose their substance when they go, but they bequeath it; the image of the lord, of the wise man, or of the orator does not disappear, nor is it lost, but he leaves it to the daughters and to the sons which he begets. I have done the same with you. Go up, then, to the surface of the earth, that you may not die. Believe in my words that it will be so," said the head of Hun-Hunahpú and of Vucub-Hunahpú.[3]

And all that they did together was by order of Huracán, Chipi-Caculhá, and Raxa-Caculhá.

After all of the above talking, the maiden returned directly to her home, having immediately conceived the sons in her belly by virtue of the spittle only. And thus Hunahpú and Xbalanqué were begotten.

And so the girl returned home, and after six months had passed, her father, who was called Cuchumaquic, noticed her condition. At once the maiden's secret was discovered by her father when he observed that she was pregnant.[4]

Then the lords, Hun-Camé and Vucub-Camé, held council with Cuchumaquic.

"My daughter is pregnant,[5] Sirs; she has been disgraced,"[6] exclaimed Cuchumaquic when he appeared before the lords.

"Very well," they said. "Command her to tell the truth,[7] and

[2] *Naol, Ahuchan,* "orator," title of one of the officials who served in the court and who were called Lolmay, Atzihuinac, Galel, and Ahuchan. They were the agents, accountants, and treasurers, according to the text of the *Petición de los principales de Santiago Atitlán al Rey Felipe II,* insert in *Ternaux Compans, Recueil de pièces relatives á la conquête du Mexique* (Paris, 1838), 415. *Naoh ah uchan,* "he who knows," master of discourse, according to Father Pantaleón de Guzmán.

[3] There was only the head of Hun-Hunahpú. As will be noted, this passage reminds one of the Mexican myth of the birth of Huitzilopochtli, the Aztec god of war, who was begotten by a little ball of feathers which fell on his mother, Coatlicue, who in turn placed it on her breast and "from which she became pregnant," according to Sahagún (*Historia general de las cosas de Nueva España,* Book III, Chap. I).

[4] *Ta x-il ri r'al,* literally, "when he saw the son."

[5] *Qo chi r'al,* literally, "she is with child."

[6] *Xa u hoxbal,* literally, "is nothing more than a prostitute."

[7] *Ch'a qoto u chi ri,* literally, "search her mouth."

if she refuses to speak, punish her; let her be taken far from here and sacrifice her."

"Very well, Honorable Lords," he answered. Then he questioned his daughter:

"Whose are the children that you carry, my daughter,"[8] And she answered, "I have no child, my father, for I have not yet known a youth."[9]

"Very well," he replied. "You are really a whore. Take her and sacrifice her, Ahpop Achih; bring me her heart in a gourd and return this very day before the lords," he said to the two owls.

The four messengers took the gourd and set out carrying the young girl in their arms and also taking the knife of flint with which to sacrifice her.[10]

And she said to them: "It cannot be that you will kill me, oh, messengers, because what I bear in my belly is no disgrace, but was begotten when I went to marvel at the head of Hun-Hunahpú which was in Pucbal-Chah. So, then, you must not sacrifice me, oh, messengers!" said the young girl, turning to them.

"And what shall we put in place of your heart? Your father told us: 'Bring the heart, return before the lords, do your duty, all working together, bring it in the gourd quickly,[11] and put the heart in the bottom of the gourd.' Perchance, did he not speak to us so? What shall we put in the gourd? We wish too, that you should not die," said the messengers.

"Very well, but my heart does not belong to them. Neither is your home here, nor must you let them force you to kill men.[12] Later, in truth, the real criminals will be at your mercy and I will overcome Hun-Camé and Vucub-Camé. So, then, the blood and only the blood shall be theirs and shall be given to them.[13] Neither

---

[8] *Apa ahchoc e ri av'al qo ch' a pam, at nu meal?*

[9] *Ma-habi achih v'etaam u vach.* "I have not known the face of a man."

[10] The *Zaquitoc,* the flint knife used to open the breast of the victim sacrificed to the Indian gods.

[11] *Ch'anim ch'y cama uloc pa zel.*

[12] *Ma cu xa ch'y chih vinac chi camic.*

[13] *Xa quic xa holomax rech ch'uxoc are chicut chuvach.* Ximénez translates this difficult passage thus: "Only the blood and skull shall be theirs." The sentence contains the possessive pronoun, singular, following the custom of the

shall my heart be burned before them.[14] Gather the product of this tree," said the maiden.

The red sap gushing forth from the tree fell in the gourd and with it they made a ball which glistened and took the shape of a heart. The tree gave forth sap similar to blood, with the appearance of real blood. Then the blood, or that is to say the sap of the red tree, clotted, and formed a very bright coating inside the gourd, like clotted blood; meanwhile the tree glowed at the work of the maiden. It was called the "red tree of cochineal,"[15] but [since then] it has taken the name of Blood Tree because its sap is called Blood.[16]

---

Quiché writer to consider as only one person the group of two, in this case Hun-Camé and Vucub-Camé. The word *holomax* is not found in the *Tesoro* by Ximènez, nor in the other Quiché and Cakchiquel vocabularies which I have consulted; but it is very similar to the Maya word *yolomal*, which is a compound of *o'om*, "blood" in the ancient Maya of Yucatán. *Yo omal uinic*, "blood of man," the *Diccionario de Motul*. It is possible, therefore, that *holomax* may be derivative of the Maya *o'om*, *yolomal*, a synonym for "blood," and for that reason the author, who was very fond of using synonyms, employs it here to give emphasis to the language.

[14] Although it had not been mentioned before, Xquic knew very well that the lords wanted her heart in order to burn it. This was an ancient custom of the Maya. Father Landa says that in the month Mac "they threw the hearts of birds into the fire to burn them, and if they had no large animals, such as jaguars, pumas, or alligators, they made hearts with incense (*pom* or copal); and if there were animals and they killed them, they brought their hearts for that fire."

[15] *Chuh Cakché.* The tree which the Mexicans called *ezquahuitl*, "tree of blood," and which the Europeans also know by the name "blood," *Sangre de Dragón*, *Croton sanguifluus*, a tropical plant, the sap of which has the color and density of blood. Vásquez de Espinosa describes it as follows: "There is another tree in this province of Chiapa and of Guatemala which is called dragon. They are tall like almonds, the leaf is white and the stem is of the same color, and if a knife is stuck into the tree anywhere it weeps blood which looks as natural as though it were human." *Compendio y Descripción de las Indias Occidentales*, Part I, Book V. In the *Relación* of his expedition to the Petén, Father Agustín Cano, cited by Ximénez (*Historia de la Provincia de San Vicente de Chiapa y Guatemala*, III, 17), says that to the north of Cahabón in Verapaz, "there are certain large trees which, when they are pierced, bleed like the dragon, and in the language of Cahabón they are called *Pilix*, and in chol *Cancanté*."

[16] *Rumal quic holomax ch'u chaxic.* Here the words which we have examined in a previous note are repeated, but in a slightly different sense. *Quic* is blood, the sap and resin of a tree, especially of the India rubber, or elastic

"There on earth you shall be beloved and you shall have all that belongs to you," said the maiden to the owls.

"Very well, girl. We shall go there, we go up to serve you; you, continue on your way, while we go to present the sap, instead of your heart, to the lords," said the messengers.

When they arrived in the presence of the lords, all were waiting.

"You have finished?" asked Hun-Camé.

"All is finished, my lords. Here in the bottom of the gourd is the heart."

"Very well. Let us see," exclaimed Hun-Camé. And grasping it with his fingers he raised it, the shell broke and the blood flowed bright red in color.

"Stir up the fire and put it on the coals," said Hun-Camé.

As soon as they threw it on the fire, the men of Xibalba began to sniff and drawing near to it, they found the fragrance of the heart very sweet.

And as they sat deep in thought, the owls, the maiden's servants, left, and flew like a flock of birds from the abyss toward earth and the four became her servants.

In this manner the Lords of Xibalba were defeated. All were tricked by the maiden.

CHAPTER 4

Well, then, Hunbatz and Hunchouén were with their mother[1] when the woman called Xquic arrived.

When the woman Xquic came before the mother of Hunbatz

rubber, which the ancient Maya and Quiché sometimes used as incense for their gods. The ball with which they played was also called *quic*. The name of the heroine of this episode was likewise Xquic, that of the feminine blood, or that of elastic rubber. Brasseur de Bourbourg (1869) calls it *"la vierge Xquic, celle de la gomme élastique."*

[1] The grandmother of these boys, who also acted as a mother to them.

and Hunchouén,[2] she carried her sons in her belly and it was not long before Hunahpú and Xbalanqué, as they were called, were to be born.

When the woman came to the old lady, she said to her: "I have come, mother; I am your daughter-in-law and your daughter, mother." She said this when she entered the grandmother's house.

"Where did you come from? Where are my sons? Did they, perchance, not die in Xibalba? Do you not see these two who remain, their descendants and blood, and are called Hunbatz and Hunchouén? Go from here! Get out!" the old lady screamed at the girl.

"Nevertheless, it is true that I am your daughter-in-law; I have been for a long time. I belong to Hun-Hunahpú. They live in what I carry, Hun-Hunahpú and Vucub-Hunahpú are not dead; they will return to show themselves clearly, my mother-in-law. And you shall soon see their image in what I bring to you," she said to the old woman.

Then Hunbatz and Hunchouén became angry. They did nothing but play the flute and sing, paint, and sculpture all day long and were the consolation of the old woman.

Then the old woman said:

"I do not wish you to be my daughter-in-law, because what you bear in your womb is fruit of your disgrace. Furthermore, you are an impostor; my sons of whom you speak are already dead."

Presently the grandmother added: "This, that I tell you is the truth; but well, it is all right, you are my daughter-in-law, according to what I have heard. Go, then, bring the food for those who must be fed. Go and gather a large net [full of corn] and return at once, since you are my daughter-in-law, according to what I hear," she said to the girl.

"Very well," the girl replied, and she went at once to the

[2] In transcribing the Quiché text, Brasseur de Bourbourg omitted several words at this point, thinking, perhaps, that it was unnecessary to repeat them. The complete text is as follows: *Arecut e qo ri u chuch Hunbatz, Hunchouen, ta x-ul ri ixoc Xquic u bi. Ta x-ul cut ri ixoc Xquic ruq ri u chuch Hunbatz, Hunchouen.*

cornfield[3] which Hunbatz and Hunchouén had planted. They had opened the road and the girl took it and so came to the cornfield; but she found only one stalk of corn; there were not two or three, and when she saw that there was only one stalk with an ear on it, the girl became very anxious.

"Ah, sinner that I am, unfortunate me! Where must I go to get a net full of corn[4] as she told me to do?" she exclaimed. Immediately she began to beg Chahal[5] for the food which she had to get and must take back.

"Xtoh, Xcanil, Xcacau,[6] you who cook the corn; and you, Chahal, guardian of the food of Hunbatz and Hunchouén!" said the girl. And then she seized the beards, the red silk of the ears of corn and pulled them off without picking the ear. Then she arranged the silk in the net like ears of corn and the large net was completely filled.

The girl returned immediately; the animals of the field went along carrying the net, and when they arrived, they went to put the load in a corner of the house, as though she might have carried it. The old woman came and when she saw the corn in the large net she exclaimed:

"Where have you brought all this corn from? Did you, perchance, take all the corn in our field and bring it all in? I shall go at once to see," said the old woman, and she set out on the road to the cornfield. But the one stalk of corn was still standing there, and she saw too where the net had been at the foot of the stalk.[7] The old woman quickly returned to her house and said to the girl:

"This is proof enough that you are really my daughter-in-law. I shall now see your little ones, those whom you carry and who also are to be soothsayers,"[8] she said to the girl.

[3] *Milpa*, field planted with corn; the same name is also given to a stalk of corn.

[4] *Echá*, food, nourishment, particularly corn.

[5] Guardian of the cornfields.

[6] Brasseur de Bourbourg interprets these names as follows: Xtoh, goddess of rain; Xcanil, goddess of grain (from *ganel*, stalk of yellow corn); and Xcacau, goddess of cacao.

[7] *U qolibal cat chuxe*. Neither Brasseur de Bourbourg nor Ximénez translated *chuxe*, "at the foot of."

[8] *E nauinac chic*, sages, magicians, or soothsayers in Quiché.

Now we shall tell of the birth of Hunahpú and Xbalanqué. Here, then, we shall tell about their birth.

When the day of their birth arrived, the girl named Xquic gave birth; but the grandmother did not see them when they were born. Instantly the two boys called Hunahpú and Xbalanqué were born. There in the wood they were born.

Then they came to the house, but they could not sleep.

"Go throw them out!" said the old woman, "because truly they cry very much." Then they went and put them on an ant-hill. There they slept peacefully. Then they took them from the ant-hill and laid them on thistles.

Now, what Hunbatz and Hunchouén wished was that they [Hunahpú and Xbalanqué] would die there on the ant-hill, or on the thistles. They wished this because of the hatred and envy[1] Hunbatz and Hunchouén felt for them.

At first they refused to receive their younger brothers in the house; they would not recognize them and so they were brought up in the fields.

Hunbatz and Hunchouén were great musicians and singers; they had grown up in the midst of trials and want and they had had much trouble, but they became very wise. They were flautists, singers, painters, and carvers; all of this they knew how to do.

They had heard about their birth and knew also that they were the successors of their parents, those who went to Xibalba and died there. Hunbatz and Hunchouén were diviners, and in their hearts they knew everything concerning the birth of their two younger brothers. Nevertheless, because they were envious, they did not show their wisdom, and their hearts were filled with bad will for them, although Hunahpú and Xbalanqué had not offended them in any way.

These two [last] did nothing all day long but shoot their blowguns; they were not loved by their grandmother, nor by

---

[1] *X-c'ah rumal qui chaquimal, qui gag vachibal puch cumal Hunbatz, Hunchouen.*

Hunbatz, nor by Hunchouén; they were given nothing to eat; only when the meal was ended and Hunbatz and Hunchouén had already eaten, then the younger brothers came to eat. But they did not become angry, nor did they become vexed, but suffered silently, because they knew their rank, and they understood everything clearly.[2] They brought their birds when they came, and Hunbatz and Hunchouén ate them without giving anything to either of the two, Hunahpú and Xbalanqué.

The only thing that Hunbatz and Hunchouén did was to play the flute and sing.

And once when Hunahpú and Xbalanqué came without bringing any bird at all, they went into the house and their grandmother became furious.

"Why did you bring no birds?" she said to Hunahpú and Xbalanqué.

And they answered: "What happened, grandmother, is that our birds were caught in the tree and we could not climb up to get them, dear grandmother. If our elder brothers so wish, let them come with us to bring the birds down," they said.

"Very well," the older brothers answered, "we shall go with you at dawn."

The two younger brothers then discussed the way to overcome Hunbatz and Hunchouén.[3] "We shall only change their nature, their appearance; and so let our word be fulfilled,[4] for all the suffering that they have caused us. They wanted us to die, that we might be lost, we, their younger brothers. In their hearts[5] they really believe that we have come to be their servants. For these reasons we shall overcome them and teach them a lesson." Thus they spoke.

[2] *Xere qu'etaam ri qui qoheic, queheri zac ca qu'ilo.*

[3] *X-caminac cut qui naoh qui cabichal chirech qui chaquic Hunbatz, Hunchouen.* This passage was not understood by Brasseur de Bourbourg. Of the translators of the *Popol Vuh;* only Ximénez has interpreted it correctly as: "And the two having talked to each other, about the overthrowal of Hun-batz and Hun-chouen."

[4] *Ca tzih ta ch'uxoc,* literally, "that our word and command be fulfilled."

[5] *Chi qui qux,* literally, "in their hearts."

127

Then they went toward the foot of the tree called Canté.[6] They were accompanied by their two elder brothers and they were shooting their blowguns. It was not possible to count the birds which sang in the tree, and their elder brothers marveled to see so many birds. There were birds, but not one fell at the foot of the tree.

"Our birds do not fall to the ground. Go and fetch them down," they said to their elder brothers.

"Very well," the latter answered. And then they climbed the tree; but the tree became larger and the trunk swelled. Then Hunbatz and Hunchouén wanted to come down but they could not come down from the top of the tree.

Then they called from the treetop. "What has happened to us, our brothers? Unfortunate we. This tree frightens us only to look at it. Oh, our brothers!" they called from the treetop. And Hunahpú and Xbalanqué answered: "Loosen your breechclouts;[7] tie them below your stomach, leaving the long ends hanging and pull these from behind, and in this way you can walk easily." Thus said the younger brothers.

"Very well," they answered, pulling the ends of their belts back, but instantly these were changed into tails and they took on the appearance of monkeys. Then they hopped over the branches of the trees, among the great woods and little woods, and they buried themselves in the forest, making faces and swinging in the branches of the trees.

In this way Hunbatz and Hunchouén were overcome by Hunahpú and Xbalanqué; and only because of their magic could they have done it.

Then they returned to their home, and when they arrived they spoke to their grandmother and their mother, and said to them: "What could it be, grandmother, that has happened to our elder

[6] *Canté*, yellow wood, *Gliricidia sepium*. A tree from the roots of which the Maya obtained a substance which yielded a yellow color, according to the *Diccionario de Motul*. In Yucatán it is known by the name *Zac-yab*, and in Central America as *Madre de cacao*. Standley, *Flora of Yucatán*.

[7] *Ch'y quira y vex*. Unfasten your trousers, or breechclout; probably a simple loin cloth similar to the *maxtatl* of the Mexican Indians and the *ex* of the Maya is meant here.

brothers, that suddenly their faces turned into the faces of animals?" So they said.

"If you have done any harm to your elder brothers, you have hurt me and have filled me with sadness. Do not do such a thing to your brothers, oh, my children," said the old woman to Hunahpú and Xbalanqué.

And they replied to their grandmother:

"Do not grieve, our grandmother. You shall see our brothers' faces again; they shall return, but it will be a difficult trial for you, grandmother. Be careful that you do not laugh at them. And now, let us cast our lot," they said.

Immediately they began to play their flutes, playing the song of Hunahpú-Qoy.[8] Then they sang, playing the flute and drum, picking up their flutes and their drum. Afterward they sat down close to their grandmother and continued playing and calling back [their brothers] with music and song, intoning the song, called Hunahpú-Qoy.

At last, Hunbatz and Hunchouén came and began to dance; but when the old woman saw their ugly faces, she began to laugh, unable to control her laughter, and they went away at once and she did not see their faces again.

"Now you see, grandmother! They have gone to the forest. What have you done, grandmother of ours? We may make this trial but four times and only three are left. Let us call them [back again] with flute and with song, but you, try to control your laughter. Let the trial begin!" said Hunahpú and Xbalanqué.

Immediately they began again to play. Hunbatz and Hunchouén returned dancing, and came as far as the center of the court of the house[9] grimacing and provoking their grandmother to laughter, until finally she broke into loud laughter. They were really very amusing with their monkey-faces, their broad bottoms, their narrow tails, and the hole of their stomach,[10] all of which made the old woman laugh.

Again the [elder brothers] went back to the woods. And

[8] The monkey of Hunahpú.
[9] X-e ul chic u nicahal u va ha, literally, "they came to the edge of the house."
[10] U chi qui qux, literally, "the mouth of their stomachs."

Hunahpú and Xbalanqué said: "And now what shall we do, little grandmother? We shall try once again, this third time."

They played the flute again, and the monkeys returned dancing. The grandmother contained her laughter. Then they went up over the kitchen; their eyes gave off a red light; they drew away and scrubbed their noses and frightened each other with the faces they made.

And as the grandmother saw all of this, she burst into violent laughter; and they did not see the faces [of the elder brothers] again because of the old woman's laughter.

"Only once more shall we call them, grandmother, so that they shall come for the fourth time," said the boys. They began again, then, to play the flute, but [their brothers] did not return the fourth time, instead they fled into the forest as quickly as they could.

The boys said to their grandmother: "We have done everything possible, dear grandmother; they came once, then we tried to call them again. But do not grieve; here we are, your grandchildren; you must look to us, oh, our mother! Oh, our grandmother! to remind you of our elder brothers, those who were called and have the names of Hunbatz and Hunchouén," said Hunahpú and Xbalanqué.

They were invoked by the musicians and singers, and by the old people. The painters and craftsmen also invoked them in days gone by.[11] But they were changed into animals and became monkeys because they became arrogant and abused their brothers.

---

[11] The painters and carvers of Yucatán invoked Hunchevén and Hunahau, who were the younger sons of Ixchel and Itzammá (a god and goddess whom the Maya of the peninsula venerated), according to Bishop Las Casas "*De los libros y de las tradiciones religiosas que había en Guatemala,*" *Apologética Historia de las Indias,* Chap. CCXXXV). Those younger sons—the chronicler says—were not gods but divine men. Their names are evidently those of the days of the Maya calendar, 1 Chuén and 1 Ahau. The reader will easily notice the similarity between the Quiché youths and the Maya demigods. Bishop Las Casas writes in this connection: "All the trained workmen like the painters, the workers in feathers, the carvers, silversmiths, and others like them, worshiped and made sacrifice to those younger sons called Hunchevén and Hunahau, so that they would grant them the talent and skill needed to do a finished, perfect piece of work."

In this way they were disgraced; this was their loss; in this way Hunbatz and Hunchouén were overcome and became animals. They had always lived in their home; they were musicians and singers and also did great things when they lived with their grandmother and with their mother.

CHAPTER 6

Then they [Hunahpú and Xbalanqué] began to work, in order to be well thought of by their grandmother and their mother. The first thing they made was the cornfield. "We are going to plant the cornfield, grandmother and mother," they said. "Do not grieve; here we are, your grandchildren, we who shall take the place of our brothers," said Hunahpú and Xbalanqué.

At once they took their axes, their picks, and their wooden hoes and went, each carrying his blowgun on his shoulder. As they left the house they asked their grandmother to bring them their midday meal.

"At midday, come and bring our food, grandmother," they said.

"Very well, my grandsons," the old woman replied.

Soon they came to the field. And as they plunged the pick into the earth, it worked the earth; it did the work alone.

In the same way they put the ax in the trunks of the trees and in the branches, and instantly they fell and all the trees and vines were lying on the ground. The trees fell quickly, with only one stroke of the ax.

The pick also dug a great deal. One could not count the thistles and brambles which had been felled with one blow of the pick. Neither was it possible to tell what it had dug and broken up, in all the large and small woods.

And having taught an animal, called Xmucur,[1] they had it climb to the top of a large tree and Hunahpú and Xbalanqué said to it: "Watch for our grandmother to come with our food, and

[1] The turtledove, *mucuy* in Maya.

as soon as she comes, begin at once to sing, and we shall sieze the pick and the ax."

"Very well," Xmucur answered.

And they began to shoot with their blowguns; certainly they did none of the work of clearing and cultivating. A little later, the dove sang, and they ran quickly, grabbing the pick and ax. And one of them covered his head and also deliberately covered his hands with earth[2] and in the same way smeared his face to look like a real laborer, and the other purposely threw splinters of wood over his head as though he really had been cutting the trees.

Thus their grandmother saw them. They ate at once, but they had not really done the work of tilling the soil, and without deserving it they were given their midday meal. After a while, they went home.

"We are really tired, grandmother," they said upon arriving, stretching their legs and arms before her, but without reason.

They returned the following day, and upon arriving at the field, they found that all the trees and vines were standing again and that the brambles and thistles had become entangled again.

"Who has played this trick on us?" they said. "No doubt all the small and large animals did it, the puma, the jaguar, the deer, the rabbit, the mountain-cat, the coyote, the wild boar, the coati, the small birds, the large birds; they, it was, who did it; in a single night, they did it."

They began again to prepare the field and to prepare the soil and cut the trees. They talked over what they would have to do with the trees which they had cut, and the weeds which they had pulled up.

"Now we shall watch over our cornfield; perhaps we can surprise those who come to do all of this damage," they said, talking it over together. And later they returned home.

"What do you think of it, grandmother? They have made fun of us. Our field, which we had worked, has been turned into a field of stubble and a thick woods. Thus we found it, when we got there, a little while ago, grandmother," they said to her and to

[2] *Xalog* in the original; literally means "in vain" as Ximénez translates it, or "gratuitously," as Brasseur de Bourbourg renders it.

132

their mother. "But we shall return there and watch over it, because it is not right that they do such things to us," they said.

Then they dressed and returned at once to their field of cut
trees, and there they hid themselves, stealthily, in the darkness.

Then all the animals gathered again; one of each kind came
with the other small and large animals. It was just midnight when
they came, all talking as they came, saying in their own language:
"Rise up, trees! Rise up, vines!"[3]

So they spoke when they came and gathered under the trees,
under the vines, and they came closer until they appeared before
the eyes [of Hunahpú and Xbalanqué].

The puma and the jaguar were the first, and [Hunahpú and
Xbalanqué] wanted to seize them, but [the animals] did not let
them. Then the deer and the rabbit came close, and the only parts
of them which they could seize were their tails,[4] only these, they
pulled out. The tail of the deer remained in their hands, and for
this reason the deer and the rabbit have short tails.

Neither the mountain-cat, the coyote, the wild boar, nor the
coati fell into their hands. All the animals passed before Hunahpú
and Xbalanqué, who were furious because they could not catch
them.

But, finally, another animal came hopping along, and this one
which was the rat, [which] they seized instantly, and wrapped
him in a cloth. Then when they had caught him, they squeezed
his head and tried to choke him, and they burned his tail in the
fire, and for that reason the rat's tail has no hair. So, too, the boys,
Hunahpú and Xbalanqué, tried to poke at his eyes.

The rat said: "I must not die at your hands. And neither is it
your business to plant the cornfield."

"What are you telling us now?" the boys asked the rat.

"Loosen me a little, for I have something which I wish to tell
you, and I shall tell you immediately, but first give me something
to eat," said the rat.

[3] *Are puch tiquil u qux agab ta x-e petic, x-e chauiheic conohel ta x-e petic.
Are qui chabal ri: Yaclin che, yaclin caam.*

[4] The original is: *Xa cuch u he x-qui chap vi.* It seems to me that this is an
error, and that it should read *xa cu u he,* etc., and I have so translated it.

"We will give you food afterward, but first speak," they answered.

"Very well. Do you know, then, that the property of your parents Hun-Hunahpú and Vucub-Hunahpú, as they were called, those who died in Xibalba, or rather the gear with which they played ball, has remained[5] and is hanging from the roof of the house: the ring, the gloves, and the ball? Nevertheless, your grandmother does not want to show them to you for it was on account of these things that your parents died."

"Are you sure of that?" said the boys to the rat. And they were very happy when they heard about the rubber ball. And as the rat had now talked, they showed the rat what his food would be.

"This shall be your food: corn, chili-seeds, beans, pataxte, cacao;[6] all this belongs to you, and should there be anything stored away or forgotten, it shall be yours also. Eat it," Hunahpú and Xbalanqué said to the rat.

"Wonderful, boys," he said; "but what shall I tell your grandmother if she sees me?"

"Do not worry, because we are here and shall know what to say to our grandmother. Let us go! We shall go quickly to the corner of the house, go at once to where the things hang; we shall be looking at the garret of the house and paying attention to our food," they said to the rat.

And having arranged it thus, during the night after talking together, Hunahpú and Xbalanqué arrived at midday. When they arrived, they brought the rat with them, but they did not show it; one of them went directly into the house, and the other went to the corner and there let the rat climb up quickly.

Immediately they asked their grandmother for food. "Pre-

[5] In his transcription from the Quiché text, Brasseur de Bourbourg omitted the words *ri qu'etzabal x-e quel canoc*, which I have translated as it is here. *Etzan* is "to play" and *etzabal* is the playing gear.

[6] These were practically the daily foods of the ancient Quiché. Of cacao beans (*cacau* in Maya and in Quiché), they made a very nourishing drink, and in the same way they used a kind of cacao, *Theobroma bicolor*, which the Quiché called *pec* and which is commonly known by the Mexican name of *pataxte*.

pare our food,[7] we wish a chili-sauce,[8] grandmother," they said. And at once the food was prepared for them and a plate of broth was put before them.

But this was only to deceive their grandmother and their mother. And having dried up the water which was in the water jar, they said, "We are really dying of thirst; go and bring us a drink," they said to their grandmother.

"Good," she said and went. Then they began to eat, but they were not really hungry; it was only a trick. They saw then by means of their plate of chile[9] how the rat went rapidly toward the ball which was suspended from the roof of the house. On seeing this in their chile-sauce, they sent to the river a certain xan, an animal called *xan*, which is like a mosquito, to puncture the side of their grandmother's water jar, and although she tried to stop the water which ran out, she could not close the hole made in the jar.

"What is the matter with our grandmother? Our mouths are dry with thirst,[10] we are dying of thirst," they said to their mother and they sent her out.[11] Immediately the rat went to cut [the cord which held] the ball and it fell from the garret of the house together with the ring and the gloves and the leather pads. The boys seized them and ran quickly to hide them on the road which led to the ball-court.

After this they went to the river to join their grandmother and their mother, who were busily trying to stop the hole in the water jar. And arriving with their blowgun, they said when they came to the river: "What are you doing? We got tired [of waiting] and we came," they said.

"Look at the hole in my jar which I cannot stop," said the

[7] *Xa ch'y cutu ca ti*, literally, "grind our food." The food of the Quiché Indians consisted principally of *tortillas*, i.e., cakes of corn, which were cooked and ground on the stone which they called *caam*, the *metatl* of Mexico.

[8] *Cutum-ic*, in Quiché; *chilmulli*, in Náhuatl, chile-sauce.

[9] *Chupam cutum ic*, within the *chilmol*. The liquid red sauce served as a mirror and reflected the rat's movements on the roof, without its appearing as though the boys were watching them.

[10] *Oh hizabah chi ya.*

[11] To fetch the water.

grandmother. Instantly they stopped it, and together they returned, the two walking before their grandmother.

And in this way the ball was found.

T
## CHAPTER 7

he boys returned happily to the ball-court to play; they were playing alone a long time and cleared the court where their parents had played.

And the Lords of Xibalba, hearing them, said: "Who are they who play again over our heads and disturb us with the noise they make? Perchance Hun-Hunahpú and Vucub-Hunahpú did not die, those who wished to exalt themselves before us? Go at once and call them!"

So said Hun-Camé, Vucub-Camé, and all the lords. And sending the messengers to call them, they said to them: "Go and tell them when you get there: 'Let them come,' the lords have said; we wish to play ball with them here, within seven days we wish to play; tell them so when you arrive," thus said the lords. This was the command which they gave to the messengers. And they came then by the wide road which the boys had made that led directly to their house; by it the messengers arrived directly before [the boy's] grandmother. They were eating when the messengers from Xibalba arrived.

"Tell them to come, without fail, the lords commanded," said the messengers of Xibalba. And the messengers of Xibalba indicated the day: "Within seven days they will await them," they said to Xmucané.

"It is well, messengers; they will go," the old woman answered. And the messengers set out on their return.

Then the old woman's heart was filled with anxiety. "Whom shall I send to call my grandchildren?[1] Was it not in this same way that the messengers of Xibalba came before, when they came to

[1] *Naqui x-chi v'u chah qui taquic ri viy?* in the original.

PART II

take the [boys'] parents?" said the grandmother, entering her house, alone and grieving.

And immediately a louse fell into her lap. She seized it and put it in the palm of her hand, and the louse wriggled and began to walk.

"My child, would you like that I sent you away to call my grandchildren from the ball-court?" she said to the louse. " 'Messengers have come to your grandmother,' tell them; come within seven days, tell them to come, said the messengers of Xibalba; thus your grandmother told me to say,' " thus she told the louse.

At once the louse swaggered off. Sitting on the road was a boy called Tamazul,[2] or the toad.

"Where are you going?" the toad said to the louse.

"I am carrying a message in my stomach, I go to find the boys," said the louse to Tamazul.

"Very well, but I see that you do not go quickly," said the toad to the louse. "Do you not want me to swallow you? You shall see how I run, and so we shall arrive quickly."

"Very well," the louse said to the toad. Immediately the toad swallowed him. And the toad walked a long time, but without hurrying. Soon he met a large snake, called Zaquicaz.[3]

"Where are you going, young Tamazul?" said Zaquicaz to the toad.

"I go as a messenger; I carry a message in my stomach," said the toad to the snake.

"I see that you do not walk quickly. Would I not arrive sooner?" the snake said to the toad. "Come here," he said. At once Zaquicaz swallowed the toad. And from then on this was the food of snakes, who still today swallow toads.

The snake went quickly and having met Vac,[4] which is a very large bird, the hawk, [the latter] instantly swallowed the snake. Shortly afterward it arrived at the ball-court. From that time,

[2] *Tamazul u bi, ri xpek.* The author here uses the Náhuatl word *Tamazul* to designate this particular toad, thus showing the old Toltec influence still remaining in the minds of the Indians of Guatemala.

[3] Literally, white armadillo. A very large snake which makes a great deal of noise when it crawls away. Santa María, *Diccionario Cakchiquel.*

[4] A hawk which eats snakes. *Vocabulario de los P. P. Franciscanos.*

this has been the food of hawks, who devour snakes in the fields.

And upon arrival, the hawk perched upon the cornice of the ball-court where Hunahpú and Xbalanqué were amusing themselves playing ball. Upon arriving, the hawk began to cry: *"Vac-có! Vac-có!"* it said cawing. ["Here is the hawk! Here is the hawk!"]

"Who is screaming? Bring our blowguns!" the boys exclaimed. And shooting at the hawk, they aimed a pellet at the pupil of the eye[5] and [the hawk] spiraled to the ground. They ran to seize it and asked: "What do you come to do here?" they asked the hawk.

"I bring a message in my stomach. First cure my eye and afterward I shall tell you," the hawk answered.

"Very well," they said, and taking a bit of the rubber of the ball with which they were playing, they put it in the hawk's eye. Lotzquic[6] they called it, and instantly the hawk's eye was perfectly healed.

"Speak, then," they said to the hawk. And immediately it vomited a large snake.

"Speak, thou," they said to the snake.

"Good," the [snake] said and vomited the toad.

"Where is the message that you bring?" they asked the toad.

"Here in my stomach is the message," answered the toad. And immediately he tried, but could not vomit; his mouth only filled with spittle but he did not vomit. The boys wanted to hit him then.

"You are a liar," they said, kicking him in the rump, and the bone of the haunches gave way. He tried again, but his mouth only filled with spittle. Then the boys opened the toad's mouth

[5] There is a play on words in the original here: *qui cu tacal u bac uub chu bac u vach*, they aimed the pellet (*bac*) of the blowgun at the ball (*bac*) of the eye.

[6] *Lotz*, sorrel; *lotzquic*, rubber, or juice of the sorrel. An herb which the Mexicans call *xocoyolli*, and which seems to be *oxalis*, according to our classification of natural history, says Brasseur de Bourbourg. He adds that the natives of Central America assured him that they still used it to remove cataracts from their eyes. Garcilaso de la Vega, the Inca, speaks in the same way of a similar plant used by the Indians of Peru. According to the *Vocabulario de los P. P. Franciscanos, lotz* is also the *sapuyulo*, or stone of the *zapote* which sometimes is covered with a white or amber-colored gum.

138

and once open, they looked inside of it. The louse was stuck to the toad's teeth; it had stayed in its mouth and had not been swallowed, but only pretended to be swallowed.[7] Thus the toad was tricked, and the kind of food to give it is not known. It cannot run; and it became the food of the snakes.

"Speak," they said to the louse, and then it gave its message. "Your grandmother has said, boys: 'Go call them; the messengers of Hun-Camé and Vucub-Camé have come to tell them to go to Xibalba, saying: "They must come here within seven days to play ball with us, and they must also bring their playing gear, the ball, the rings, the gloves, the leather pads, in order that they may amuse themselves here," said the lords. They have really come,' said your grandmother. That is why I have come. For truly your grandmother said this and she cries and grieves, for this reason I have come."

"Is it true?" the boys asked themselves when they heard this. And running quickly they arrived at their grandmother's side; they went only to take their leave of her.

"We are going, grandmother, we came only to say good-bye. But here will be the sign which we shall leave of our fate: each of us shall plant a reed, in the middle of the house we shall plant it; if it dries, this shall be the sign of our death. 'They are dead!' you shall say, if it begins to dry up. But if it sprouts again: 'They are living!' you shall say, oh, our grandmother. And you, mother, do not weep, for here we leave the sign of our fate," thus they said.

And before going, Hunahpú planted one [reed] and Xbalanqué planted another; they planted them in the house and not in the field, nor did they plant them in moist soil, but in dry soil; in the middle of their house, they left them planted.

CHAPTER 8

Then they went, each one carrying his blowgun, and went down in the direction of Xibalba. They descended the

[7] *Xa quehe xa bic.*

steps quickly and passed between several streams and ravines. They passed among some birds and these birds were called Molay.[1]

They also passed over a river of corruption, and over a river of blood, where they would be destroyed, so the people of Xibalba thought; but they did not touch it with their feet, instead they crossed it on their blowguns.

They went on from there, and came to a crossway of four roads. They knew very well which were the roads to Xibalba; the black road, the white road, the red road, and the green road. So, then, they sent an animal called Xan.[2] It was to go to gather information which they wanted. Sting them, one by one; first sting the one seated in the first place and then sting all of them, since this is the part you must play: to suck the blood of the men on the roads," they said to the mosquito.

"Very well," answered the mosquito. And immediately it flew on to the dark road and went directly toward the wooden men which were seated first and covered with ornaments. It stung the first, but this one said nothing; then it stung the next one, it stung the second, who was seated, but this one said nothing, either.

After that it stung the third; the third of those seated was Hun-Camé. "Ah!" he exclaimed when it stung him. "What is this, Hun-Camé? What is it that has stung you? Do you not know who has stung you?" said the fourth one of the lords, who were seated.[3]

"What is the matter, Vucub-Camé? What has stung you?" said the fifth.

"Ah! Ah!" then said Xiquiripat. And Vucub-Camé asked him, "What has stung you?" and when they stung the sixth who was seated [he cried], "Ah!"

[1] *Molay* and its derivatives in Maya mean "together," "flock," "herd," derived from *mol*, "to gather." The text possibly refers here to the large flocks of birds which are still to be found in the tropical woods and fields of Guatemala.

[2] Mosquito. The same ally of Hunahpú and Xbalanqué who made a hole in the water jar of Xmucané.

[3] Brasseur de Bourbourg corrected the text of this passage, which in the original manuscript reads as follows: *¿Naqui Hun-Came, naquila mi-x-i tiouic? ¿Xah i na qu'i chila mi x-i tionic? x-cha chic u cah culel.*

"What is this, Cuchumaquic?" asked Xiquiripat. "What is it that has stung you?" And the seventh one seated said "Ah" when he was stung.

"What is the matter, Ahalpuh?" said Chuchumaquic. "What has stung you?" And when it stung him, the eighth of those seated said, "Ah!"

"What is the matter, Ahalcaná?" said Ahalpuh. "What has stung you?" And when he was stung the ninth of those seated said, "Ah!"

"What is this, Chamiabac?" said Ahalcaná. "What has stung you?" And when the tenth of those seated was stung, he said "Ah!"

"What is the matter, Chamiaholom?" said Chamiabac. "What has stung you?" And when the eleventh of those seated was stung he said, "Ah!"

"What happened?" said Chamiaholom. "What has stung you?" And when the twelfth of those seated was stung, he said "Alas!"

"What is this, Patán?" they said. "What has stung you?" And the thirteenth of those seated said "Alas!" when he was stung.

"What is the matter, Quicxic?" said Patán. "What has stung you?" And the fourteenth of those seated when he was stung said, "Alas!"

"What has stung you, Quicrixcac?" said Quicré.

In this way they told their names, as they all said them one to the other.[4] So they made themselves known[5] by telling their names, calling each chief, one by one. And in this manner each of those seated in his corner told his name.

Not a single one of the names was missed. All told their names when Hunahpú pulled out a hair of his leg, which was what had

[4] In the list of the Lords of Xibalba given here, some names appear which differ from those in Chapter 1 of this Part II, while others are omitted altogether. It is true that between one and another of these episodes a generation in time has elapsed and these changes are natural. Or is this still another version of these histories? The following are the new names: *Quicxic* (bloody wing), *Quicrixcac* (bloody claw), *Quicré* (teeth covered with blood). In the composition of all of these names, the word *quic* (blood) very appropriately appears.

[5] *X qui cut u vach*, literally, "they showed their faces."

stung them. It was really not a mosquito which stung them which went for Hunahpú and Xbalanqué to hear the names of all of them.

They [the youths] continued on their way and arrived where the Lords of Xibalba were.

"Greet the lord, the one who is seated," said one in order to deceive them.

"That is not a lord. It is nothing more than a wooden figure," they said, and went on. Immediately they began to greet them:

"Hail, Hun-Camé! Hail, Vucub-Camé! Hail, Xiquiripat! Hail, Cuchumaquic! Hail, Ahalpuh! Hail, Ahalcaná! Hail, Chamiabac! Hail, Chamiaholom! Hail, Quicxic! Hail, Patán! Hail, Quicré! Hail, Quicrixcac!" they said coming before them. And looking in their faces, they spoke the name of all, without missing the name of a single one of them.

But what the lords wished was that they should not discover their names.

"Sit here," they said, hoping that they would sit in the seat [which they indicated].

"That is not a seat for us; it is only a hot stone," said Hunahpú and Xbalanqué, and they [the Lords of Xibalba] could not overcome them.

"Very well, go to that house," the lords said. And they [the youths] went on and entered the House of Gloom. And neither there were they overcome.

CHAPTER 9

This was the first test of Xibalba. The Lords of Xibalba thought that [the boys'] entrance there would be the beginning of their downfall. After a while [the boys] entered the House of Gloom; immediately lighted sticks of fat pine were given them and the messengers of Hun-Camé also took a cigar to each one.

" 'These are their pine sticks,' said the lord; 'they must return them at dawn, tomorrow, together with the cigars, and you must bring them back whole,' said the lord." So said the messengers when they arrived.

"Very well," [the boys] replied. But they really did not [light] the sticks of pine, instead they put a red-colored thing in place of them, or some feathers from the tail of the macaw, which to the night watches[1] looked like lighted pine sticks. And as for the cigars, they attached fireflies to their end.[2]

All night [everybody] thought they were defeated. "They are lost," said the night watchmen. But the pine sticks had not been burned and looked the same, and the cigars had not been lighted and looked the same as before.

They went to tell the lords.

"How is this? Whence have they come? Who conceived them? Who gave birth to them? This really troubles us, because it is not well what they do. Their faces are strange, and strange is their conduct," they said to each other.

Soon all the lords summoned [the boys].

"Eh! Let us play ball, boys!" they said. At the same time they were questioned by Hun-Camé and Vucub-Camé:

"Where did you come from? Tell us, boys!" said the Lords of Xibalba.

"Who knows whence we came! We do not know," they said, and nothing more.

"Very well. Let us play ball, boys," said the Lords of Xibalba.

"Good," they replied.[3]

[1] *Varanel*, the "night guards."

[2] *Caca chicop*, insect of fire, glowworms. As in English, the firefly.

[3] In order to understand better the passages of the *Popol Vuh* in which the ball game is spoken of, it is well to read Sahagún's description of it (*Historia general de las cosas de Nueva España*, Vol. II, Book VIII, Chap. X, p. 297), which follows: " . . . At other times the lord played ball for his pastime, and for this balls of *ulli* were kept; these balls were about the size of some large balls for bowling [and] they were solid, of a certain resin or gum which they called *ulli*, which is very light and bounces like an inflated ball; and he also brought with him good ball players who played before him and other principal men played on the opposite [team] and they won gold and *chalchiguites* and beads of gold, and turquoise, and slaves, and rich mantles, and *maxtles*, and cornfields and houses, etc. [feathers, cacao, cloaks of feather]. . . . the ballcourt was called

"We shall use our ball," said the Lords of Xibalba.[4]

"By no means, shall you use [your ball], but ours," the boys answered.

"Not that one, but ours we shall use," insisted the Lords of Xibalba.

"Very well," said the boys.

"Let us play for a worm, the *chil*,"[5] said the Lords of Xibalba.

"No, but instead, the head of the puma shall speak,"[6] said the boys.

"Not that," said those of Xibalba.

"Very well," said Hunahpú.

Then the Lords of Xibalba seized the ball; they threw it directly at the ring of Hunahpú. Immediately, while those of Xibal-

---

*tlaxtli* or *tlachtli* and consisted of two walls, twenty or thirty feet apart, and were up to forty or fifty feet in length; the walls and the floor were whitewashed, and were about eight and a half feet high, and in the middle of the court was a line which was used in the game. In the middle of the walls, in the center of the court, were two stones, like millstones hollowed out, opposite each other, and each one had a hole wide enough to contain the ball for each one of them. And the one who put the ball in it won the game; they did not play with their hands, but instead struck the ball with their buttocks; for playing, they wore gloves on their hands and a belt of leather on their buttocks, with which to strike the ball."

[4] Brasseur de Bourbourg intentionally changes the order of this part of the dialogue. The order has been re-established here according to the original Quiché, to which both Ximénez and I adhere, as may be seen in the former's first version (1857).

[5] *Chil*, a caterpillar which, according to Ximénez in his *Tesoro*, clings. This may be the centipede, according to the *Vocabulario Maya-Quiché-Cakchiquel que se habla en la laguna de Atitlán*.

[6] This passage is very vague, and Brasseur de Bourbourg even says that it is unintelligible. There is an evident play of words concerned in it. The original says: "He bala xa hù chil, x-e cha Xibalba. Ma bala, xa holom coh cha chic, x-e cha qaholab. Bala is an indefinite word used to give emphasis to the account, and is sometimes also an adverb of place. It seems, nevertheless, that here it is repeated in the text to appear like *balam*, as though wishing to say: "The head of the jaguar [*balam*] does not rule here, but the head of the puma [*coh*]." These seem to be terms of the ancient ball game. Surmounting the side of the imposing ball-court of Chichén-Itzá is the Temple of the Jaguars, so called because of the figures of these animals which are engraved on its walls. Undoubtedly the jaguar had some connection with the ball game.

ba grasped the handle of the knife of flint,[7] the ball rebounded and bounced all around the floor of the ball-court.

"What is this?" exclaimed Hunahpú and Xbalanqué. "You wish to kill us? Perchance you did not send to call us? And your own messengers did not come? In truth, unfortunate are we! We shall leave at once," the boys said to them.

This was exactly what those of Xibalba wanted to have happen to the boys, that they would die immediately, right there in the ball-court and thus they would be overcome. But it did not happen thus, and it was the Lords of Xibalba who were defeated by the boys.

"Do not leave, boys, let us go on playing ball, but we shall use your ball," they said to the boys.

"Very well," the boys answered and then they drove their ball[8] through [the ring of Xibalba], and with this the game ended.

And offended by their defeat, the men of Xibalba immediately said: "What shall we do in order to overcome them?" And turning to the boys they said to them: "Go gather and bring us, early tomorrow morning,[9] four gourds of flowers." So said the men of Xibalba to the boys.

"Very well. And what kind of flowers?" they asked the men of Xibalba.

"A branch of red *chipilín*, a branch of white *chipilín*, a branch of yellow *chipilín*, and a branch of *carinimac*," said the men of Xibalba.[10]

"Very well," replied the boys.

Thus the talk ended; equally strong and vigorous were the

[7] *Catepuch ta x-qu il Xibalba ri zaqui tog, ta x-el chupam ri quic.* The Lords of Xibalba, without losing time, wanted to kill their guests with the sacrificial knife and only were deterred from this intention by the just complaint which may be read in the following paragraph.

[8] *Are cu x-oc ri quic.* Playing with their own ball, the youths had no difficulty in driving it through the ring of their opponents and thus winning the game.

[9] *Xa cacha ca cah cah zel cotzih.* Cah is the numeral "four" and also the adverb "early."

[10] *Caca-muchih.* Muchih or muchit is the name of a certain plant called *chipilín*, says Ximénez. It is a plant of the leguminous family, *Crotalaria longirostrata*. It has not been possible to identify the plant which the text calls *Carinimac*.

words of the boys. And their hearts were calm when they gave themselves up to be overcome.

The Lords of Xibalba were happy, thinking that they had already defeated them.

"This has turned out well for us. First they must cut them [the flowers],"[11] said the Lords of Xibalba. "Where shall they go to get the flowers?" they said to themselves.

"Surely you will give us our flowers tomorrow early;[12] go, then, to cut them,"[13] the Lords of Xibalba said to Hunahpú and Xbalanqué.

"Very well," they replied. "At dawn[14] we shall play ball again," they said upon leaving.

And immediately the boys entered the House of Knives, the second place of torture in Xibalba. And what the lords wanted was that they would be cut to pieces by the knives, and would be quickly killed; that is what they wished in their hearts.

But the [boys] did not die. They spoke at once to the knives[15] and said to them:

"Yours shall be the flesh of all the animals," they said to the knives. And they did not move again, but all the knives were quiet.

Thus they passed the night in the House of Knives, and calling all the ants, they said to them: "Come, Cutting Ants,[16] come, zompopos,[17] and all of you go at once, go and bring all the kinds of flowers that we must cut for the lords."

[11] *Nabe mi x-e ca chaco.*

[12] *Quitzih ta agab ch'y ya ri ca cotzih.* Here *agab, agabá* means at dawn, or daybreak, when night is over, and only by following this interpretation does this part of the story agree with that which appears farther on.

[13] *Ca chacom puch.* Until now, the meaning of the verb *chacón* from *chacá* and *chaqué*, "to cut bunches of flowers," has escaped translators of the *Popol Vuh*.

[14] *Agabá* the same as in the previous paragraph.

[15] *Ta x-e cha chire cha.* Brasseur de Bourbourg observes here that the Quiché delighted in these plays on words. In this entire chapter the author uses the word *cha*, which means to talk, to say, lance, knife, glass, etc. The same may be said of the word *cah* used, as has been said in a previous note, as an adjective, a verb, and an adverb.

[16] *Chai-zanic,* cutting ants.

[17] *Chequen-zanic,* red or black ants which travel by night and cut the tender leaves and flowers. In Guatemala they are commonly known as *zompopos,* a Mexican word.

"Very well," they said, and all the ants went to bring the flowers from the gardens of Hun-Camé and Vucub-Camé.

Previously [the lords] had warned the guards of the flowers of Xibalba: "Take care of our flowers, do not let them be taken by the boys who shall come to cut them. But how could [the boys] see and cut the flowers?[18] Not at all. Watch, then, all night!"

"Very well," they answered. But the guards of the garden heard nothing. Needlessly they shouted up into the branches of the trees in the garden. There they were all night, repeating their same shouts and songs.

"*Ixpurpuvec! Ixpurpuvec!*" one shouted.

"*Puhuyú! Puhuyú!*" the other answered.[19]

Puhuyú was the name of the two who watched the garden of Hun-Camé and Vucub-Camé.[20] But they did not notice the ants who were robbing them of what they were guarding, turning around and moving here and there, cutting the flowers, climbing the trees to cut the flowers, and gathering them from the ground at the foot of the trees.

Meanwhile the guards went on crying, and they did not feel the teeth which were cutting their tails and their wings.

And thus the ants carried, between their teeth, the flowers which they took down, and gathering them from the ground, they went on carrying them with their teeth.

Quickly they filled the four gourds with flowers, which were moist [with dew] when it dawned.[21] Immediately the messengers

18 ¿*Ana-vi x-pe vi r'ilo ca chacón cumal?* Again the verb *chacón*, in the sense of cutting branches or flowers.

19 *Purpuvec* and *puhuy* are the names which the Quiché and Cakchiquel still give to the red or barn owl. They are words which imitate the call of these birds. "*Puhuy, Pupuek*, a night bird which travels when the moon is up, at night," says the *Vocabulario de los P.P. Franciscanos*. The birds of which the text speaks here seem to be rather the bird commonly called the churn owl. This word imitates the choppy call of those birds which are to be heard at a distance in the night. Puhuy is the Maya name of one of these night birds. The *Vocabulario de las lenguas Quiché y Cakchiquel* defines these words as follows: *Xpurpugüek*, cuerpo-ruin; *Puhuyú*, chotacabra. Both names apply to the same bird, a member of the Caprimulgidae family.

20 *Ri Puhuyú u bi e caib chi chahal ticon, u ticon Hun-Camé, Vucub Camé.*

21 *Tiquitoh chicut ta x-zaquiric.*

arrived to get them. " 'Tell them to come,' the lord has said, 'and bring here instantly what they have cut,' " they said to the boys.

"Very well," the [boys] answered. And carrying the flowers in the four gourds, they went, and when they arrived before the lord [of Xibalba] and the other lords, it was lovely to see the flowers they had brought. And in this way the Lords of Xibalba were overcome.

The boys had only sent the ants [to cut the flowers], and in a night the ants cut them and put them in the gourds.

Instantly the Lords of Xibalba paled and their faces became livid because of the flowers. They sent at once for the guardians of the flowers: "Why did you permit them to steal our flowers? These which we see here are our flowers," they said to the guardians.

"We noticed nothing, my lord. Our tails also suffered," they answered. And then the [lords] tore at their mouths as a punishment for having let that which was under their care be stolen.

Thus were Hun-Camé and Vucub-Camé defeated by Hunahpú and Xbalanqué. And this was the beginning of their deeds. From that time the mouth of the owl is divided, cleft as it is today.

Immediately they went down to play ball, and also they played several tie-matches. Then they finished playing and agreed to play again the following day at dawn. So said the Lords of Xibalba.

"It is well," said the boys upon finishing.


CHAPTER 10

Afterward they entered the House of Cold. It is impossible to describe how cold it was. The house was full of hail; it was the mansion of cold. Soon, however, the cold was ended because with [a fire of] old logs the boys made the cold disappear.

That is why they did not die; they were still alive when it dawned. Surely what the Lords of Xibalba wanted was that they would die; but it was not thus, and when it dawned, they were still full of health, and they went out again, when the messengers came to get them.

"How is this? They are not dead yet?" said the Lords of Xibalba. They were amazed to see the deeds of Hunahpú and Xbalanqué.

Presently the [boys] entered the House of Jaguars. The house was full of jaguars. "Do not bite us! Here is what belongs to you,"[1] [the boys] said to the jaguars. And quickly they threw some bones to the animals, which pounced upon the bones.

"Now surely they are finished. Now already they have eaten their own entrails. At last they have given themselves up. Now their bones have been broken," so said the guards, all happy because of this.

But they [the boys] did not die. As usual, well and healthy, they came out of the House of Jaguars.

"What kind of people are they? Where did they come from?" said all the Lords of Xibalba.

Presently they [the boys] entered into the midst of fire in the House of Fire, inside which there was only fire; but they were not burned. Only the coals and the wood burned. And, as usual, they were well when it dawned. But what they [the Lords of Xibalba] wished was that [the boys] would die rapidly, where they had been. Nevertheless, it did not happen thus, which disheartened the Lords of Xibalba.

Then they put them into the House of Bats. There was nothing but bats inside this house, the house of Camazotz,[2] a large animal, whose weapons for killing were like a dry point,[3] and instantly those who came into their presence perished.[4]

[1] *Qo yvech ch'uxic*, literally, "yours shall be what is here." Ximénez translates this passage thus: "This must be your food!" reading *yvecha* instead of the possessive *yvech*, "yours."

[2] Death Bat. The vampire bat god of the Maya *códices* appears with the sacrificial knife in one hand and his victim in the other.

[3] *Chaqui tzam*, "dry point"; it may be understood here as referring to the burnt staff, hardened in the fire.

[4] *Huzu ch'utzinic ch'opon chi qui vach*, in the original. *Chupan* in Brasseur de Bourbourg through an error in copying.

They [the boys] were in there, then, but they slept inside their blowguns. And they were not bitten by those who were in the house. Nevertheless, one of them had to give up because of another Camazotz that came from the sky, and made him come into sight.

The bats were assembled in council all night, and flew about: "*Quilitz, quilitz*," they said: So they were saying all night. They stopped for a little while, however, and they did not move and were pressed against the end of one of the blowguns.

Then Xbalanqué said to Hunahpú: "Look you, has it begun already to get light?"

"Maybe so. I am going to see," [Hunahpú] answered.

And as he wished very much to look out of the mouth of the blowgun, and wished to see if it had dawned, instantly Camazotz cut off his head and the body of Hunahpú was decapitated.

Xbalanqué asked again: "Has it not yet dawned?" But Hunahpú did not move. "Where have you gone, Hunahpú? What have you done?" But he did not move, and remained silent.

Then Xbalanqué felt concerned and exclaimed: "Unfortunate are we. We are completely undone."

They went immediately to hang the head [of Hunahpú] in the ball-court by special order of Hun-Camé and Vucub-Camé, and all the people of Xibalba rejoiced for what had happened to the head of Hunahpú.

CHAPTER II

Immediately he [Xbalanqué] called all the animals, the coati, the wild boar, all the animals small and large, during the night, and at dawn he asked them what their food was.

"What does each of you eat? For I have called you so that you may choose your food," said Xbalanqué to them.

"Very well," they answered. And immediately each went to take his [own food] and they all went together. Some went to take rotten things; others went to take grasses; others went to get stones. Others went to gather earth. Varied was the food of the [small] animals and of the large animals.

Behind them the turtle was lingering,[1] it came waddling along to take its food. And reaching at the end [of Hunahpú's body] it assumed the form of the head of Hunahpú, and instantly the eyes were fashioned.

Many soothsayers came, then, from heaven. The Heart of Heaven, Huracán, came to soar over the House of Bats.

It was not easy to finish making the face, but it turned out very well; the hair had a handsome appearance and [the head] could also speak.

But as it was about to dawn and the horizon reddened: "Make it dark again, old one!" the buzzard was told.[2]

"Very well," said the old one,[3] and instantly the old one dark-

[1] *Ri tiz coc*, literally, "the turtle squeezed or compressed" (inside its shell).

[2] This passage is very difficult to understand in Brasseur de Bourbourg's transcription. The text may be read as follows: *Are cut ta chi r'ah zaquiric chi cactarin u xecah, "¡Ca zaquinu chic, ama!", x-u chax ri vuch*, since farther on, one reads *x-u chax umul*, which is said to the rabbit. When transcribing the primitive text, Ximéenz wrote *chux* and not *chax*, but in his literal translation it is "was said to the buzzard."

It seems to me that those who in this place have translated the verb *xaquin* as "to open the legs" have also erred. *Xaquin* in Quiché means to darken, to stain, to soil with soot or coal. Ximénez wisely translates it here as "darken."

Note, also, that following Ximénez, I have translated *vuch* as "buzzard" (vulture), and not as a fox bitch or *tacuatzin*, as do Brasseur de Bourbourg and others. "Vulture" in Quiché is *cuch* or *kuch,* that the Spanish clerics sometimes wrote *guch*, which has the same sound of *vuch* or *uuch*. The meaning in this passage corresponds more nearly to "vulture" or "buzzard," a bird of black plumage. The picture of the buzzard spreading its wings in order to darken the sky and to hide the secret fashioning of the artificial head of Hunahpú belongs to the most genuine expression of aboriginal American mythology.

[3] "*ve*," *x-cha ri mama*. The Quiché call the male buzzard *mama cuch*, "old buzzard." The identity of the creature mentioned here, however, is of no importance. The ancient Indians made use of objects and beings in nature with which to represent imaginary ideas and immaterial things, by means of the similarity of their names. In the present case they were trying, without doubt, to represent the idea of the darkness which immediately precedes the dawn, which they called *vuch*. Father Thomas Coto thus explains the significance of the word *vuch*: "It signifies that darkening of the sky when it is about to dawn." In order to represent this idea, the Indians traced the figure of the animal whose name sounded like the word they were trying to suggest.

ened [the sky]. "Now the buzzard has darkened it," the people say nowadays.

And so, during the cool of dawn, the [Hunahpú] began his existence.

"Will it be good?" they said. "Will it turn out to look like Hunahpú?"

"It is very good," they answered. And really it seemed that the skull had changed itself back into a real head.

Then they [the two boys] talked among themselves and agreed: "Do not play ball; only pretend to play; I shall do everything alone," said Xbalanqué.[4]

At once he gave his orders to a rabbit: "Go and take your place over the ball-court; stay there within the oak grove,"[5] the rabbit was told by Xbalanqué; "when the ball comes to you, run out immediately, and I shall do the rest," the rabbit was told, when they gave him these instructions during the night.

Presently day broke and the two boys were well and healthy. Then they went down to play ball. The head of Hunahpú was suspended over the ball-court.

"We have triumphed! [said the Lords of Xibalba]. You worked your own destruction,[6] you have delivered yourselves," they said. In this way they annoyed Hunahpú.

"Hit his head with the ball,"[7] they said. But they did not bother him with it;[8] he paid no attention to it.[9]

Then the Lords of Xibalba threw out the ball. Xbalanqué went out to get it; the ball was going straight to the ring, but it

---

[4] The text here should read: *Mana qui c'at chaahic, xaqui ch'a yecuh avib. Xa in hun qui qui banouic, x-cha xbalanqué chire.*

[5] *Chupam pixc.* Ximénez translates "in the tomato patch," taking *pixc* for *pix*. Brasseur de Bourbourg translates *entre les glands de la corniche.* Villacorta and Rodas say, "Inside the hole of the roof." Schultze Jena says "cornice." *Pixc,* in Quiché and Cakchiquel, is the evergreen oak and its fruit, the acorn, *gland* in French.

[6] *Mi-x-y bano qui yan,* in the original.

[7] *Ch'a caca ri holom chi quic.* Brasseur de Bourbourg interprets this sentence fancifully, according to his whim. *Cac* means "to stone," "to hit."

[8] In the original: *Ma cu chi qui ca caxou chic.*

[9] *Chi yecoub quib,* literally, to "pretend" or "dissimulate."

stopped, bounced, and passed quickly over the ball-court and with a jump went toward the oak grove.

Instantly the rabbit ran out and went hopping; and the Lords of Xibalba ran after it. They went, making noise and shouting after the rabbit. It ended by all of the Lords of Xibalba going.

At once Xbalanqué took possession of the head of Hunahpú; and taking the turtle he went to suspend it over the ball-court. And that head was actually the head of Hunahpú and the two boys were very happy.

Those of Xibalba ran, then, to find the ball and having found it between the oaks, called them, saying:

"Come here. Here is the ball. We found it," they said, and they brought it.

When the Lords of Xibalba returned, they exclaimed, "What is this we see?"

Then they began to play again. Both of them tied.

Presently Xbalanqué threw a stone at the turtle, which came to the ground and fell in the ball-court, breaking into a thousand pieces like seeds, before the lords.

"Who of you shall go to find it? Where is the one who shall go to bring it?" said the Lords of Xibalba.

And so were the Lords of Xibalba overcome by Hunahpú and Xbalanqué. These two suffered great hardships, but they did not die despite all that was done to them.

H ere is the account of the death of Hunahpú
and Xbalanqué. Now we shall tell of the way they died.

CHAPTER 12

Having been forewarned of all the suffering which the [Lords of Xibalba] wished to impose upon them, they did not die of the tortures of Xibalba, nor were they overcome by all the fierce animals which were in Xibalba.

Afterward they sent for two soothsayers who were like prophets; they were called Xulú and Pacam[1] and were diviners, and they said unto them:

"You shall be questioned by the Lords of Xibalba about our deaths, for which they are planning and preparing because of the fact that we have not died, nor have they been able to overcome us, nor have we perished under their torments, nor have the animals attacked us. We have the presentiment in our hearts that they shall kill us by burning us. All the people of Xibalba have assembled, but the truth is, that we shall not die. Here, then, you have our instructions as to what you must say:

"If they should come to consult you about our death and that we may be sacrificed, what shall you say then, Xulú and Pacam? If they ask you: 'Will it not be good to throw their bones into the ravine?' 'No, it would not be well,' tell them, 'because they would be brought to life again, afterward!' If they ask you: 'Would it not be good to hang them from the trees?' you shall answer: 'By no means would it be well, because then you shall see their faces again.' And when for the third time they ask you: 'Would it be good to throw their bones into the river?' If you were asked all the above by them, you should answer: 'It would be well if they were to die that way; then it would be well to crush their bones on a grinding stone, as corn meal is ground; let each one be ground [separately]; throw them into the river immediately, there where the spring gushes forth, in order that they may be carried away among all the small and large hills.' Thus you shall answer them when the plan which we have advised you is put into practice," said Hunahpú and Xbalanqué. And when they [the boys] took leave of them, they already knew about their approaching death.

They made then, a great bonfire, a kind of oven; the men of Xibalba made it and filled it with thick branches.

Shortly afterward the messengers arrived who had to accompany [the boys], the messengers of Hun-Camé and Vucub-Camé.

" 'Tell them to come. Go and get the boys; go there so that

---

[1] *Xulú*, little devils who appear near the rivers, according to Father Barela. Ahxulú is the same as *ahquib*, "soothsayer." *Pacam*, "distinguished."

they may know we are going to burn them.' This the lords said, oh, boys!" the messengers exclaimed.

"It is well," they answered. And setting out quickly, they arrived near the bonfire. There [the Lords of Xibalba] wanted to force the boys to play a mocking game with them.

"Let us drink our *chicha* and fly four times, each one, [over the bonfire] boys!" was said to them by Hun-Camé.

"Do not try to deceive us," [the boys] answered. "Perchance, we do not know about our death, oh lords! and that this is what awaits us here?" And embracing each other, face to face, they both stretched out their arms, bent toward the ground and jumped into the bonfire, and thus the two died together.

All those of Xibalba were filled with joy, shouting and whistling they exclaimed: "Now we have overcome them. At last they have given themselves up."

Immediately they called Xulú and Pacam, to whom they [the boys] had given their instructions, and asked them what they must do with their bones, as they [the boys] had foretold. Those of Xibalba then ground their bones and went to cast them into the river. But the bones did not go very far, for settling themselves down at once on the bottom of the river, they were changed back into handsome boys. And when again they showed themselves, they really had their same old faces.[2]

O
CHAPTER 13

n the fifth day they appeared again and were seen in the water by the people. Both had the appearance of fishmen;[1] when those of Xibalba saw them, after having hunted them all over the river.

[2] That is, those of Hunahpú and Xbalanqué.

[1] *Vinac-car*, literally "fish man." The author no doubt plays with these words to give the idea that the heroes of the story were sons of the water. *Vinac car* is really the common name of a variety of fish, "a very large fish," says Barela, "which is caught with *barbasco* [a poisonous plant]." However, the *Vocabulario de las lenguas Quiché y Cakchiquel*, closely following the literal meaning of the words, interprets them as "a large fish or mermaid."

And the following day, two poor men presented themselves with very old-looking faces and of miserable appearance, [and] ragged clothes, whose countenances did not commend them. So they were seen by all those of Xibalba.

And what they did was very little. They only performed the dance of the *puhuy* [owl or churn-owl], the dance of the *cux* [weasel], and the dance of the *iboy* [armadillo], and they also danced the *xtzul* [centipede] and the *chitic* [that walks on stilts].[2]

Furthermore, they worked many miracles. They burned houses as though they really were burning and instantly they were as they had been before.[3] Many of those of Xibalba watched them in wonder.

Presently they cut themselves into bits; they killed each other; the first one whom they had killed stretched out as though he were dead, and instantly the other brought him back to life. Those of Xibalba looked on in amazement at all they did, and they performed it, as the beginning of their triumph over those of Xibalba.

Presently word of their dances came to the ears of the lords Hun-Camé and Vucub-Camé. Upon hearing it they exclaimed: "Who are these two orphans? Do they really give you so much pleasure?"

"Surely their dances are very beautiful, and all that they do," answered he who had brought the news to the lords.

Happy to hear this, the [lords] then sent their messengers to call [the boys] with flattery. " 'Tell them to come here, tell them to come so that we may see what they do; that we may admire them and regard them with wonder,' this the lords said. 'So you shall say unto them,' " this was told to the messengers.

They arrived at once before the dancers and gave them the message of the lords.

"We do not wish to," the [boys] answered, "because, frankly, we are ashamed. How could we not but be ashamed to appear in the house of the lords with our ugly countenances, our eyes which

[2] In the dance of Xtzul, the dancers wear small masks, and tails of the macaw on the napes of their necks, according to Barela. Landa says that when the New Year fell on the day Muluc, the Maya of Yucatán danced a dance on very tall stilts during the corresponding fiestas.

[3] *Vinaquir chic*, literally, "they were created again."

are so big, and our poor appearance? Do you not see that we are nothing more than some [poor] dancers? What shall we tell our companions in poverty who have come with us and wish to see our dances and be entertained by them? How could we do our dances before the lords?[4] For that reason, then, we do not want to go, oh, messengers," said Hunahpú and Xbalanqué.

Finally, with downcast faces and with reluctance and sorrow they went; but for a while they did not wish to walk, and the messengers had to beat them in the face many times, when they led them to the house of the lords.

They arrived, then, before the lords, timid and with head bowed; they came prostrating themselves, making reverences and humiliating themselves.[5] They looked feeble, ragged, and their appearance was really that of vagabonds when they arrived.

They were questioned immediately about their country and their people; they also asked them about their mother and their father.

"Where do you come from?" [the lords] said.

"We do not know, Sir. We do not know the faces of our mother and father; we were small when they died," they answered, and did not say another word.

"All right. Now do [your dances] so that we may admire you. What do you want? We shall give you pay," they told them.

"We do not want anything; but really we are very much afraid," they said to the lord.

"Do not grieve, do not be afraid. Dance! And do first the part in which you kill yourselves; burn my house, do all that you know how to do. We shall marvel at you, for that is what our hearts desire. And afterwards, poor things, we shall give help for your journey," they told them.

[4] The exact sentence in the original is as follows: *Ma quehe la cu x-chi ca ban chique ri ahauab?*

[5] Here there is a repetition of the same idea expressed in a series of synonymous verbs: *que mocho chic, chi qui xule la qui vach, x-qui quemelah quib, chi qui luc quib, chi qui pach quib.* This last word was omitted by Brasseur de Bourbourg. All these sentences have identical meaning and are undoubtedly used to emphasize the respect which the youthful heroes, so cleverly disguised as vagabonds, wished to feign before their enemies, the Lords of Xibalba.

Then they began to sing and dance. All the people of Xibalba arrived and gathered together in order to see them. Then they performed the dance of the *cux*, they danced the *puhuy*, and they danced the *iboy*.

And the lord said to them: "Cut my dog into pieces and let him be brought back to life by you," he said to them.

"Very well," they answered, and cut the dog into bits. Instantly they brought him back to life. The dog was truly full of joy when he was brought back to life, and wagged his tail when they revived him.

The Lord said to them then: "Burn my house now!" Thus he said to them. Instantly they put fire to the lord's house, and although all the lords were assembled together within the house, they were not burned. Quickly it was whole again, and not for one instant was the house of Hun-Camé destroyed.

All of the lords were amazed, and in the same way the [boys'] dances gave them much pleasure.

Then they were told by the lord: "Now kill a man, sacrifice him, but do not let him die," he told them.

"Very well," they answered. And seizing a man, they quickly sacrificed him, and raising his heart on high, they held it so that all the lords could see it.

Again Hun-Camé and Vucub-Camé were amazed. A moment afterward the man was brought back to life by them [the boys], and his heart was filled with joy when he was revived.

The lords were astounded. "Sacrifice yourselves now, let us see it! We really like your dances!" said the lords. "Very well, Sirs," they answered. And they proceeded to sacrifice each other. Hunahpú[6] was sacrificed by Xbalanqué; one by one his arms and his legs were sliced off; his head was cut from his body and carried away; his heart was torn from his breast and thrown onto the grass. All the Lords of Xibalba were fascinated.[7] They looked on in wonder, but really it was only the dance of one man; it was Xbalanqué.

---

[6] *Xhunahpú* in the original.

[7] *Que gabar cu ri ronohel rahaual Xibalba*, literally, "all the Lords of Xibalba were drunk."

"Get up!" he said, and instantly[8] [Hunahpú] returned to life. They [the boys] were very happy and the lords were also happy. In truth, what they did gladdened the hearts of Hun-Camé and Vucub-Camé, and the latter felt as though they themselves were dancing.[9]

Then their hearts were filled with desire and longing by the dances of Hunahpú and Xbalanqué;[10] and Hun-Camé and Vucub-Camé gave their commands.

"Do the same with us! Sacrifice us!" they said. "Cut us into pieces, one by one!" Hun-Camé and Vucub-Camé said to Hunahpú and Xbalanqué.[11]

"Very well; afterward you will come back to life again. Perchance, did you not bring us here in order that we should entertain you, the lords, and yours sons, and vassals?" they said to the lords.[12]

And so it happened that they first sacrificed the one, who was the chief and [Lord of Xibalba], the one called Hun-Camé, king of Xibalba.

And when Hun-Camé was dead, they overpowered Vucub-Camé, and they did not bring either of them back to life.

[8] *Libah chicut*, omitted in the Brasseur de Bourbourg transcription.

[9] This juggling, which brings to mind the deceptions of the fakirs of India, was also well known by the Maya Indians of Mexico. Sahagún, describing the customs of the Huasteca, a Mexican tribe related to the Maya of Yucatán, says that when they returned to Panutla, or Pánuco, "they took with them the old songs which they used when they danced and all the adornment which they used in the dance or *areyto*. They were also fond of trickery, with which they deceived the people, making them believe as true that which is false, as they made them believe that they burned the houses, when it was not so; that they made a fountain with fishes appear, and it was nothing but an optical illusion; that they killed each other, slicing their flesh into pieces, and other things which were apparent but not true. . . ." As Brasseur de Bourbourg observes, this paragraph seems to have been taken from the *Popol Vuh*. Cf. Sahagún, *Historia general . . . de Nueva España*, Book X, Chap. XXIX, par. 12.

[10] Xhunahpú, and Xbalanqué in the original.

[11] *Hunal tah coh i puzu x-e cha cut*, omitted by Brasseur de Bourbourg.

[12] *Ma pa yx qo cam oh pu quicotirizay yve*, etc. The verb *cam* means "to die" and "to bring." Brasseur de Bourbourg translates this passage as follows: *est-ce que pour vous peut exister la mort?* but the complete meaning of the sentence justifies the interpretation which Ximénez gives it and which, in the main, is the same as mine.

159

The people of Xibalba fled as soon as they saw that their lords were dead and sacrificed. In an instant both were sacrificed. And this they [the boys] did in order to chastize them. Quickly the principal lord was killed. And they did not bring him back to life.

And another lord humbled himself then, and presented himself before the dancers. They had not discovered him, nor had they found him. "Have mercy on me!" he said when they found him.

All the sons and vassals of Xibalba fled to a great ravine, and all of them were crowded into this narrow, deep place. There they were crowded together and hordes of ants came and found them and dislodged them from the ravine. In this way [the ants] drove them to the road, and when they arrived [the people] prostrated themselves and gave themselves up; they humbled themselves and arrived, grieving.

In this way the Lords of Xibalba were overcome. Only by a miracle and by their [own] transformation could [the boys] have done it.[13]

I
CHAPTER 14

mmediately [the boys] told their names and they extolled themselves before all the people of Xibalba.

"Hear our names. We shall also tell you the names of our fathers. We are Hunahpú and Xbalanqué;[1] those are our names. And our fathers are those whom you killed and who were called Hun-Hunahpú and Vucub-Hunahpú. We, those whom you see here, are, then, the avengers of the torments and suffering of our fathers.[2] That is the reason why we resent all the evil you have done to them. Therefore, we shall put an end to all of you, we shall kill you, and not one of you shall escape," they said.

[13] This refers naturally to the changing of Hunahpú and Xbalanqué into two poor boys who tragically deceived the Lords of Xibalba with their magic art.

[1] Xhunahpú, Xbalanqué, in the original. The initial X denotes the diminutive in Quiché. Here it serves to establish the relationship of father and son between Hun-Hunahpú and Xhunahpú.

[2] *Oh cu pacol re vae qui rail, qui caxcol ri ca cahau*, in the original.

Instantly all the people of Xibalba fell to their knees, crying.

"Have mercy on us, Hunahpú and Xbalanqué! It is true that we sinned against your fathers as you said, and that they are buried in Puchbal-Chah," they said.

"Very well. This is our sentence, that we are going to tell you. Hear it, all you of Xibalba:

"Since neither your great power nor your race any longer exist, and since neither do you deserve mercy, your rank shall be lowered.[3] Not for you shall be the ball game.[4] You shall spend your time making earthen pots and tubs and stones to grind corn.[5] Only the children of the thickets and desert shall speak with you. The noble sons, the civilized vassals shall not consort with you, and they will foresake your presence.[6] The sinners, the evil ones, the sad ones, the unfortunate ones, those who give themselves up to vice, these are the ones who will welcome you. No longer will you seize men suddenly [for sacrifice]; remember your rank has been lowered."

Thus they spoke to all the people of Xibalba.

In this way their destruction and their lamentations began. Their power in the olden days was not much. They only liked to do evil to men in those times. In truth, in those days, they did not have the category of gods. Furthermore, their horrible faces frightened people. They were the enemies, the owls.[7] They incited to evil, to sin and to discord.

[3] *X-zaquin chic ch'y quic holomax*. I believe I give an approximate interpretation of this expression. In another place I have explained that both *quic* and *holomax* have the meaning of "blood." Here, says Brasseur de Bourbourg, there is a mysterious play on words which escapes translation.

[4] *Mavi chahom quic yve*, in the original. It is to be remembered that the ball game was reserved for the important people.

[5] These were occupations of the common people.

[6] *Xa noh chi tzaco rib ch'y vach*. This sentence is very difficult to understand and has been translated in many different ways. The verb *tzaca* has, among other meanings, that of fleeing, frightening away, or chasing.

[7] *Ah-Tza*, "those of the war." *Ah-Tucur*, "the owls." As Brasseur de Bourbourg indicates, there may be a relation between these names and those of the Itzá, a Maya tribe which lived in the northern part of Guatemala, in the region called Petén-Itzá, and the settlers of Tucurú, people of Verapaz. Undoubtedly the Quiché and Cakchiquel emigrated from the north, fleeing from the tyranny of these tribes, in order to live in freedom in a new land.

They were also false in their hearts, black and white at the same time,[8] envious and tyrannical,[9] according to what was said of them. Furthermore, they painted and greased their faces.

In this way, then, occurred the loss of their grandeur and the decadence of their empire.

And this was what Xhunahpú and Xbalanqué did.[10]

Meanwhile, the grandmother was crying and lamenting before the reeds which they had left planted. The reeds sprouted, then they dried up when [the boys] were consumed in the bonfire; afterward [the reeds] sprouted again. Then the grandmother lighted the fire and burned incense before the reeds in memory of her grandchildren. And the grandmother's heart filled with joy when, for the second time, the reeds sprouted. Then they were worshiped by the grandmother, and she called them the Center of the House, *Nicah* [the center] they were called.

"Green reeds growing in the plains" [*Cazam Ah Chatam Uleu*] was their name. And they were called the Center of the House and the Center, because in the middle of the house they planted the reeds. And the reeds, which were planted, were called the plains, Green Reeds growing on the plains. They also were called Green Reeds because they had resprouted. This name was

8 *E quecail, zaquiil*, with the appearance of blacks and whites, double appearance, symbol of their duplicity.

9 *Ahmoxvach, Ahlatzab*. Other synonyms which mean originators of evil, wicked, evildoers, oppressors.

10 Among the legends which Bishop Bartolomé de las Casas gathered in Verapaz, there is one of a god who had been born in that province and who was called Exbalanquén. "They say of him, among other tales," says the chronicler, "that he went to the inferno to make war, fought with all the people there, overcame them, and seized the king and many of his army. On his return to earth, Exbalanquén brought the king of the inferno with him, but when they were a few steps from the surface, he [the king] begged not to be taken up and giving him a kick he [Exbalanquén] said to him: 'Go back and let yours be all that is rotten and cast away and stinks.'" Las Casas adds that "in Verapaz, Exbalanquén was not received with the feasting and songs which he wished, and he therefore went to another kingdom, where he was received in a manner pleasing to him, and they say that this vanquisher of the inferno began to sacrifice men." *Apologética Historia de las Indias*, Chap. CXXIV, p. 330. It is too bad that this historian has not transcribed in his work the "other fables" which the people of Verapaz told, and which possibly coincided with the legends contained in the *Popol Vuh*, judging from this version of the deeds of Exbalanquén or Xbalanqué.

given them by Xmucané [given] to those [reeds] which Hunahpú
and Xbalanqué left planted in order that they should be remembered by their grandmother.

Well, now, their fathers, those who died long ago, were Hun-
Hunahpú and Vucub-Hunahpú. They also saw the faces of their
fathers there in Xibalba and their fathers talked with their descendants, that is the ones who overthrew those of Xibalba.

And here is how their fathers were honored by them. They
honored Vucub-Hunahpú; they went to honor him at the place
of sacrifice of the ball-court.[11] And at the same time they wanted
to make Vucub-Hunahpú's face. They hunted there for his entire body, his mouth, his nose, his eyes. They found his body, but
it could do very little.[12] It could not pronounce his name, this
Hunahpú.[13] Neither could his mouth say it.

And here is how they extolled the memory of their fathers,
whom they had left there in the place of sacrifice at the ball-court:
"You shall be invoked," their sons said to them, when they forti-
fied their heart. "You shall be the first to arise, and you shall be the
first to be worshiped by the sons of the noblemen, by the civilized
vassals. Your names shall not be lost. So it shall be!" they told their
fathers and thus consoled themselves. "We are the avengers of
your death, of the pains and sorrows which they caused you."

Thus was their leave-taking, when they had already overcome all the people of Xibalba.

Then they rose up in the midst of the light, and instantly they
were lifted into the sky. One was given the sun, the other, the
moon. Then the arch of heaven and the face of the earth were
lighted. And they dwelt in heaven.

11 *Pucbal-Chah.*

12 *Xa cu zcaquin chic x-cha tah vi xere,* in the original.

13 *Hunahpuil* in the original, probably by a *lapsus calami.* Brasseur de Bourbourg thought that this was a plural form and that it meant the union of the
Hunahpú, but it is evident that the text refers to Vucub-Hunahpú, that is, the
second of the Hunahpú. As will be seen, the two young heroes found only the
head of Vucub-Hunahpú buried in the ball-court, and spoke only with it. It
must be remembered that the head of Hun-Hunahpú was taken from his body
and fastened in the branches of the calabash tree where it was confused with the
fruit of the tree.

Then the four hundred boys whom Zipacná had killed, also ascended, and so they again became the companions of [the boys] and were changed into stars in the sky.

# PART III

Here, then, is the beginning of when it was decided to make man, and when what must enter into the flesh of man was sought.

And the Forefathers, the Creators and Makers, who were called Tepeu and Gucumatz said: "The time of dawn has come, let the work be finished, and let those who are to nourish and sustain us appear, the noble sons, the civilized vassals; let man appear, humanity, on the face of the earth." Thus they spoke.

They assembled, came together and held council in the darkness and in the night; then they sought and discussed, and here they reflected and thought. In this way their decisions came clearly to light and they found and discovered what must enter into the flesh of man.

It was just before the sun, the moon, and the stars appeared over the Creators and Makers.

From Paxil, from Cayalá,[1] as they were called, came the yellow ears of corn and the white ears of corn.

[1] *Paxil* means separation, spreading of the waters, inundation. *Cayalá*, derived from *cay*, "rotten," may also be interpreted as putrid matter in the water. These legendary places which gave to the Middle American people the native fruits which are the base of their subsistence and economic development, were found, in the opinion of Brasseur de Bourbourg in the region of Tabasco, where the Usumacinta River, after watering northern Guatemala, divides into various branches and overflows this entire region during the period when the rivers rise. This phenomenon is similar in its cause and effects to the inundations by the Nile, that spread the fertile sediment which produces the rich harvests of Egypt. Bancroft believed that Paxil and Cayalá were in the region of Palenque and the

These are the names of the animals which brought the food:[2] *yac* (the mountain cat), *utiú* (the coyote), *quel* (a small parrot), and *hoh* (the crow). These four animals gave tidings of the yellow ears of corn and the white ears of corn, they told them that they should go to Paxil and they showed them the road to Paxil.[3]

And thus they found the food, and this was what went into the flesh of created man, the made man; this was his blood; of this the blood of man was made. So the corn entered [into the formation of man] by the work of the Forefathers.

And in this way they were filled with joy, because they had found a beautiful land, full of pleasures, abundant in ears of yellow corn and ears of white corn, and abundant also in *pataxte* and cacao,[4] and in innumerable *zapotes, anonas, jocotes, nantzes, matasanos,* and honey.[5] There was an abundance of delicious food in

---

Usumacinta. Both opinions would have some foundation, if it were possible to establish the location of these mythological places, for that was, without doubt, the region which was inhabited for some time by the Guatemalan tribes in their wanderings toward the lands of the south.

[2] *Echá*, "food," "nourishment." In the case of man, *echá* is the cooked and ground corn which was the common food of the American Indian, and which the Quiché thought, logically, had been used to fashion the first men.

[3] "Which was the paradise," Ximénez adds in his first version, of their own harvest. The Cakchiquel Manuscript says that, when the Creator and the Maker made man, they had nothing with which to feed him until they found corn in Paxil, fighting for it with two animals, the coyote and the crow, who knew where it was raised. The coyote was killed in the middle of the cornfield. From the dough of the corn, mixed with the blood of the snake, the flesh of man was made. The Mexican legend tells of the discovery of corn in a similar way. According to the *Códice Chimalpopoca*, Azcatl, the ant, told Quetzalcoatl that there was corn in Tonacatepetl (mountain of our subsistence). Quetzalcoatl immediately changed himself into a black ant and went with Azcatl, entered that place, and brought the corn to Tamoanchán.

[4] *Cacau* in Maya and Quiché, a well-known plant of tropical America. A variety of cacao, *Theobroma bicolor*, called *pec* in Quiché, commonly known under the Mexican name *pataxte*.

[5] *Tulul*, zapote, mamey in Yucatán, *Lucuma mammosa*. The *anona* is well known by this name and also as *chirimoya*, the Quiché name is *cavex*. The *jocote*, a name derived from the Náhuatl *xocotl*, *Spondias purpurea*, L., is the *quinom* of the Quiché and Cakchiquel. The *nantze*, so called in Náhuatl, *Byrsonima crassifolia*, is the *tapal* in the languages of Guatemala. The *matasano, ahaché* in these languages, *Casimiroa edulis*, *Llave*, and *Lex.*, completes the list of those fruits which abound in the hot and temperate lands of Guatemala.

those villages called Paxil and Cayalá. There were foods of every kind, small and large foods, small plants and large plants.

The animals showed them the road. And then grinding the yellow corn and the white corn, Xmucané made nine drinks, and from this food came the strength and the flesh, and with it they created the muscles and the strength of man. This the Forefathers did, Tepeu and Gucumatz, as they were called.

After that they began to talk about the creation and the making of our first mother and father; of yellow corn and of white corn they made their flesh; of corn meal dough they made the arms and the legs of man. Only dough of corn meal went into the flesh of our first fathers, the four men, who were created.

CHAPTER 2

These are the names of the first men who were created and formed: the first man was Balam-Quitzé, the second, Balam-Acab, the third, Mahucutah, and the fourth was Iqui-Balam.[1]

These are the names of our first mothers and fathers.[2]

It is said that they only were made and formed, they had no mother, they had no father. They were only called men.[3] They were not born of woman, nor were they begotten by the Creator

---

[1] Ximénez explains the significance of these names as follows: *Balam-Quitzé* means jaguar of sweet laughter, or much laughter, or fatal laughter, like poison. *Balam-Acab*, jaguar of the night. *Mahucutah*, not brushed. *Iqui-Balam*, jaguar of moon or of chile, black jaguar, in Maya. The god of the people of Yucatán, was worshiped under the name of "Ek-Balam or Equebalam, black jaguar." (*Relaciones de Yucatán*, II, 53). It is very difficult, if not impossible, to find the true origin of these names. Ximénez' explanation has been generally accepted, although it is not entirely satisfactory. It must be noted that *balam* also has the meaning of "sorcerer," and that the ancient Quiché, who believed in sorcery and incantations, saw their first fathers as sorcerers and wizards.

[2] Meaning the forefathers, the ancestors. In the next chapter the author begins to call them mothers, in the same generic sense.

[3] *Xa utuquel achih.* They had no family name. They had no ancestors. They were the beginning of the human race.

nor by the Maker, nor by the Forefathers.[4] Only by a miracle, by means of incantation were they created and made by the Creator, the Maker, the Forefathers,[5] Tepeu and Gucumatz. And as they had the appearance of men, they were men; they talked, conversed, saw and heard, walked, grasped things; they were good and handsome men, and their figure was the figure of a man.

They were endowed with intelligence; they saw and instantly they could see far, they succeeded in seeing, they succeeded in knowing all that there is in the world. When they looked, instantly they saw all around them, and they contemplated in turn the arch of heaven and the round face of the earth.

The things hidden [in the distance] they saw all, without first having to move; at once they saw the world, and so, too, from where they were, they saw it.

Great was their wisdom; their sight reached to the forests, the rocks, the lakes, the seas, the mountains, and the valleys. In truth, they were admirable men, Balam-Quitzé, Balam-Acab, Mahucutah, and Iqui-Balam.

Then the Creator and the Maker asked them: "What do you think of your condition? Do you not see? Do you not hear? Are not your speech and manner of walking good? Look, then! Contemplate the world, look [and see] if the mountains and the valleys appear! Try, then, to see!" they said to [the four first men].

And immediately they [the four first men] began to see all that was in the world. Then they gave thanks to the Creator and the Maker: "We really give you thanks, two and three times![6] We have been created, we have been given a mouth and a face, we speak, we hear, we think, and walk; we feel perfectly, and we know what is far and what is near. We also see the large and the small in the sky and on earth. We give you thanks, then, for having created us, oh, Creator and Maker! for having given us being, oh, our grandmother! oh, our grandfather!" they said, giving thanks for their creation and formation.

4 *Rumal ri Ahtzac, Ahbit, ri Alom, Qaholom.*

5 *Rumal ri Tzacol, Bitol, Alom, Qaholom.*

6 *Chi camul camo, oxmul camo.* Like the expression "a thousand and one times" in modern languages.

They were able to know all, and they examined the four corners, the four points of the arch of the sky and the round face of the earth.

But the Creator and the Maker did not hear this with pleasure. "It is not well what our creatures, our works say; they know all, the large and the small," they said. And so the Forefathers held counsel again. "What shall we do with them now? Let their sight reach only to that which is near; let them see only a little of the face of the earth! It is not well what they say. Perchance, are they not by nature simple creatures of our making? Must they also be gods? And if they do not reproduce and multiply when it will dawn, when the sun rises? And what if they do not multiply?"[7] So they spoke.

"Let us check a little their desires, because it is not well what we see. Must they perchance be the equals of ourselves, their Makers, who can see afar, who know all and see all?"

Thus spoke the Heart of Heaven, Huracán, Chipi-Caculhá, Raxa-Caculhá, Tepeu, Gucumatz, the Forefathers, Xpiyacoc, Xmucané, the Creator and the Maker. Thus they spoke, and immediately they changed the nature of their works, of their creatures.

Then the Heart of Heaven blew mist into their eyes, which clouded their sight as when a mirror is breathed upon. Their eyes were covered and they could see only what was close, only that was clear to them.

In this way the wisdom and all the knowledge of the four men, the origin and beginning[8] [of the Quiché race], were destroyed.

In this way were created and formed our grandfathers, our fathers, by the Heart of Heaven, the Heart of Earth.

[7] *Que q̇uiritahic,* "they multiply"; *qui iaric,* as it is in the original, literally, "they bear many," "they propagate," are synonyms, derived from the adverb of quantity *qui,* "many." Like *multos, multiplicare* in Latin.

[8] *U xe u ticaribal.*

# T

hen their wives had being, and their women were made. God himself made them carefully.[1] And so, during sleep, they came, truly beautiful, their women, at the side of Balam-Quitzé, Balam-Acab, Mahucutah, and Iqui-Balam.

There were their women when they awakened, and instantly their hearts were filled with joy because of their wives.

Here are the names of their wives: Cahá-Paluna was the name of the wife of Balam-Quitzé; Chomihá was the wife of Balam-Acab; Tzununihá, the wife of Mahucutah; and Caquixahá was the name of the wife of Iqui-Balam. These are the names of their wives, who were distinguished women.[2]

They conceived the men, of the small tribes and of the large tribes, and were the origin of us; the people of Quiché.

There were many priests and sacrificers; there were not only four, but those four were the Forefathers[3] of us, the people of the Quiché.

The names of each one were different when they multiplied there in the East, and there were many names of the people: Tepeu, Olomán, Cohah, Quenech, Ahau, as they called those men there in the East, where they multiplied.[4]

The beginning is known, too, of those of Tamub and those of Ilocab who came together from there in the East.[5]

[1] *Xavi Cabahuil x-naohin chic. Naohin* means to make something carefully.

[2] Ximénez (*Historia . . . de Chiapa y Guatemala*, I, 35) interprets these names as follows: Cahá-Paluna, standing water (vertical) falling from above; *Chomihá*, beautiful, chosen water; *Tzununihá*, water of hummingbirds; *Caquixahá*, water of the macaw. The *Título de los Señores de Totonicapán* gives the names of the wives of those Quiché heroes with some differences: "The wife of Balam-Quitzé was called Zaka-Paluma, the wife of Balam-Agab was Tzununi-há; that of Mahucutah, Cakixa-ha; Iqi-Balam was single."

[3] *Ri qui chuch oh quiche vinac*, literally "the mothers of us, the Quiché." *Chuch*, "mothers," here has the generic meaning, as the word "fathers" has in Spanish, and both are understood as the forefathers.

[4] It is possible to recognize among these names that of Tepeu, which in other places in this book is applied to the Yaquis, Yaqui-Tepeu, one of the tribes of Toltec origin who emigrated together with the Quiché. The people of Olomán, who are the Olmeca, Olmeca-xicalanca, who lived at the south of Veracruz, may be identified as those with whom the Quiché were likewise intimately united.

Balam-Quitzé was the grandfather and the father of the nine great houses of the Cavec; Balam-Acab was the grandfather and father of the nine great houses of the Nimhaib; Mahucutah, the grandfather and father of the four great houses of Ahau-Quiché.

Three groups of families existed; but they did not forget the name of their grandfather and father, those who propagated and multiplied there in the East.

The Tamub and Ilocab also came, and thirteen branches of peoples, the thirteen of Tecpán, and those of Rabinal, the Cakchiquel, those from Tziquinahá, and the Zacahá and the Lamaq, Cumatz, Tuhalhá, Uchabahá, those of Chumilahá, those of Quibahá, of Batenabá, Acul-Vinac, Balamihá, the Canchahel, and Balam-Colob.[6]

These are only the principal tribes, the branches of the people which we mention; only of the principal ones shall we speak. Many others came from each group of the people, but we shall not write their names. They also multiplied there in the East.

[5] Copichoch, Cochochlam, Mahquinalon, and Ahcanabil were the chiefs of the tribe of Tamub whose names are found in the *Título de los Señores de Totonicapán* and in the *Historia Quiché de D. Juan de Torres,* an unpublished manuscript which also describes the succession of these chiefs. Brasseur de Bourbourg (*Popol Vuh,* p. CCLXI) makes known the names of the chiefs of the tribe of Ilocab, which he took from another manuscript, the *Título de los Señores de Sacapulas,* which was in his possession. These names, which also appear in the *Título de Totonicapán,* are as follows: *Chi-Ya-Toh, Chi-Ya-Tziquin, Xol-Chi-Tum, Xol-Chi-Ramag,* and *Chi-Pel-Camuhel.*

[6] These thirteen tribes of Tecpán, which the *Título de Totonicapán* calls *Vukamag Tecpam,* are the Pocomam and Poconchi tribes, according to Brasseur de Bourbourg. The tribe of Rabinal was established in the interior of the present Republic of Guatemala, and its descendants still form an important center of Quiché population. The Cakchiquel constituted a strong and numerous kingdom, a rival of the Quiché Kingdom, which had as its capital, Iximché (native name of the tree now called bread-nut or *ramón* in Spanish). The Mexicans called *Iximché Tecpán-Quauhtemállan,* from which comes the present name of Guatemala. The tribe of Tziquinahá took as its capital the city of Atitlán, and occupied the western part of the territory surrounding the lake of this same name. Zacahá is the present Salcaja, close to the modern city of Quetzaltenango. *Lamac, Cumatz, Tuhalhá,* and *Uchabahá* were on the outskirts of Sacapulas, according to Brasseur de Bourbourg. It has not been possible to identify the rest of the tribes. That of *Balamihá* may be the tribe which established itself in the place now called Balamyá, in the department of Chimaltenango.

Many men were made and in the darkness they multiplied. Neither the sun nor the light had yet been made when they multiplied. All lived together, they existed in great number and walked there in the East.

Nevertheless, they did not sustain nor maintain [their God]; they only raised their faces to the sky, and they did not know why they had come so far as they did.

There they were then, in great number, the black men and the white men, men of many classes, men of many tongues, that it was wonderful to hear them.[7]

There are generations in the world, there are country people, whose faces we do not see, who have no homes, they only wander through the small and large woodlands, like crazy people. So it is said scornfully of the people of the wood. So they said there, where they saw the rising of the sun.

The speech of all was the same. They did not invoke wood nor stone,[8] and they remembered the word of the Creator and the Maker, the Heart of Heaven, the Heart of Earth.

In this manner they spoke, while they thought about the coming of the dawn.[9] And they raised their prayers, those worshipers of the word [of God], loving, obedient, and fearful, raising their faces to the sky when they asked for daughters and sons:

[7] In the original this paragraph reads as follows: *Ta x-qohe pa qui chiri queca vinac, zaqui vinac, qui vachibal vinac, qui u chabal vinac, cay u xiquin.* Brasseur de Bourbourg changed the meaning of *qui,* "much," for *quiy,* "sweet," and says in his translation that "sweet was the appearance of those peoples, sweet the language of those peoples." *Qui vachibal vinac* means literally "men of many forms, aspects, or appearances." *Qui u chabal vinac,* "many were the tongues of the men." Evidently the author was trying to give the idea of the multitude of different people, strange to each other, blacks and whites, that is, of light skin and of dark skin, and of the many different tongues which were in the East. The Quiché, however, maintained their ethnic unity and their common tongue in the midst of this Babylon, as is seen farther on. Ximénez translates the end of the paragraph saying "there were many languages and of two ears," which lacks meaning. In his second version (*Historia . . . de Chiapas y Guatemala,* I, 36) he tries to explain the sentence and says "that they hear and understand each other through the diversity of languages." *Cay, cab,* or *caíb* is the number "2," but the first form, which is the one used in the text also means to see or hear with wonder, and this is probably the idea which it means to express here.

[8] That is, the idols.

[9] "They were only waiting for the sunrise" is Ximénez' interpretation.

"Oh thou, Tzacol, Bitol![10] Look at us, hear us! Do not leave us, do not forsake us, oh, God, who art in heaven and on earth, Heart of Heaven, Heart of Earth! Give us our descendants, our succession, as long as the sun shall move and there shall be light. Let it dawn; let the day come! Give us many good roads, flat roads! May the people have peace, much peace, and may they be happy; and give us good life and useful existence![11] Oh, thou Huracán, Chipi-Caculhá, Raxa-Caculhá, Chipi-Nanauac, Raxananauac, Voc, Hunahpú, Tepeu, Gucumatz, Alom, Qaholom, Xpiyacoc, Xmucané, grandmother of the sun, grandmother of the light, let there be dawn, and let the light come!"[12]

Thus they spoke while they saw and invoked the coming of the sun, the arrival of day; and at the same time that they saw the rising of the sun, they contemplated the Morning Star, the Great Star, which comes ahead of the sun, that lights up the arch of the sky and the surface of the earth, and illuminates the steps of the men who had been created and made.

CHAPTER 4

Balam-Quitzé, Balam-Acab, Mahucutah, and Iqui-Balam said, "Let us await the break of day." So said those great wise men, the enlightened men, the priests and sacrificers. This they said.

Our first mothers and fathers did not yet have wood nor stones to keep;[1] but their hearts were tired of waiting for the sun. Al-

[10] Creator and Maker.

[11] *Utzilah qazlem, vinaquirem ta puch coh a ya vi.*

[12] The Quiché pantheon appears complete in this paragraph with the addition of the two new names, Voc and the large and small Nanauac. The first, Voc or *vac*, the hawk, was the messenger of Huracán who came to be present at the ball game of Hun-Hunahpú and Vucub-Hunahpú, according to the account in a previous chapter of the Quiché book. Nanauac, the Omniscient, according to Brasseur de Bourbourg is the same person who, with the name Nanahuatl (the disfigured), appears in the *Códice Chimalpopoca*.

[1] Which means idols.

173

ready all the tribes and the Yaqui people,² the priests and sacrificers, were very many.

"Let us go, let us go to search and see if our [tribal] symbols are in safety; if we can find what we must burn before them.³ For being as we are, there is no one who watches for us," said Balam-Quitzé, Balam-Acab, Mahucutah, and Iqui-Balam.

And having heard of a city, they went there.

Now then, the name of the place where Balam-Quitzé, Balam-Acab, Mahucutah, and Iqui-Balam and those of Tamub and Ilocab went was Tulán-Zuiva, Vucub-Pec, Vucub-Ziván.⁴ This was the name of the city where they went to receive their gods.

So, then, all arrived at Tulán. It was impossible to count the men who arrived; there were very many and they walked in an orderly way.

² *Yaqui-Vinac, ahqixb, ahcahb*, the Mexicans, the ancient Tolteca, the Náhuatl tribe, which united with the Maya of the south, were the origin of the Indian nations of Guatemala. The author calls the Yaquis the priests and sacrificers, and these same names are given in various places to the Quiché chiefs, Balam-Quitzé and his companions. In describing the death of these chiefs, the text designates them in this way: "the chiefs and sacrificers, so called." Cf. end of Chap. 5, Part IV.

³ *Chi ca ric ri coh tzihón ta chuvach*, evidently they searched for the incense to burn before the gods.

⁴ This passage of the *Popol Vuh* is very interesting as proof of the common origin of the Quiché and the other peoples of Guatemala, and of the tribes which established themselves in ancient times in various parts of Mexico and Yucatán. Tulán-Zuivá, the Cave of Tulán, Vucub-Pec, Seven Caves, and Vucub-Ziván, Seven Ravines, are the Quiché names of the place to which Mexican tradition gives the name of Chicomoztoc, which in Náhuatl also means Seven Caves. In the Manuscript of Sahagún from the *Academia de la Historia* these words are found: "Our fathers had news that from Chicomoztoc they had come, as they themselves said, the seven tribes who proceeded from there, born there." (*Cf.* Seler, *Los Cantares de los dioses*, in Sahagún, *Historia General*, 1938 ed., V, 84). According to Maya tradition, the name of the cradle of the human race is similar to that which was given by the Quiché, Holtún Çuuyva, the Zuiva Cave, according to the *Books of Chilan Balam*. Although it has not been possible to locate exactly the site of ancient Tulán of the caves or ravines, the common tradition preserved in Mexico and Guatemala gives all the people of this vast region an origin which, although purely legendary, marks the beginning of their historical evolution. The ancient chronicles of Guatemala are remarkable in this sense, for the clarity with which they show the movement of the tribes from their place of reunion to the places where they finally settled and reached the state of civilization in which the Spaniards found them in the early sixteenth century.

Then was the appearance of their gods; first those of Balam-Quitzé, Balam-Acab, Mahucutah, and Iqui-Balam, who were filled with joy: "At last we have found that for which we searched!" they said.

And the first that appeared was Tohil, as this god was called, and Balam-Quitzé put him on his back, in his chest.[5] Instantly the god called Avilix appeared, and Balam-Acab carried him. The god called Hacavitz was carried by Mahucutah; and Iqui-Balam carried the one called Nicahtacah.[6]

And together with the people of the Quiché, they also received those of Tamub. And in the same way Tohil was the name of the god of the Tamub who received the grandfather and father of the Lords of Tamub, whom we know today.

In the third place were those of Ilocab. Tohil was also the name of the god who was received by the grandfathers and the fathers of the lords, whom we also know today.

In this way, the three Quiché [families] were given their names and they did not separate, because they had a god of the same name, Tohil of the Quiché, Tohil of the Tamub and [Tohil] of the Ilocab; one only was the name of the god,[7] and therefore the three Quiché [families] did not separate.

[5] *U coc*, in this case is the chest or wooden frame which the Indians bear on their backs and in which they carry their products, or burdens, from one place to another. The common name in Guatemala is *cacaxte*, taken, like many others, from the Mexicans.

[6] Tohil gets his name from *toh*, "rain," according to Ximénez. The people of Rabinal called him Huntoh, 1 Toh, which is a day of the calendar. Farther on, the author writes that Tohil and Quetzalcoatl were the same being. The Cakchiquel Manuscript calls Tohohil the principal god of the Quiché. There is no satisfactory etymology for the names of Avilix and Hacavitz. Nicahtacah, literally "in the middle of the plain," does not appear again in the narration, probably because Iqui-Balam had a very secondary part, and did not leave descendants. Explaining the origin of the name Tohohil, the Cakchiquel Manuscript says that when the tribes were in the region of the Laguna de Términos, before going southward into the mountains of Guatemala, the Quiché said: *Xaqui tohoh quihilil xibe chi cah*, or "thus like it thundered and resounded in the sky," and adds, "in truth in the sky is our salvation. Thus they said and for that reason they were called those of Tohohil." The name *Tohil*, is, in effect, associated with the idea of rain and thunder, as stated at the beginning of this note.

[7] *Xahun u bi u cabauil*, in the original.

175

Great indeed was the virtue of the three, Tohil, Avilix, and Hacavitz.

Then all the people arrived, those from Rabinal, the Cakchiquel, those from Tziquinahá, and the people who now are called the Yaqui. And there it was that the speech of the tribes changed; their tongues became different. They could no longer understand each other clearly after arriving at Tulán. There also they separated, there were some who had to go to the East,[8] but many came here.

And their clothing was only the skins of animals; they had no good clothes to put on, the skins of animals were their only dress. They were poor, they possessed nothing, but they had the nature of extraordinary men.

When they arrived at Tulán-Zuiva, Vucub-Pec, Vucub-Ziván, the old traditions say that they had traveled far in order to arrive there.

CHAPTER 5

And they did not have fire. Only the people of Tohil had it. He was the god of the tribes which first created fire. It is not known how it was made, because it was already burning when Balam-Quitzé and Balam-Acab saw it.

"Ah, we have no fire yet! We shall die of cold," they said. Then Tohil said to them: "Do not worry! Yours shall be the lost fire which is talked of. Yours shall be what is spoken of as lost fire," Tohil said to them.

"Really? Oh, God, our support, our maintenance, thou, our God!" they said, returning thanks.

And Tohil answered: "Very well, certainly I am your God; so shall it be! I am your Lord; so let it be!" Thus it was told to the priests and sacrificers by Tohil. And in this manner the tribes received fire and they were joyful because of it.

Instantly a great shower began to fall when the fire of the

[8] To Yucatán.

tribes was burning. Much hail fell on all the tribes and the fire was put out because of it, and again the fire was extinguished.

Then Balam-Quitzé and Balam-Acab again asked Tohil for fire. "Oh, Tohil, we are truly dying of cold!" they said to Tohil.

"Very well, do not worry," Tohil answered, and instantly he made fire, turning about in his shoe.[1]

Balam-Quitzé, Balam-Acab, Mahucutah, and Iqui-Balam were at once happy and immediately they became warm.

Now, the fire of the peoples [of Vucamag] had also gone out and they were dying of cold. Immediately they came to ask Balam-Quitzé, Balam-Acab, Mahucutah, and Iqui-Balam for fire. They could no longer bear the cold nor the ice; they were shivering and their teeth were chattering; they were numb; their legs and hands shook and they could not hold anything in them, when they came.

"We are not ashamed to come before you, to beg for a little of your fire," they said. But they were not well received.[2] And then the tribes were very sad.

"The speech of Balam-Quitzé, Balam-Acab, Mahucutah, and Iqui-Balam is different! Oh! We have given up our speech! What have we done? We are lost. How were we deceived? We had only one speech when we arrived there at Tulán; we were created and educated in the same way. It is not good what we have done," said all the tribes under the trees, under the vines.

Then a man came before Balam-Quitzé, Balam-Acab, Mahucutah, and Iqui-Balam and [this man], who was a messenger of Xibalba, spoke thus: "This is, in truth, your God; this is your support; this is, furthermore, the representation, the memory of your Creator and Maker. Do not give your fire to the tribes until they present offerings to Tohil. It is not necessary that they give any-

[1] *X-u bac uloc chupan u xahab.* I give the Ximénez version. The expression undoubtedly refers to the primitive way of making fire by means of a stick which the Indians twirled rapidly in a hole in another stick. According to the *Título de los Señores de Totonicapán,* Balam-Quitzé and his companions were "beginning to rub wood and stones, those who first made fire." The tribes of Vukamag only succeeded in having the Quiché give them "a little" of their fire by offering them their daughters.

[2] *Ma cu habi x-e culaxic.*

177

thing to you.[3] Ask Tohil what they should give when they come to receive fire," said the man from Xibalba. He had wings like the wings of a bat.[4] "I am sent by your Creator, your Maker," said the man of Xibalba.

They were filled with joy then, and Tohil, Avilix, and Haca-vitz were also gladdened when the man from Xibalba spoke, who disappeared instantly from their presence.[5]

But the tribes did not perish when they came, although they were dying of cold.[6] There was much hail, black rain and mist, and indescribable cold.

All the tribes were trembling and shivering with cold when they came where Balam-Quitzé, Balam-Acab, Mahucutah, and Iqui-Balam were. Their hearts were greatly troubled and their mouths and eyes were sad.

In a moment the beggars[7] came before Balam-Quitzé, Balam-Acab, Mahucutah, and Iqui-Balam and said: "Will you not have pity on us, we only ask a little of your fire? Perchance, were we not [once] together and reunited? Did we not have the same home and one country when we were created, when we were made? Have mercy, then, on us!" they said.

[3] *M'yv ahauah chi qui ya ch'yve.* The verb *ahauax*, according to Ximénez, means "to be convenient," "to be necessary."

[4] *Qo uxic queheri uxic zotz.* I follow Ximénez in his interpretation of this phrase, which he reads *Qo u xic queheri u xic zotz.* Brasseur de Bourbourg trans-lates it that the form of the messenger was like a bat. The text, however, clearly says that the one who presented himself before Balam-Quitzé and his companions was a man; a man who had wings like those of a vampire.

[5] The appearance of this "man of Xibalba," *demonium loquens eis,* or demon of which they spoke, is curious, according to what Ximénez says of him in the original manuscript. Evidently, and in a general sense, Xibalba was for the Quiché the world of ghosts and phantoms. In the present episode the messenger, who comes to advise the priests, presents himself as one sent from the Creator and Maker, but there is reason to suspect his identity.

[6] *Mavi x-mainic ta x-e ul chicut ri amag que utzin rumal teu,* as it is in the original.

[7] *E elegom,* in the original. *Elegom* is a substantive derived from the verb "to rob," but here it may be an error in the text of the primitive copy. Brasseur de Bourbourg interprets the word as meaning *à la dérobée;* other translators render it as meaning "in secret," "desolate." Ximénez translates directly as "the thieves." From the Quiché verb *elahic,* "to pray, supplicate, humiliate" themselves, the substantive *elahom* is formed, giving the idea I prefer in this place, and which seems to conform more nearly to the meaning of the passage concerned.

"What will you give us so that we shall have mercy on you? they were asked.

"Well, then, we shall give you money," the tribes answered.

"We do not want money," said Balam-Quitzé and Balam-Acab.

"And what do you want?" [asked the tribes]

"We shall ask now." [said Balam-Quitzé]

"Very well," said the tribes.

"We shall ask Tohil and then we shall tell you," they answered.

"What must the tribes give, oh, Tohil! who have come to ask for your fire?" said Balam-Quitzé, Balam-Acab, Mahucutah, and Iqui-Balam.

"Well! Are they willing to give their waist and their armpits?[8] Do they want me to embrace them? For if they do not want to do that, neither shall I give them fire," answered Tohil.

"Tell them that this shall come later, that they do not have to come now to give me their waist and their armpits. This is what Tohil orders us to tell you, you will say." This was the answer to Balam-Quitzé, Balam-Acab, Mahucutah, and Iqui-Balam.

Then they took Tohil's message. "Very well, we shall join you and we shall embrace him," they [the people] said when they heard and were told the message from Tohil. And they did not delay in acting. "Good," they said, "but may it be soon!" And immediately they received the fire. Then they became warm.

## CHAPTER 6

There was nevertheless a tribe who stole the fire in the smoke;[1] and they were from the house of Zotzil.[2] The god of

[8] *Ma chi c'ah qui tunic xe qui toloc, xe pu qui mezquel?* That is to say, deliver up the victims in order that they may be sacrificed, in the Mexican style, by opening their breasts with the flint knife and offering their hearts to the god. The same idea is repeated farther on in more unequivocal terms.

[1] *Xa x-relecah ubic gag pa zib,* in the original.

[2] *Zotzilá-ha,* the house of the *zotziles* or bats. Thus the royal house of the Cakchiquel was called, and its king boasted the title of Ahpo-zotzil, King or Lord Bat.

the Cakchiquel was called *Chamalcán*[3] and he had the form of a bat.

When they passed through the smoke, they went softly and then they seized the fire. The Cakchiquel did not ask for the fire, because they did not want to give themselves up to be overcome, the way that the other tribes had been overcome when they offered their breasts and their armpits so that they would be opened. And this was the opening [of the breasts] about which Tohil had spoken; that they should sacrifice all the tribes before him, that they should tear out their hearts from their breasts.

And this had not yet begun when the taking of power and sovereignty by Balam-Quitzé, Balam-Acab, Mahucutah, and Iqui-Balam was prophesied by Tohil.[4]

There in Tulán-Zuiva, whence they had come, they were accustomed to fast, they observed a perpetual fast while they awaited the coming of dawn and watched for the rising sun.

They took turns at watching the Great Star called *Icoquih*,[5] which rises first before the sun, when the sun rises, the brilliant Icoquih, which was always before them in the East, when they were there in the place called Tulán-Zuiva, whence came their god.

[3] The present Cakchiquel call a serpent of great size *chamalcán*.

[4] *Maha chi tihou oc u banic ta x-nicvachixic rumal Tohil u camic puch gagal tepeual cumal ri Balam-Quitzé*, etc. In interpreting this sentence, the translators of the *Popol Vuh* have given the word *camic* the common meaning of "death," suggested to them, no doubt, by the idea of the human sacrifices of which the previous paragraph speaks. Brasseur de Bourbourg translates this paragraph as follows: *On n'avait pas tenté cette pratique, quand fut énigmatiquement proposée par Tohil leur mort dans l'épouvante et la majesté*. Nevertheless, the sentence in Quiché is very simple, and it becomes clear by reading *camic* as the substantive derived from the verb *cam*, "to take," "to receive." The first sentence of the third paragraph following confirms this interpretation. The verb *nicvachin* means "to see at a distance." The prophet, augur, sorcerer, or seer is *nicvachinel* in Quiché. The words *gagal*, *tepeual*, signify sovereignty, divine or royal majesty, says the *Vocabulario de las lenguas Quiché y Kakchiquel. Tepeual* is a word of Náhuatl origin.

[5] *Icoquih*, Venus, the precursor of the sun, literally, "who carries the sun on her back." "The star of the aurora," says the *Vocabulario de los P. P. Franciscanos*, and the Manuscript Yzquin which Fuentes y Guzmán cites calls it *Nimá Chumil*, "Great Star," which is exact equivalent to the Maya *Noh Ek*.

It was not here, then, where they received their power and sovereignty, but there they subdued and subjected the large and small tribes when they sacrificed them before Tohil, and offered him the blood, the substance, breasts, and sides of all the men.

In Tulán power came instantly to them; great was their wisdom in the darkness and in the night.

Then they came, they pulled up stakes there and left the East. "This is not our home; let us go and see where we should settle," Tohil said then.

In truth, he was accustomed to talk to Balam-Quitzé, Balam-Acab, Mahucutah, and Iqui-Balam: "Give thanks before setting out; do what is necessary to bleed your ears, prick your elbows, and make your sacrifices, this shall be your thanks to God."

"Very well," they said, and took blood from their ears. And they wept in their chants[6] because of their departure from Tulán; their hearts mourned when they left Tulán.

"Pity us! We shall not see the dawn here, when the sun rises and lights the face of the earth," they said at leaving. But they left some people on the road which they followed so that they would keep watch.

Each of the tribes kept getting up to see the star which was the herald of the sun. This sign of the dawn they carried in their hearts when they came from the East, and with the same hope they left there, from that great distance, according to what their songs now say.[7]

[6] *X-oc cut chupan qui bix.* Here the verb *oc* means "to cry."

[7] Las Casas (*Apologética Historia de las Indias,* Chap. CLXXIV, p. 459) says that, next to the sun, whom they had as their principal lord, they honored and worshiped the Morning Star "more than any other heavenly or earthly creature, because they believed it as true that their god Quetzalcoatl, when he died, had been changed into that star." And Las Casas adds that each day they waited for it to rise in order to venerate it, offering it incense and shedding their own blood to honor it.

CHAPTER 7

They came at last to the top of a mountain and there all the Quiché people and the tribes were reunited. There they all held council to make their plans. Today this mountain is called Chi-Pixab,[1] this is the name of the mountain.

There they reunited and there they extolled themselves: "I am, I, the people of the Quiché! And thou, Tamub, that shall be thy name." And to those from Ilocab they said: "Thou, Ilocab, this shall be thy name. And these three Quiché [peoples] shall not disappear, our fate is the same,"[2] they said when they gave them their names.

Then they gave the Cakchiquel their name: Gagchequeleb[3] was their name. In the same way they named those of Rabinal, which was their name, and they still have it. And also those of Tziquinahá,[4] as they are called today. Those are the names which they gave to each other.

There they were come together to await the dawn and to watch for the coming of the star, which comes just before the sun, when it is about to rise. "We came from there, but we have separated," they said to each other.

And their hearts were troubled; they were suffering greatly; they did not have food; they did not have sustenance; they only smelled the ends of their staffs and thus they imagined they were eating; but they did not eat when they came.[5]

[1] "The mandate, or council." Probably it is the same place which the *Título de los Señores de Totonicapán* calls *Chi-Quiché*. According to this document, the tribes left Tulán Pa Civán (between ravines), crossed the sea, arrived at the edge of a lake where they made huts (houses with roof of straw), but disgusted with the place, they continued on to the place called Chicpach, where they lived, and leaving a stone there as a monument, they continued their wanderings, nourishing themselves with roots. They arrived at another place which they named Chi-Quiché and finally came to a hill which they called Hacavitz-Chipal, "where they settled."

[2] *Xa hunam ca tzih*. *Tzih* has several meanings: word, opinion, history, fate, or destiny.

[3] Those of the red tree, or of fire.

[4] The people of Rabinal still preserve their old name. Tziquinahá is the present town of Santiago Atitlán and was the capital of the Zutuhil.

It is not quite clear, however, how they crossed the sea; they crossed to this side, as if there were no sea; they crossed on stones, placed in a row over the sand. For this reason they were called Stones in a Row, Sand Under the Sea,[6] names given to them when they [the tribes] crossed the sea, the waters having parted when they passed.

And their hearts were troubled when they talked together, because they had nothing to eat, only a drink of water and a handful of corn they had.[7]

There they were, then, assembled on the mountain called Chi-Pixab. And they had also brought Tohil, Avilix, and Hacavitz. Balam-Quitzé and his wife Cahá-Paluna, which was the name of his wife, observed a complete fast. And so did Balam-Acab and his wife, who was called Chomihá; and Mahucutah and his wife, called Tzununihá, also observed a complete fast, and Iqui-Balam with his wife, called Caquixahá, likewise.

And there were those who fasted in the darkness, and in the night. Great was their sorrow when they were on the mountain, called Chi-Pixab.

CHAPTER 8

And their gods spoke to them again. Thus Tohil, Avilix, and Hacavitz spoke to Balam-Quitzé, Balam-Acab, Mahucutah, and Iqui-Balam: "Let us go, let us get up, let us not stay here, take us to a secret place! Already dawn draws near. Would it not be a disgrace for you if we were imprisoned by our enemies within these walls where you, the priests and sacrificers, keep us?

[5] The Cakchiquel Manuscript describes in similar terms the hardship and hunger suffered by the tribes: "There was nothing to eat. . . . everything was lacking, we nourished ourselves with the bark of trees, we only smelled the end of our canes and with this felt satisfied"; *xa ca ti ca zec ru xe ca chamey ti cuquer vi ca cux ruma,* in the Cakchiquel tongue.

[6] *Cholochic-Abah, Bocotahinac-Zanaieb.*

[7] *Hu uq chi qui cumeh ri, xa huma ixim,* in the original.

Put each of us, then, in a safe place,"[1] they said when they spoke.

"Very well. We shall go on, we shall go in search of the forests," all answered.

Immediately after, they took up their gods and put them on their backs. In this way they carried Avilix to the ravine called Euabal-Ziván,[2] so named by them, to the large ravine of the forest, now called Pavilix,[3] and there they left him. In this ravine he was left by Balam-Acab.

They were left one by one. The first one left was Hacavitz, he was left on a large red pyramid,[4] on the mountain now called *Hacavitz*. There they founded their town, there in the place where the god called Hacavitz, was.

In the same way, Mahucutah left his god, who was the second one hidden by them.

Hacavitz was not in the forest, but on a hill cleared of trees, Hacavitz was hidden.

Then Balam-Quitzé came, he came there to the large forest; Balam-Quitzé came to hide Tohil at the hill which is today called *Patohil*. Then they celebrated the hiding of Tohil in the ravine, in his refuge. A great quantity of snakes, jaguars, vipers, and *cantiles*[5] were in the forest where they were hidden by the priests and sacrificers.

Balam-Quitzé, Balam-Acab, Mahucutah, and Iqui-Balam were together; together they awaited the dawn, there on the mountain, called Hacavitz.

And a short distance away, was the god of the people of

---

[1] *Huhun ta cut y ya vi*. The verb *ya, yac,* is used here in the sense of guarding, to have custody, to insure, *Diccionario Cakchiquel*.

[2] Ravine of the hiding place.

[3] In Avilix.

[4] *Hun nima caq ha*, a large mound, painted red, an artificial pyramid such as the Indians constructed as a base for their temples. On some of these the red paint is still preserved. They lived for many years in Hacavitz-Chipal, says the *Título de Totonicapán*. According to Brasseur de Bourbourg, the mountain Hacavitz is one of those which rises to the north of Rabinal three leagues from the Chixoy River. In the Cuchumatan Mountains, to the east of the Chixoy River, and at an altitude of 5,900 feet, there is the archaeological site of Chipal which might be the ancient Hacavitz-Chipal.

[5] *Canti*, a variety of poisonous serpent, *Trigonocephalus specialis*. The ancient Indians thought that these serpents were minor gods of their mythology.

Tamub and of the people of Ilocab. *Amac-Tan*,[6] the place is called, where the god of the Tamub [people] was, and there dawn came to the tribes. The place where those from Ilocab awaited the dawn was called *Amac-Uquincat*;[7] there was the god of those of Ilocab, a short distance from the mountain.

There, too, were all the people of Rabinal, the Cakchiquel, the Tziquinahá, all the small tribes, and the large tribes. Together they stayed, awaiting the coming of the dawn and the rising of the large star called Icoquih, which rises just before the sun, when it dawns, according to the legend.

There they were together, then, Balam-Quitzé, Balam-Acab, Mahucutah, and Iqui-Balam. They did not sleep; they remained standing and great was the anxiety of their hearts and their stomachs for the coming of dawn and the day. There, too, they felt shame; they were overcome with great sorrow, great suffering, and they were oppressed with pain.

They had come that far. "Oh, we have come without joy! If only we could see the rising of the sun! What shall we do now? If we lived in harmony in our country, why did we leave it?" they said to each other, in the midst of their sadness and affliction, and with mournful voices.

They talked, but they could not calm their hearts which were anxious for the coming of the dawn. "The gods are seated in the ravines, in the forests, they are among the air-plants, among the mosses,[8] not even a seat of boards were they given," they said.

First there were Tohil, Avilix, and Hacavitz. Great was their

[6] The tribe of Tan, Amagtán in the *Título de Totonicapán.*

[7] The name Uquincat might mean "net of gourds," from *uqui*, a tree which produces a fruit resembling the gourd, and *cat*, "net." The *Título de los Señores de Totonicapán* mentions this place under the name of Uquín, and adds that together with the tribes of Tamub and Ilocab there were the thirteen tribes called Vucamag-Tecpan.

[8] *Xa pa ec, xa pa atziac e qo vi. Ec* is the *Tillandsia Species pluribus*, a bromeliaceous plant which lives on trees, as was said before. *Atziac* is another bromeliaceous plant which also grows on trees, and its thick fibres, similar to gray hair, hang to the ground. Ist common name in Guatemala is *paxte*, derived from the Náhuatl word *paxtle*. An epiphyte *Dendropogon usneoides*, incorrectly called moss of Florida and Spanish moss in the southern part of the United States.

glory, their strength, and their power over the gods of all the tribes. Many were their miracles, and countless their journeys, and their pilgrimages in the midst of the cold; and the hearts of the tribes were filled with fear.

But calm were the hearts of Balam-Quitzé, Balam-Acab, Mahucutah, and Iqui-Balam with respect to them [the gods]. They felt no anxiety in their hearts for the gods whom they had received, and had carried on their backs when they came there from Tulán-Zuiva, from there in the East.

They were there, then, in the forest, now called Zaquiribal, Pa-Tohil, P'Avilix, Pa-Hacavitz.[9]

And next came the dawn, and light shone for our grandparents and our parents.

Now we shall tell of the coming of the dawn and the appearance of the sun, the moon, and the stars.

# CHAPTER 9

Here, then, is the dawn, and the coming of the sun, the moon, and the stars.

Balam-Quitzé, Balam-Acab, Mahucutah, and Iqui-Balam were very happy when they saw the Morning Star. It rose first, with shining face, when it came ahead of the sun.

Immediately they unwrapped the incense[1] which they had brought from the East, and which they had planned to burn, and then they untied the three gifts which they had planned to offer.

The incense which Balam-Quitzé brought was called Mixtán-

[9] The coming of dawn in the mountains of Tohil, of Avilix, and of Hacavitz. The *Titulo de los Señores de Totonicapán* says that when the chiefs of the Quiché nation disappeared, their children found themselves, by a miracle, in the mountains where the gods were, and that since that time these mountains are called Zaquiribal-Tohil, Zaquiribal-Avilix, and Zaquiribal-Hacavitz.

[1] The Maya and Quiché Indians give the name *Pom* to the incense or white aromatic resin which oozes from a tree, and they used it in their religious ceremonies. This resin is commonly known as *copal,* from the Náhuatl *copalli* (*Protium copal,* Engl.).

Pom; the incense which Balam-Acab brought was called Cavixtán-Pom; and that which Mahucutah brought was called Cabauil-Pom.[2] The three had their incense and burned it when they began to dance facing toward the East.

They wept for joy as they danced and burned their incense, their precious incense. Then they wept because they did not yet behold nor see the sunrise.

But, then, the sun came up. The small and large animals were happy; and arose from the banks of the river, in the ravines, and on the tops of the mountains, and all turned their eyes to where the sun was rising.

Then the puma and the jaguar roared. But first the bird called Queletzú[3] burst into song. In truth, all the animals were happy, and the eagle, the white vulture;[4] the small birds and the large birds stretched their wings.

The priests and the sacrificers were kneeling; great was the joy of the priests and sacrificers and of the people of Tamub and Ilocab and the people of Rabinal, the Cakchiquel, those from Tziquinahá, and those from Tuhalhá, Uchabahá, Quibahá, from Batená, and the Yaqui Tepeu, all those tribes which exist today. And it was not possible to count the people. The light of dawn fell upon all the tribes at the same time.

Instantly the surface of the earth was dried by the sun. Like

[2] These names have a marked Mexican flavor and seem to come from the Aztec tongue. *Mixtán-Pom* might be the copal, or incense, which they burned to Mictán Ahau, and *Cavixtán-Pom* that which they offered to Cavestán Ahau. Father Guzmán (*Compendio de nombres en lengua Cakchiquel*) mentions as gods of this tribe, among other minor deities, Mictán Ahau and Cavestán Ahau. The Aztec word *Mictlán* serves to designate the inferno. *Cabauil-Pom* is clearly the incense of the Quiché divinity in general, which is expressed with the word *Cabauil*, probably derived from the Maya *Kauil*, "god." The variety of incense of the offerings seems to be explained by the fact that the Quiché liked to offer "incense of a certain fragrance" to their gods.

[3] A climbing bird of the parrot family; *quel* in Quiché is a kind of parrot or magpie known in Guatemala as the *chocoyo*.

[4] *Zaccuch*, literally a vulture or white buzzard, "white-breasted buzzard," says Father Coto. The one called king buzzard, *Gypargus papa*, is larger than the ordinary vulture. It is also distinguished by the combination of its black and white feathers.

a man was the sun when it showed itself, and its face glowed when it dried the surface of the earth.

Before the sun rose, damp and muddy was the surface of the earth, before the sun came up; but then the sun rose, and came up like a man. And its heat was unbearable.[5] It showed itself when it was born and remained fixed [in the sky] like a mirror. Certainly it was not the same sun which we see, it is said in their old tales.

Immediately afterward Tohil, Avilix, and Hacavitz were turned to stone, together with the deified beings,[6] the puma, the jaguar, the snake, the *cantil*, and the hobgoblin. Their arms became fastened to the trees when the sun, the moon, and the stars appeared. All alike, were changed into stone. Perhaps we should not be living today[7] because of the voracious animals, the puma, the jaguar, the snake, and the *cantil*, as well as the hobgoblin; perhaps our power would not exist if these first animals had not been turned into stone by the sun.

When the sun arose, the hearts of Balam-Quitzé, Balam-Acab, Mahucutah, and Iqui-Balam were filled with joy. Great was their joy when it dawned. And there were not many men at that place; only a few were there on the mountain Hacavitz.[8] There dawn came to them, there they burned their incense and danced, turning their gaze toward the East, whence they had come. There were their mountains and their valleys, whence had come Balam-

---

[5] *Ma cu x-chihtahic u qatanal.* All the translators have followed the interpretation of Ximénez, who translates these words as: "The heat was not great." *Chihtahic,* however, means "to bear," "to suffer," and the negative sentence must be understood in the sense that the heat of the sun was unbearable or insufferable. If the heat of the sun had not been intense, it would not have dried the damp and muddy surface of the earth. In the recent edition of the *Popol Vuh,* Schultze Jena gives the correct translation of this passage in German.

[6] *U cabauilal coh, balam,* etc.

[7] *Ma ta oh yacamarinac,* "Perhaps we would not be standing." The transformation of the animals into stone, according to Chavero, is a symbol of the change of religion, their abandoning the old animal nature cult for the worship of the heavenly bodies.

[8] *Mana e ta quiá vinac chi qui qoheic, xa e chutin ta x-e qohe chiri chuvi huyub Hacavitz.* Ximénez gives a different interpretation to this sentence, as follows: "And the men were not large then, but they were small when they were on the hills of Hacavitz."

Quitzé, Balam-Acab, Mahucutah, and Iqui-Balam, as they were called.

But it was here where they multiplied, on the mountain, and this was their town; here they were, too, when the sun, the moon, and the stars appeared, when it dawned and the face of the earth and the whole world was lighted. Here, too, began their song, which they call *camucú*;[9] they sang it, but only the pain in their hearts and their innermost selves they expressed in their song. "Oh pity us! In Tulán we were lost, we were separated, and there our older and younger brothers stayed. Ah, we have seen the sun! but where are they now, that it has dawned?" so said the priests and the sacrificers of the Yaqui.

Because, in truth, the so-called Tohil is the same god of the Yaqui, the one called Yolcuat-Quitzalcuat.[10]

"We became separated there in Tulán, in Zuyvá, from there we went out together, and there our race was created when we came," they said to each other.

Then they remembered their older brothers and their younger brothers, the Yaqui, to whom dawn came there in the land which today is called Mexico. Part of the people remained there in the East, those called Tepeu Olimán, who stayed there, they say.

They felt much grief in their hearts, there in Hacavitz; and sad, too, were the people from Tamub and Ilocab, who were also there in the forest called Amac-Tan,[11] where dawn came to the priests and sacrificers of Tamub and to their god, who also was Tohil, because one and the same was the name of the god of the three branches of the Quiché people. And this is also the name of the god of the people of Rabinal, for there is little difference between that and the name of Huntoh, as the god of the people of

[9] "We see," or "our dove," *mucuy* in Maya.

[10] The great civilizer was worshiped as a divinity by the ancient Mexicans, who gave him different names. They called him Ehecatl, or God of the Wind; Yolcuat, or the Rattle Snake; Quetzalcoatl, or serpent covered with green feathers. The last meaning corresponds also to the Maya name Kukulcán, and to the Quiché, Gucumatz. Here the text shows that the Quiché also identified Quetzacoatl with their own god Tohil. Both were actually rain gods.

[11] *Pa quechelah Amac Dan ubi.* This place was already named in Chapter 8 of Part III, as the residence of the tribe of Tamub.

Rabinal is called; for that reason, it is said, they wanted to make their speech the same as that of the Quiché.

Well, the speech of the Cakchiquel is different, because the name of their god was different when they came from there, from Tulán-Zuyva. Tzotzihá Chimalcán was the name of their god, and today they speak a different tongue; and also from their god the families of Ahpozotzil and Ahpoxa,[12] as they are called, took their names.

The speech of the god was also changed when they were given their god there, in Tulán, near the stone;[13] their speech was changed when they came from Tulán in the darkness. And being together, dawn came to them and the light shone on all the tribes, in the order of the names of the gods of each of the tribes.

CHAPTER 10

And now we shall tell of their stay and abode there on the mountain, where the four called Balam-Quitzé, Balam-Acab, Mahucutah, and Iqui-Balam were together. Their

[12] Tzotzihá, the house of the zotzils or bats, that is to say of the Cakchiquel, who like the Zotzil of Chiapas also had the bat as a symbol. Chimalcán or Chamalcán, as explained in Chapter 6 of Part III was the name of a serpent, a sacred animal among the peoples of Middle America. Ahpozotzil and Ahpoxahil were the names of the king of the Cakchiquel and of his principal assistant and heir. The Spaniards gave the former, who was governing in 1524, the name Sinacán, from the Náhuatl Tzinacán, which also means "bat." Xahil, which may be translated as "dancer," from xah, "to dance," was the name of the second reigning house, and one of its descendants, Francisco Hernández Arana, wrote the *Memorial de Sololá*, which contains the history of the Cakchiquel nation.

[13] *Chirih abah*. The meaning of these words is vague. However, it becomes clearer if one recalls the constant association of the ancient American divinity with stone. The *Book of Chilan Balam of Chumayel* says, describing the creation of the world, that God was hidden in the stone when there was neither sky nor earth, and that later he came from the stone and fell into a second stone, and then he declared his divinity (*Kuil*). The Quiché documents speak of the stone which Nacxit gave to those tribes when they left Tulán, and which "they used for their incantations." And they add that in Qotuhá or Tzutuhá they also found a stone similar to that which Nacxit gave them, which they, the kings and the people, worshiped. As for the Manuscript of the Cakchiquel, it speaks of the obsidian stone, or *Chay Abah* to which that nation rendered homage.

hearts mourned for Tohil, Avilix, and Hacavitz, whom they had placed among the air-plants and the moss.

We shall tell now how they made the sacrifices at the foot of the place where they had carried Tohil, when they arrived in the presence of Tohil and Avilix. They went to see them, to greet them, and also to give them thanks for the arrival of the dawn. They were in the thicket[1] amidst the stones, there in the woods. And only by magic art did they speak when the priests and sacrificers came before Tohil. They did not bring great gifts, only resin, the remains of the gum, called *noh*, and *pericón*,[2] they burned before their gods.

Then Tohil spoke; only by a miracle he gave counsel to the priests and sacrificers. And they [the gods] spoke and said: "Truly here shall be our mountains and our valleys. We are yours; great shall be our glory and numerous our descendents, through the work of all men. Yours are all the tribes and we, your companions. Care for your town, and we shall give you your learning.

"Do not show us before the tribes when we are angered by the words of their mouths, or because of their conduct. Neither shall you permit us to fall into a snare. Give us, instead, the creatures of the woods and of the fields, and also the female deer, and the female birds.[3] Come and give us a little of your blood, have pity upon us. You may have the skins of the deer[4] and guard us from those whose eyes have deceived us.[5]

[1] *E cu vonovoh*, in the dense and thick.

[2] *Xa col xa r'achac noh ruq yiá.* Instead of the incense of the East, the Quiché burned a kind of aromatic substance on the altars of their gods: turpentine, or the resin from the pine, which they called *col; pom*, which is the *copalli* of Mexico; the gum called *noh*, which is another resin, according to Ximénez, and the large fan-grass, or *hyperitum, Tagetes lucida*, of the composite family made up of them. According to Sahagún, the Aztecs used the grass called *yiauhtli*, dried and ground, which burned like incense and which seems to be the same grass which the Quiché called *yiá*. The gum *noh* which the text mentions may be the same that the Maya of Yucatán call *xnoh*, "resin which drips from the pine" or turpentine, according to Roys.

[3] As has been said in another part, by the word *queh*, "deer," all quadrupeds are understood.

[4] *Ch'y canah cut r'izmal ri queh.* The text probably refers to the skin of the deer covered with hair, which the priests must show to the people instead of the real gods of the Quiché, thus obeying the command of Tohil.

[5] *Ch'y chahih are e ri u mucuvach chi mich canoc*, in the original.

"So, then, [the skin of] the deer shall be our symbol which you shall show before the tribes. When they ask 'Where is Tohil?' show the deerskin before their eyes. Neither shall you show yourselves, for you shall have other things to do. Great shall be their position; you shall dominate all the tribes; you shall bring your blood and their substance before us, and those who come to embrace us, shall be ours also," thus spoke Tohil, Avilix, and Hacavitz.[6]

They had the appearance of youths, when those who came to offer gifts saw them. Then the persecution of the young of the birds and of the deer began, and the fruit of the chase was received by the priests and sacrificers. And when they found the young of the birds and the deer, they went at once to place the blood of the deer and of the birds in the mouths of the stones, that were Tohil and Avilix.

As soon as the blood had been drunk by the gods, the stones spoke, when the priests and the sacrificers came, when they came to bring their offerings. And they did the same before their symbols, burning *pericón* and *holom-ocox.*[7]

The symbols of each one were there where they had been placed on the top of the mountain. But they [the priests] did not live in their houses by day, but walked over the mountains, and ate only the young horseflies, and the wasps, and the bees which they hunted; they had neither good food nor good drink. And neither were the roads from their homes known, nor did they know where their wives had remained.

[6] It will be noted here that the three gods spoke together to the tribes.

[7] "Which is a grass," says Ximénez; literally, head of a mushroom.

# PART IV

Now, then, many towns were being founded, one by one, and the different branches of the tribes were being reunited and settled close to the roads, their roads which they had opened.

As for Balam-Quitzé, Balam-Acab, Mahucutah, and Iqui-Balam, it was not known where they were. But when they saw the tribes that passed on the roads, instantly they began to shout on the mountain-tops, howling like a coyote, screaming like a mountain cat, and imitating the roaring of the puma and the jaguar.

And the tribes seeing these things, as they walked, said: "Their screams are like those of the coyote, of the mountain cat, of the puma, and of the jaguar. They want to appear to the tribes as though they are not men, and they only do this to deceive us, we the people. Their hearts wish something. Surely, they do not frighten us with what they do. They mean something with the roaring of the puma, with the noise of the jaguar which they break into when they see one or two men walking; what they want is to make an end of us."

Every day they [the priests] came to their houses and to their women, carrying only the young of the bumblebees and the wasps, and the honeybees to give to their women.

Every day, too, they came before Tohil, Avilix, and Hacavitz and said in their hearts: "Here are Tohil, Avilix, and Hacavitz. We can offer them only the blood of the deer and the birds; we

193

take only blood from our ears and our arms. Let us ask Tohil, Avilix, ánd Hacavitz for strength and vigor. What will [the tribes] say about the deaths of the people, which, one by one, we are killing?" they said to one another as they went into the presence of Tohil, Avilix, and Hacavitz.

Then they punctured their ears and their arms before the divinities; they caught their blood and put it in a vase near the stones.[1] They were not really stones, but each one appeared in the likeness of a youth.

They were happy with the blood of the priests and sacrificers when they arrived with this example of their work.

"Follow their tracks [those of the animals which they sacrificed], there is your salvation!

"From there, from Tulán, whence you brought us, they were told, came the skin, called Pazilizib, which was given to you, smeared with blood: spill your blood and let this be the offering of Tohil, Avilix, and Hacavitz."[2]

CHAPTER 2

Here is how Balam-Quitzé, Balam-Acab, Mahucutah, and Iqui-Balam began the abduction of the men of the tribes [of Vuc Amag].

Then came the killing of the tribes. They seized a man as he walked alone, or two when they were walking together, and it was not known when they were seized, and then they went to sacrifice them before Tohil and Avilix. Afterward they sprinkled the blood on the road and placed the heads separately on the road.

[1] X-*qui hic u coc pu chi abah*. U *coc* is the gourd or squash, the *xicalli* in which the Mexicans received the blood of their victims. *Pu chi abah*, near the stone, or in the mouth of the stone, that is to say, in the stone statutes of their gods.

[2] Despite its incoherency and its obscure meaning, this chapter seems to be the prologue to the destruction of the tribes of *Vuc Amag*, enemies of the Quiché, whom the priests decided to sacrifice in the way they had learned in the north, as will be seen in the chapters which follow.

And the tribes said, "The jaguar ate them." And they spoke thus because like footprints of the jaguar were the tracks which they had left, although they did not show themselves.

Already, many were the men who had been carried off, but the tribes did not notice it until later. "Could it be Tohil and Avilix who have been here among us? It must be they who are nourished by the priests and the sacrificers. Where are their homes? Let us follow their footprints!" said all the people.

Then they held a council among themselves. Then they began to follow the footprints of the priests and the sacrificers, but they were not clear. There were only tracks of wild animals, tracks of jaguars that they saw, but the tracks were not distinct. The first ones were not clear because they were reversed, as though made so that the people went astray, and their way was not clear. A mist formed, a black rain fell and made much mud; and it began to drizzle. This was what the people saw before them. And their hearts became weary of searching and following them on the roads, because the beings of Tohil, Avilix, and Hacavitz were so great that the latter withdrew to the summit of the mountains, in the vicinity of the people, whom they killed.

Thus began the abduction of the people when the sorcerers caught the tribes in the roads and sacrificed them before Tohil, Avilix, and Hacavitz; but their [own] sons they saved there on the mountain.

Tohil, Avilix, and Hacavitz had the appearance of three youths and walked by virtue of the magic stone. There was a river in which they bathed, at the edge of the water, and only there did they appear. For this reason it was called "In the Bathing Place of Tohil," and this was the name of the river.[1] Often the tribes saw them, but they disappeared immediately, when they were seen by the people.

Then they had tidings of where Balam-Quitzé, Balam-Acab, Mahucutah, and Iqui-Balam were, and at once the tribes held council as to the way in which they could be killed.

[1] *Chi r'atinibal Tohil.* Brasseur de Bourbourg locates the river of this name thirteen to fifteen miles to the southeast of Cubulco, on the road to Joyabaj, on the summit of the mountain which separates both towns.

In the first place the tribes wanted to discuss the way to overcome Tohil, Avilix, and Hacavitz. And all the priests and sacrificers [of the tribes] said to the people: "Arise, all of you, call everyone, let there be not one group, nor two groups, among us who remain behind the others."

All assembled, they assembled in great numbers and deliberated among themselves. And they said, asking each other: "What shall we do to overcome the Quiché of *Cavec*[2] by whose hands our sons and vassals are being killed? It is not known how our people are being destroyed. If we must perish, because of these abductions, so let it be; and if the power of Tohil, Avilix, and Hacavitz is so great then let our god be this Tohil, and God grant that you take him captive. It is not possible that they shall overcome us. Are there not, perchance, enough men among us? And the Cavec are not many," they said, when all were assembled.

And some said, turning to the tribes, when they spoke: "Who has seen those who bathe in the river every day? If they are Tohil, Avilix, and Hacavitz, then we shall overcome them first, and afterward, we shall begin the destruction of the priests and sacrificers." This, many of them said, when they talked.

"But how shall we overcome them?" they asked again.

"This shall be our way of overcoming them. Since they have the appearance of youths when they let themselves be seen in the water, then let two maidens who are really beautiful, and very lovely, go and provoke in them desire to possess them," they said.

"Very well. Let us go, then; let us find two beautiful maidens," they exclaimed, and then they went to find their daughters. And truly beautiful were the maidens.

Then they instructed the maidens: "Go, our daughters, go to wash clothes at the river, and if you see the three youths, undress before them, and if their hearts desire you, call to them. If they say to you, 'May we come to you?' answer, 'Yes.' And when they ask: 'Where do you come from, whose daughters are you?' tell them, 'We are daughters of the lords.' "[3]

[2] The family of Cavec was the most important and numerous in the Quiché kingdom.

[3] The chiefs of the tribes of Vucamag, who were enemies of the Quiché

"Then you shall say: 'Give us a token of yours.' And if after they have given you something, they want to kiss your faces, really give yourselves to them. And if you do not give yourselves to them, we shall kill you. Afterward our hearts shall be satisfied. When you have the token, bring it here, and this shall be proof, in our judgment, that they were joined with you."

Thus spoke the lords when they advised the two maidens. Here are their names: Xtah was the name of one of the maidens, and the other was Xpuch.[4] And the two maidens, Xtah and Xpuch, were sent to the river, to the bathing place of Tohil, Avilix, and Hacavitz. This is what was decided by all the tribes.

They went at once, well adorned, and they were truly very beautiful when they went there where Tohil[5] was bathing, so that they would be seen, when they were washing. When they went, the lords were happy because they had sent their two daughters.

As soon as the latter arrived at the river, they began to wash. The two had already taken off their clothes and were bending over the stones when Tohil, Avilix, and Hacavitz came. They came there to the edge of the river and paused a moment, surprised to see the two young girls who were washing, and the girls became ashamed at the moment when Tohil came. But the two girls did not appeal to Tohil. And then he asked them: "Where did you come from?" Thus he asked the two maidens, and added: "What do you want that you come here to the edge of our water?"

And they answered: "The lords have sent us to come here. 'Go look at the faces of Tohil and speak with them,' the lords

and fathers of the maidens, were called Rotzhaib, Uxab, Qibahá, and Quebat-Zunuhá, according to the *Título de los Señores de Totonicapán*.

[4] *Are qui bi va Xtah u bi hun gapoh, Xpuch chicut u bi hunchic*, in the original. *Xtán* is "girl" in Cakchiquel. *Ichpoch* also means "girl" in Náhuatl, according to Brasseur de Bourbourg. The *Título de los Señores de Totonicapán* adds a third maiden called *Quibatzunah* ("well arranged," or "polished"). It is more logical to believe that the mission sent out by the tribes was composed of three sirens, since the gods whom they were trying to seduce were three in number. Another version of the legend in the *Título de Totonicapán* is that Balam-Quitzé, Balam-Acab, and Mahucutah, and not the gods of the Cavec, were the youths whom they tried to tempt.

[5] Here Tohil again becomes a collective noun.

197

told us; and 'then bring proof that you have seen their faces,' they told us." Thus the two girls spoke, making known the purpose of their coming.

Well, what the tribes wanted was that the two maidens would be violated by the incarnation of Tohil.[6] But Tohil, Avilix, and Hacavitz said, speaking again to Xtah and Xpuch, as the two maidens were called: "Very well, with you shall go proof of our conversation. Wait a little and then you shall give it to the lords," they said.

Then they held council with the priests and sacrificers and they said to Balam-Quitzé, Balam-Acab, Mahucutah, and Iqui-Balam:[7] "Paint three capes, paint on them the symbol of your being in order that it may be recognized by the tribes, when the maidens who are washing carry them back. Give the capes to them," Balam-Quitzé, Balam-Acab, and Mahucutah were told.

At once the three began to paint. First, Balam-Quitzé painted a jaguar; the figure was made and painted on the surface of the cape. Then Balam-Acab painted the figure of an eagle on the surface of a cape; and then Mahucutah painted bumblebees and wasps all over, figures and drawings of which he painted on the cloth. And the three finished their paintings, three pieces they painted.

Then they went to give the capes to Xtah and Xpuch, as they were called, and Balam-Quitzé, Balam-Acab, and Mahucutah said to them: "Here is proof of your conversation [with us]; take these before the lords: Say to them, 'In truth, Tohil has talked to us; here we bring the proof,' tell them, and have them dress themselves in the clothes which you will give them." This they told the maidens when they bade them farewell. The latter went at once, carrying the above-mentioned painted capes.[8]

[6] According to the Quiché belief, these youths who appeared in the Bath of Tohil were the reincarnation of the gods in human form, their bodily representatives, their *alter egos*. The *nagual* was the person or animal into which the Indians could be transformed at will.

[7] The name of Iqui-Balam appears here with that of the other Quiché chiefs, but later the manuscript says that there were only the other three who painted the capes.

[8] *Ta x-e be cut x-cu caah u bi ri tziban cul*, in the original.

When they arrived, the lords were filled with joy to see their faces and their hands, from which hung the things the maidens had gone for.

"Did you see the face of Tohil?" they asked them.

"Yes, we saw it," answered Xtah and Xpuch.

"Very well. And you bring the token, do you not?" the lords asked, thinking that this was the proof of their sin.

Then the maidens held out the painted capes, all covered with [the figures] of jaguars and eagles, and covered with bumblebees and wasps, painted on the surface of the cloth and which shone before them. At once they felt a desire to put the capes on.

The jaguar did nothing when the lord threw the first painting on his back. Then the lord put on the second painting, with the figure of the eagle. The lord felt very well wrapped within it. And he turned about before all of them. Then he undressed before all, and put on the third painted cape. And now he had on himself, the bumblebees and wasps which were on it. Instantly the bumblebees and the wasps stung his flesh. And not being able to suffer the stings of these insects, he began to scream because of the insects whose figures were painted on the cloth, the painting of Mahucutah, which was the third one that had been painted.

Thus they were overcome. Then the lords reprimanded the two maidens named Xtah and Xpuch: "What kind of clothes are those which you have brought? Where did you go to bring them, you devils?" they said to the maidens when they reprimanded them. All the people were overcome by Tohil.

Well, what they [the lords] wanted was that Tohil should have gone to amuse himself with Xtah and Xpuch, and that the [maidens] would have become whores, for the tribes believed that they would serve to tempt them. But it was not possible that they should overcome them, thanks to those miraculous men, Balam-Quitzé, Balam-Acab, Mahucutah, and Iqui-Balam.

## CHAPTER 3

Afterwards the tribes held council again.

"What shall we do with them? In truth, their estate is very great," they said when they assembled again in council.

"Well, then, we shall waylay them, we shall kill them, we shall arm ourselves with bows and with shields. Perchance, are we not many? Let there not be one or two among us who remains behind." This they said when they held council. And all the people armed. Many were the warriors when all the people gathered together for the killing.

Meanwhile, there were Balam-Quitzé, Balam-Acab, Mahucutah, and Iqui-Balam, they were on the mountain Hacavitz, on the hill of this name. They were there in order to save their sons who were on the mountain.

And they did not have many people, they did not have multitudes such as the multitudes of the tribes. The summit of the mountain where they had their place was small, and for that reason when the tribes assembled together and rose, they decided to kill all of them.

In this manner, then, took place the reunion of all the people, all armed with their bows and their shields. It is impossible to describe the richness of their arms; the appearance of all the chiefs and men was very beautiful, and certainly all obeyed their orders.

"They shall positively be destroyed, and as for Tohil, he shall be our god, we shall worship him, if we take him prisoner," they said to each other. But Tohil knew everything and so did Balam-Quitzé, Balam-Acab, and Mahucutah. They heard all the plans, because they did not sleep, or rest, from the time the warriors armed themselves.

Then all the warriors rose up and started out on the road, intending to enter [the town] by night. But they did not arrive, for all the warriors were watching on the road, and then they were destroyed by Balam-Quitzé, Balam-Acab, and Mahucutah.

All remained watching along the road, but they heard nothing and they finally fell asleep. Then they [Balam-Quitzé, Balam-Acab, and Mahucutah] began to pull out their eyelashes and their beards; they took off the metal ornaments from their throats—their crowns and necklaces. And they took the metal from the handles of their spears. They did this to punish them and humiliate them, and give them an example of the power of the Quiché people.

When they [the warriors] awoke, they wanted to take their crowns and their staffs, but they no longer had metal in the staff-handles, nor their crowns. "Who has stripped us? Who has torn out our beards? Whence have they come to rob us of our precious metals?" said all of the warriors. "Can it be these devils who are carrying off the men? But they shall not succeed in frightening us. We shall enter their town by force, and we shall again see the face of our silver; this we shall do," said all the tribes, and all truly intended to carry out their word.

Meanwhile the hearts of the priests and the sacrificers on the summit of the mountain were calm. And Balam-Quitzé, Balam-Acab, Mahucutah, and Iqui-Balam[1] having talked together, they built a wall at the edge of the town and enclosed it with boards and thorns. Then they made figures in the form of men, and put them in rows on the wall, armed them with shields and arrows and adorned them, putting metal crowns on their heads. These they put on the simple wooden figures, they adorned them with the metal which they had taken from the tribes on the road and with them they decorated the figures.

They made a moat around the town, and then they asked advice of Tohil: "Shall they kill us? Shall they overcome us?" their hearts said to Tohil.

"Do not be troubled! I am here. And this you will use. Do not be afraid," he [Tohil] said to Balam-Quitzé, Balam-Acab, Mahucutah, and Iqui-Balam, when they were given the bumblebees and the wasps. This is what they went to fetch. And when they came, they put them inside four big gourds which were placed around the town. They shut the bumblebees and wasps inside the gourds, in order to fight the people with them.

The city was watched from afar, spied upon and observed by

[1] *Ta x-e naohin cut Balam-Quitzé, Balam-Acab, Mahucutah, Iqui-Balam,* in the original.

201

the scouts of the tribe. "They are not many," they said. But they saw only the wooden figures which lightly moved their bows and their shields. In truth, they had the appearance of men, had in truth the appearance of warriors when the tribes looked at them, and all the tribes were happy because they saw that they were not many.

There were many tribes; it was not possible to count the people, the warriors and soldiers who were going to kill Balam-Quitzé, Balam-Acab, and Mahucutah, who were on the mountain Hacavitz, the name of the place where they were found.

Now we shall tell about their arrival.

## CHAPTER 4

They were there, then, Balam-Quitzé, Balam-Acab, Mahucutah, and Iqui-Balam, were all together on the mountain with their wives and their children when all the warriors and soldiers came. The tribes did not number sixteen thousand, or twenty-four thousand men,[1] [but even more].

They surrounded the town, crying out loudly, armed with arrows and shields, beating drums, giving war whoops, whistling, shouting, inciting them to fight, when they arrived in front of the town.

But the priests and sacrificers were not frightened; they only looked at them from the edge of the wall, where they were in good order with their wives and children. They thought only of the strength and the shouting of the tribes when they came up the side of the mountain.

Shortly before they were about to throw themselves at the

[1] *Mavi xa ca chuy, ox chuq ri amac. Chuy, chuguy,* literally the bag or sack in which the cacao was stored and which contained eight thousand beans, equivalent to the *xiquipil* of Mexico. The same word is used here also to count the troops. The text gives one to understand that the army of the tribes contained more than 24,000 men. In the *Memorial Cakchiquel de Sololá* one finds the same form of enumeration: *Maqui xa hu chuvy, ca chuvy x-pe, x-ul ca chi amag;* "neither eight thousand nor sixteen thousand came, all the people came."

entrance of the town, the four gourds which were at the edge of the town were opened and the bumblebees and the wasps came out of the gourds; like a great cloud of smoke they emerged from the gourds. And thus the warriors perished because of the insects which stung the pupils of their eyes,[2] and fastened themselves to their noses, their mouths, their legs, and their arms. "Where are they," they said, "those who went to get and bring in all the bumblebees and wasps that are here?"

They went straight to sting the pupils of their eyes, the little insects buzzing in swarms over each one of the men; and the latter, stunned by the bumblebees and wasps, could no longer grasp their bows and their shields, which were broken on the ground.

When the warriors fell, they were stretched out on the mountainside, and they no longer felt when they were hit with arrows, and wounded by the axes. Balam-Quitzé and Balam-Acab used only blunt sticks. Their wives also took part in this killing. Only a part [of them] returned and all the tribes began to flee. But the first ones caught were put to death; not a few of the men died, and those who died were not the ones they intended to kill but those who were attacked by the insects. Neither was it a deed of valor, because the warriors were not killed by arrows or by shields.

Then all the tribes surrendered. The people humbled themselves before Balam-Quitzé, Balam-Acab, and Mahucutah. "Have pity on us, do not kill us," they exclaimed.

"Very well. Although you deserve to die, you shall [instead] become [our] vassals for the rest of your lives,"[3] they said to them.

In this way were all of the tribes destroyed by our first mothers and fathers; and this happened there on the mountain Hacavitz, as it is now called. This was where they first settled, where they multiplied and increased, begot their daughters, gave being to their sons, on the mountain Hacavitz.

They were, then, very happy when they had overcome all the tribes, whom they destroyed there on the mountaintop. In

---

[2] *Tacatoh chu bac qui vach*, in the original.

[3] The Quiché expression is very picturesque: *chi be quih, chi be zac,* "so long as the sun walks, so long as there is light."

this way they carried out the destruction of the tribes, of all the tribes. After this their hearts rested. And they said to their sons that when they [the tribes] intended to kill them, the hour of their own death was approaching.

And now we shall tell of the death of Balam-Quitzé, Balam-Acab, Mahucutah, and Iqui-Balam, as they were called.

CHAPTER 5

And as they had had a presentiment of their death, they counseled their children. They were not ill, they had neither pain nor agony when they gave their advice to their children.

These are the names of their sons: Balam-Quitzé had two sons, Qocaib the first was called, and Qocavib was the name of the second son of Balam-Quitzé, the grandfather and father of those of Cavec.

And these are the two sons which Balam-Acab begot, here are their names: Qoacul the first of his sons was called, and Qoacutec was the name of the second son of Balam-Acab [the founder] of those of Nihaib.[1]

Mahucutah had but one son, who was called Qoahau.

Those three had sons, but Iqui-Balam did not have children. They were really the sacrificers, and these are the names of their sons.

So, then, they bade [their sons] farewell. The four were together and they began to sing, feeling sad in their hearts; and their hearts wept when they sang the *camucú*, as the song is called which they sang when they bade farewell to their sons.

"Oh, our sons! we are going, we are going away; sane advice and wise counsel we leave you. And you, also, who came from our distant country, oh our wives!" they said to their women, and

[1] The text calls these two branches of the Quiché family Caviquib and Nihaibab, which are the plurals of Cavec and Nihaib. The third family, that of Ahau Quiché, descended from Mahucutah.

they bade farewell to each one. "We are going back to our town, there already in his place is Our Lord of the stags,[2] to be seen there in the sky. We are going to begin our return, we have completed our mission [here], our days are ended. Think, then, of us, do not erase us [from your memory], nor forget us. You shall see your homes and your mountains again; settle there, and so let it be! Go on your way and you shall see again the place from which we came."

These words they said when they bade them farewell. Then Bàlam-Quitzé left the symbol of his being: "This is a remembrance which I leave for you. This shall be your power. I take my leave filled with sorrow," he added. Then he left the symbol of his being, the *Pizom-Gagal*,[3] as it was called, whose form was invisible because it was wrapped up and could not be unwrapped; the seam did not show because it was not seen when they wrapped it up.

[2] *C'Ahaual Queh.* Among the Maya, as well as among the Quiché, the Lord, or owner, of the Stags is a symbol of disappearance and of farewell. In Yucatán, Lord Deer is called *Yumilceh*. He was the guiding spirit of the Maya when they arrived in Xocné-Ceh, according to the *Book of Chilan Balam of Chumayel*.

[3] The bundle, symbol of power and majesty, the mysterious package which the servants of the temple guarded as a symbol of authority and sovereignty. The *Título de los Señores de Totonicapán* gives some information about this Bundle of Majesty. This document says that when the Quiché left Tulán-Civán, under the command of Balam-Quitzé, "the great father Nacxit gave them a gift called Giron-Gagal." Giron, or *quirón*, is derived from *quira*, "unfasten," "unroll," "to preserve" a thing. Farther on the same document says that it was in Hacavitz-Chipal where, for the first time, they unwrapped the gift which old Nacxit gave them when they came from the East, and that "this gift was what they feared and respected." The gift was a stone, "the stone of Nacxit, which they used in their incantations." Possibly it was the same stone of slate or obsidian which they called *Chay Abah*, and which is also mentioned in the *Memorial de Sololá*, as the symbol of the Divinity, which the Cakchiquel have worshiped from ancient times. Torquemada (*Monarquía Indiana*, Part 2, Book VI, Chap. XLII) says that the Mexican Indians used a bundle, called *Haquimilolli*, made of the mantles of the dead gods, in which they wrapped some sticks with green stones and the skins of snakes and jaguars, and that this bundle they venerated as their principal god. The *Título de los Señores de Totonicapán* says that upon taking leave of their children, Balam-Quitzé pronounced these words: "Keep the pecious gift which our father Nacxit gave us; it will be useful to us, because we have not yet found the place in which we are going to settle. Beget sons worthy of the title of Ahpop, Ahpop Camhá, Galel, Ahtzivinak; make sons filled with the fire and majesty which our father Nacxit gave us."

In this way they took their leave and immediately they disappeared there on the summit of the mountain Hacavitz.

They [the four lords] were not buried by their wives nor by their children, because they were not seen when they disappeared. Only their leaving was seen clearly, and therefore the bundle was very dear to them. It was the reminder of their fathers and at once they burned incense before this reminder of their fathers.

And then the lords, who succeeded Balam-Quitzé, begot new generations of men, and this was the beginning of the grandfathers and fathers of those of Cavec; but their sons, those called Qocaib and Qocavib, did not disappear.

In this way the four died, our first grandfathers and fathers; in this way they disappeared, leaving their children on the mountain Hacavitz, there where they have remained.

And the people being subdued already, and their grandeur ended, the tribes no longer had power, and all lived to serve daily.

They remembered their fathers; great was the glory of the bundle to them. Never did they unwrap it, but it was always wrapped, and with them. Bundle of Greatness they called it when they extolled and named that which their fathers had left in their care as a symbol of their being.

In this manner, then, came about the disappearance and end of Balam-Quitzé, Balam-Acab, Mahucutah, and Iqui-Balam, the first men who came there from the other side of the sea, where the sun rises. They had been here a long time when they died, being very old, the chiefs and sacrificers, as they were called.

CHAPTER 6

Then they decided to go to the East, thinking thus to fulfill the command of their fathers which they had not forgotten. It had been a long time since their fathers had died, when the tribes gave them their wives, and thus they acquired many relatives-in-law, when the three took wives.[1]

[1] X *qui biah*, literally, "they had fathers-in-law and brothers-in-law."

And starting on their journey, they said: "We are going to the East, there whence came our fathers." So they said when the three sons set out. One was called Qocaib, and he was the son of Balam-Quitzé, of the Cavec. The one called Qoacutec was son of Balam-Acab, of the Nihaib; and the other called Qoahau, was son of Mahucutah, of the Ahau-Quiché.[2]

These, then, are the names of those who went there to the other side of the sea; the three went then, and were endowed with intelligence and experience, but they were not common men. They took leave of all their brothers and relatives and left joyfully. "We shall not die; we shall return," said the three when they left.

Certainly they crossed the sea when they came there to the East, when they went to receive the investiture of the kingdom. And this was the name of the Lord, King of the East, where they went. When they arrived before Lord Nacxit,[3] which was the name of the great lord, the only supreme judge of all the kingdoms, he gave them the insignia of the kingdom and all its distinctive symbols. Then came the insignia of Ahpop and Ahpop-Camhá, and then the insignia of the grandeur and the sovereignty

[2] This was the second journey to the East which Diego Reynoso, author of Chapter IV of the *Título de los Señores de Totonicapán*, describes. According to this Indian writer, there were four princes who took part in the expedition; the two brothers Qocaib and Qocavib, Qoacul and Acutec, and a fifth was added afterward who had the title of Nim Chocoh Cavec, who later received the title of Chocohil-Tem.

[3] Nacxit is the abbreviated name which the Quiché and the Cakchiquel gave, in their tales, to the King of the Orient, who was no other than Topiltzin Acxitl Quetzalcoatl, the famous Toltec king who, having been obliged to abandon his dominions in the north, emigrated at the end of the tenth century to the lands of Yucatán (the Orient of the ancient chronicles), and there repopulated Chichén Itzá and founded the city of Mayapán, civilized the peninsula, and, upon finishing his mission, returned to the place whence he had come. The fabulous Tlapallan, the place to which, it is said, the great monarch migrated, was the country which extended from Xicalanco toward the east, that is, the coastal region of the modern Mexican states of Tabasco, Campeche, and Yucatán.

The Chronicles, or *Books of Chilan Balam*, of Yucatán speak of the prophecy of the return of Kukulcán-Quetzalcoatl who, in those documents, is called Nacxit-Xuchit.

of the Ahpop and the Ahpop-Camhá.[4] And Nacxit ended by giving them the insignia of royalty, which are: the canopy, the throne, the flutes of bone, the *cham-cham*, yellow beads, puma claws, jaguar claws, the heads and feet of the deer, dais, snail shells, tobacco, little gourds, parrot feathers, standards of royal aigrette feathers, *tatam*, and *caxcon*.[5] All the foregoing they car-

[4] *Ahpop* is the Maya word which has passed without variation to the languages of the interior of Guatemala; its literal meaning is "the mat." The mat, *pop*, was the symbol of royalty, and the chief or lord is represented as seated upon it on the most ancient monuments of the Maya Old Empire which had its origin in the Petén, Guatemala. The Ahpop was the Quiché king and chief of the House of Cavec; the Ahpop Camhá, also of the House of Cavec, was the second reigning prince; the Ahau Galel was the chief or king of the House of Nihaib, and the Ahtzic Vinac Ahau the chief of the House of Ahau Quiché. Another group of Quiché nobles also bore the same title as the two first, and in this place the text refers to them as Ah-popol, Ahpop-camhail, which are the plural forms.

[5] It is extremely difficult to interpret the names of the gifts of Nacxit because they belong to the archaic Quiché and Maya tongues. I believe, however, that I have made some progress in identifying these ancient objects, decreasing in number the unknown names which the venerable first translator of the *Popol Vuh* left unexplained.

"Canopy" corresponds to the Quiché *muh*, which is also the word for the royal mantle.

"Throne," *galibal*, a high seat where the king or principal lord was seated.

"Flutes of bone" is the literal translation of *zubac*.

*Cham-cham*, another flute, says Ximénez; drums, according to Brasseur de Bourbourg, Seler, and Raynaud; and in this case it brings to mind the African tom-tom.

Yellow beads, *titil canabah*. The *Diccionario Cakchiquel* interprets *canabah* as the yellow paint with which the Indians painted their bodies. According to Ximénez, the expression of the text is equivalent to *chalchihuites*, or beads of stone, usually green or yellow serpentine. In Maya the selected beads, jewels, or stones which were used in divination and as ornaments are called *tetil kan*, "fruit pits or stones which the Indians used as money and for necklaces," according to the *Diccionario de Motul*.

Puma claws, jaguar claws, *tzicvuil coh, tzicvuil balam*, through analogy with the text of the *Título de los Señores de Totonicapán* which mentions "nails of the puma and the eagle, pelts of other animals, and also stones, sticks, etc." Seler gives the same interpretation here.

*Holom, pich queh*, literally translated, are the heads and feet of the deer.

Canopies, *macutax*. In Cakchiquel, *macamic* is a tent or pavilion; *macom*, mat, like a canopy; *macubal*, canopy. (*Diccionario Cakchiquel*). The *Título de los Señores de Totonicapán* enumerates the canopies or pavilions assigned to the lords. The Ahpop had the right to use four canopies over his head; the Ahpop

ried, those who came after going to the other side of the sea to receive the paintings of Tulán, the paintings, as these were called, in which they wrote their histories.[6]

Then, having arrived at their town called Hacavitz, all the people of Tamub and of Ilocab assembled there; all the tribes were assembled and were filled with joy when Qocaib, Qoacutec, and Qoahau arrived, and there they again assumed the rule of the tribes.[7]

Camhá, three; etc. The newly created honors, according to the same document, were those of Galel-Tem, Atzivinaquil-Tem, Nim-Chocohil-Tem, Gale-Yam-hail-Tem, Nima-Yamolah-Tem, four Ah-Tohil, three Chocohib, three Utzam-Pop, three Yacolhá, and Pop-Camhá.

Snail shell, *tot*, sea-shells.

Tobacco, *quz;* little gourds, *buz*, by resemblance with the Maya words of Yucatán, the country where Nacxit lived. In Maya, tobacco is *cuz* and *kutz. Buz* may be the Maya *bux*, little gourds for keeping ground tobacco, according to the *Diccionario de Motul*. The Maya used tobacco in their incantations and sorcery. In Maya, *kutz* is also the magnificent wild turkey, *Meleagris ocellata*, which may very well be another gift worthy of princes. It is interesting to recall here that, according to the *Crónica Mexicana* by Fernando de Alvarado Tezozomoc, the Aztec upon giving the royal investiture to Moctezuma, fastened around his neck a *tecomatillo* (small gourd) in which to keep *piciete* [tobacco] "which is strength for the roads."

Parrot feathers, *chiyom*. This word is found in the *Vocabulario Kakchiquel* by Father Francisco Barela. With the green feathers of the common parrot of the Peninsula of Yucatán, ornaments were made for the finery of the princes and warriors; but here is meant the bright red and blue feathers of the macaw, also used for the same purpose.

Royal heron, *aztapulul*. This word is taken from the Aztec *aztapololli*, a derivative of *aztatl*, large white herons, very white like snow, says Sahagún, who adds that the feather workers made "standards with feathers of the royal heron."

I have been unable to interpret the words *tatam* and *caxcón*.

[6] *U tzibal Tulán.* The paintings which the Tolteca had brought from far-away Tula and in which they preserved the stories of ancient times. Although the paintings of the Quiché have not been preserved, there is a reliable proof of their former existence furnished by the Oidor Zorita, whom I have mentioned various times; he says that in Utatlán he found out "through the paintings which they had of their antiquities of more than eight hundred years, and by very old people, that there used to be among them, in the time of their paganism, three lords, and that the principal one had three canopies or mantles of very rich feathers on his seat, the second had two, and the third, one." Those paintings "of more than eight hundred years" in 1550 could well have been the paintings brought from Tulán.

[7] The *Título de los Señores de Totonicapán* speaks of two journeys which the Quiché princes made to the East. Chapter III of that manuscript says that the

The people of Rabinal, the Cakchiquel, and the people of Tziquinahá rejoiced. Before them they showed the insignia of the grandeur of the kingdom. Great, too, were the tribes, although they had not finished showing their might. And they were there in Hacavitz, all were there with those who came from the East. There they spent much time;[8] there on the summit of the mountain they were in great numbers.

There, too, the wives of Balam-Quitzé, Balam-Acab, and Mahucutah died.

Later they left, abandoning their country, and searching for

---

same Balam-Quitzé said to his companions: "It is time now to send ambassadors to our father and Lord Nacxit; that he may know the state of our affairs, that he give us means so that in the future our enemies shall never overcome us, so that never shall our noble birth be made light of; that he designate honors for us and for all our descendants, and, that, finally, he send public offices for those who deserve them." With this aim, the chiefs elected Qocaib and Qocavib, both sons of Balam-Quitzé, who received their instructions and set out. "Qocaib went in the direction of the East, and Qocavib in that of the West," says the manuscript, which must be interpreted as indicating that the first went by the east coast of Guatemala and Yucatán in order to go toward Chichén Itzá, the metropolis of the northeastern part of the peninsula, which was the court of Quetzalcoatl, Acxitl, or Kukulcán; while the second probably followed the course of ʋie Chixoy River, which flows close to Hacavitz, and the Usumacinta River, which carried him to the west coast of Yucatán. After a long journey of no less than a year, Qocaib arrived in the presence of the Emperor Nacxit Kukulcán and fulfilled his mission; but Qocavib, "encountering some obstacles on the shores of the Lake of Mexico [undoubtedly the Laguna de Términos] returned without doing anything." However, on his return to his own people and "finding a weak soul he illicitly knew [carnally] his sister-in-law, the wife of Qocaib."

Finally Qocaib returned and gave an account of his mission. "He brought the titles of Ahpop, Ahtzalam, Tzanchinamital, and many others; he showed the insignia which must accompany these titles, and they were the claws of the jaguars and eagles, skins of other animals, and also stones, sticks, etc." Seeing his wife with a newly born child in her arms, he asked whence it had come. "It is of thy blood," answered the woman, "of thy flesh and thy same bones." Qocaib accepted the explanation, and taking the child's cradle said: " 'From today on, and forever this child shall be called Balam Conaché.' And the latter began the House of Conaché and Iztayul." With respect to the second journey of the Quiché princes, the Título says that they returned satisfied to Hacavitz Chipal, and displayed the signs and symbols which they brought.

[8] Naht chicut x-qui ban, "There they lived many years," says the Título de los Señores de Totonicapán, using, it would seem, the same Quiché words. The whereabouts of the original of the Título is not known.

other places in which to settle. Innumerable were the places in which they settled, where they were, and which they named. There our first mothers and our first fathers were reunited and increased. So said the old people when they told how they left their first capital, called Hacavitz, and went to found another capital, called *Chi-Quix*.[9]

They were a long time in this other town, where they had daughters and sons. There were many of them there, and there were four other places, to each of which they gave the name of their town. Their daughters and sons married; they simply gave them away [in marriage] and the presents and favors they received they considered as the price for their daughters, and, in this way, they lived happily.[10]

Afterward they went through each one of the wards of the town, the different names of which are: Chi-Quix, Chichac, Humetahá, Culbá, and Cavinal. These were the names of the places where they settled. And they surveyed the hills and their towns and sought the uninhabited places, for, all together, they were now very many.

Those who had gone to the East to receive the sovereignty were now dead. They were already old when they arrived at each of the towns. They did not become accustomed to the different places through which they passed; they suffered many hardships and troubles and only after a long time did the grandfathers and

---

[9] "In the thorns." The *Título de Totonicapán*, which so effectively supplements the information given in the *Popol Vuh*, mentions the place of Chi-Quiché, where the tribes were before establishing themselves in Hacavitz, but it does not speak of Chi-Quix, despite the fact that it names some twenty places where the Quiché stopped after they had left Hacavitz. It seems, however, by the text which I translate, that Chi-Quix was only a suburb, or hill, which formed part of the general group of Chi-Quix, Chichac, Humetahá, Culbá, and Cavinal, and these three last names are found also in the *Título de Totonicapán* as Chi-Humet and Culba-Cavinal, "where they built houses and made huts," before continuing on to Izmachi.

[10] The Quiché married their daughters—says the *Título de Totonicapán*—with certain ceremonies and water-jars of white *batido* (a drink made of corn meal to which cacao is sometimes added), and they had a basket of little avocados, a leg of wild pig, and little tamales wrapped and tied with vines. These were the gifts, and with them the marriage was agreed upon.

fathers arrive at their town. Here is the name of the city to which they came.

CHAPTER 7

Chi-Izmachí[1] is the name of the site of their town, where they were afterward and where they settled. There, under the fourth generation of kings, they developed their power and constructed buildings of mortar and stone.[2]

And Conaché and Beleheb-Queh, the Galel-Ahau,[3] ruled. Then king Cotuhá and Iztayul reigned, as they were called the Ahpop and the Ahpop-Camhá, who reigned there in Izmachí, which was the beautiful city which they had built.[4]

Only three great houses were there in Izmachí. There were not twenty-four great houses then, only their three great houses, only a great house of the Cavec, only a great house of the Nihaib, and only one of the people of Ahau-Quiché. Only two had great houses,[5] the two branches of the family [the Quiché and the Tamub].

And there they were in Izmachí with only one thought, with-

[1] "In the beards." This city was situated to the south of Utatlán, the last capital of the Quiché.

[2] X-cah qui chun qui zahcab, literally, "they ground their lime and their chalk." Ximénez and Brasseur de Bourbourg interpret this sentence as meaning they built their houses of lime and stone.

[3] Balam-Conaché was the third king of the Quiché, according to the final chapter of the book, and according to the text, he ruled with Beleheb-Queh, king of the fourth generation of the House of Nihaib, and with Ahau-Galel, or the first of the lords of the House of Nihaib. Balam-Conaché was the son of Qocavib, conceived by the wife of his brother, Qocaib, when the latter was absent on his first journey to the East, to Chichén Itzá, according to the Título de los Señores de Totonicapán and to the document from Zapotitlán about the origin of the Quiché kings, a translation of which is included in the Appendix to this book. Qocaib recognized the son of his brother and his own wife as being of his own blood, and this was the beginning, according to the Título, of the House of those of Conaché and Iztayul, and herein the rank and office of Ahpop-Camhail, second title of the House of Iztayul, had its origin.

[4] Iztayul was the son of Balam-Conaché.

out disputes or difficulties, peaceful was the kingdom, they had no quarrels nor disputes, in their hearts were only peace and happiness. They were not envious nor jealous. Their grandeur was limited, they had not thought of aggrandizing themselves, nor of expanding. When they tried to do it, they fastened the shield there in Izmachí but only to give a sign of their empire, as a symbol of their power and a symbol of their greatness.

Seeing this, the people of Ilocab began the war; they wanted to kill King Cotuhá, wishing to have a chief of their own. And as for Lord Iztayul, they wanted to punish him, that he be punished and killed by those of Ilocab. But their evil plans against King Cotuhá did not succeed, for he fell upon them before the people of Ilocab were able to kill him.

This, then, was the beginning of the revolution and the dissensions of the war. First they attacked the town, and the warriors came. And what they wanted was to ruin the Quiché race; they wanted to reign alone. But they only came to die; they were captured and fell into captivity, and few among them succeeded in escaping.

Immediately afterward the sacrifices began; the people of Ilocab were sacrificed before the god, and this was the punishment for their sins by order of King Cotuhá. Many also fell into slavery and servitude; they only went to give themselves up to be overcome because of having arranged the war against the lords and against the town.[6] The destruction and ruin of the Quiché race and their king was what they wished, but they did not succeed in accomplishing it.

In this way the sacrifice of men began before the gods, when the war of the shields broke out, which was the reason that they began the fortifications of the city of Izmachí.

[5] *Xaqui caib chi nim ha ri ca chob chi chinamit.* In transcribing this sentence Brasseur de Bourbourg substituted the word *cumatzil,* which he translates "serpents," for *nim ha.* In the margin of the manuscript of the *Popol Vuh,* one reads *cumatzil pro nim ha,* but Ximénez translates it as "large house."

[6] *Chirih ahau, chirih civan-tinamit.* "Against the Lords, against the city of the ravines." It was an ancient custom to name the Indian towns in this way, by the fact that they were built in places surrounded by ravines, in order to protect them against attacks by their enemies.

There began and originated their power, because the empire of the King of the Quiché was really large. They were in every sense marvelous kings; there was no one who could dominate them, neither was there anyone who could humble them. And at the same time they were the builders of the grandeur of the kingdom which they had founded there in Izmachí.

There the fear of god waxed, they were inspired with awe, and the tribes large and small were filled with fear, for they saw the arrival of the captives, those who were sacrificed and killed because of the power and sovereignty of King Cotuhá, the King Iztayul, and the people of Nihaib and Ahau-Quiché.

There were only three branches of the [Quiché] family there in Izmachí, as the town was called, and there they also began the feasts and orgies for their daughters when [suitors] came to ask for them⁷ in marriage.

There the so-called three great houses gathered, and there they drank their drinks, there they also ate their food, which was the price of their sisters, the price of their daughters, and their hearts were joyful when they did it, and they ate and drank⁸ in the great houses.

"In this way we show our gratitude, and thus we open the road for our posterity and our descendents, this is the demonstration of our consent to their becoming husbands and wives," they said.

There they identified themselves,⁹ and there they took their names; they distributed themselves in clans in the seven principal tribes and in cantons.¹⁰

"Let us unite, we of the Cavec, we of the Nihaib, and we of the

---

⁷ *Ta x-qui ziih uloc*, literally, "when they carried their wood." This evidently refers to the native custom which obliged the suitor to carry a load of wood to his sweetheart's house when he went to ask her hand in marriage.

⁸ *X-e ocha*, they drank from painted gourds, like those now made in Rabinal which are called *och*.

⁹ *Chila x-cob vi uloc*, "there they distinguished themselves," that is, they were identified, one from another.

¹⁰ *Qui chinamit quib, vuc amag quib, qui ticpan quib.* These are the names of the groups into which the Quiché were divided. *Chinamit* is the family or clan. *Vuc-Amag*, literally the seven principal tribes of which the *Título de los Señores de Totonicapán* frequently speaks. The word *ticpán* comes from the Náhuatl *tecpán* and means suburb, or district of a large city.

Ahau-Quiché," said the three clans, and the three great houses. For a long time they were there in Izmachí, until they found and saw another town, and abandoned that of Izmachí.

## A

fter they had left there, they came here to the town of Gumarcaah,[1] as the Quiché named it when Kings Cotuhá

[1] The word *Gumarcaah* means "rotten huts," according to Ximénez; translating this name into their own tongue, the Mexicans called the city *Utatlán*, "place of reed fields." When the Spaniards arrived, it was the most important city in Central America. In his first letter to Cortés, Pedro de Alvarado, the conqueror of Guatemala, describes it in a few words, saying: "This city is well built and marvelously strong." Bishop Las Casas, who arrived in Guatemala a few years after the Conquest, says in his *Apologética Historia* that he saw "towns enclosed by very deep moats, as was the one called Guatemala [Iximché, capital of the Cakchiquel kingdom], and another which was indeed the head of the kingdom, called Utatlán, with marvelous buildings of stone masonry of which I saw many." Another witness of that time, Dr. Alonso de Zorita, a contemporary of Las Casas, writes in his *Historia de la Nueva España:* "Utatlán, which is in the Province of Guatimala, was also considered by the natives of that land as a great sanctuary, and there were in it and around it many and very large temples which they call *cues*, of marvelous construction, and I saw some of them when I visited that land, being there Oidor in the royal Audiencia which has its residence in Guatimala, although they were in a state of ruin."

A brief but graphic description remains from the French architect, César Daly, who visited Utatlán in 1857 and says of it that "it is one of the architectural curiosities of the world: three mounds which come from a kind of abyss or ravine and which are crowned by table-lands which support cities." Daly passed close to seven weeks in the central city and made plans and drawings of this metropolis, as well as of Iximché, the capital of the Cakchiquel. See "*Notes pouvant servir à l'exploration des anciens monuments du Mexique*," in *Archives de la Commission Scientifique du Mexique* (Paris, 1865), I, 146–61.

D. Miguel Rivera Maestre made a reconnaissance of the site of Utatlán and published a map and some pictures of the ruins of the Quiché capital in the *Atlas* of the state of Guatemala (1832). In the narrative of his trip to Central America, John L. Stephens says that he used the report of Rivera Maestre in his description of that ancient city, which he visited in 1840. The great English archaeologist Alfred P. Maudslay visited the cities of Utatlán and Iximché in January, 1887, and made surveys of the two sites. He describes the Quiché and Cakchiquel country and the Indian capitals in Volume II of *Archaeology*, of the *Biologia Centrali-Americana*, as well as in his magnificent book and that of his wife: *A Glimpse at Guatemala* (1899).

and Gucumatz and all the lords came. There had then begun the fifth generation of men, since the beginning of civilization and of the population, the beginning of the existence of the nation.

There, then, they built many houses and at the same time constructed the temple of God; in the center of the high part of the town they located it when they arrived and settled there.

---

The historians of the Colonial Period have also left more or less exact descriptions of the capital of the Quiché and of the temple of Tohil. The clearest of these is that of Ximénez (*Las Historias del Origen de los Indios de Esta Provincia de Guatemala,* 165–67) which, summarized, is as follows: The temple, or place of worship, and the rest of the buildings of Gumarcaah were constructed over a hill surrounded by a large ravine. On top of the plateau which the hill forms were the twenty-four large houses of the lords, built around so as to make small courts, each one like a large room raised about two yards from the ground, with a corridor and straw roof. In these little courts the large dances which they had during their feasts were held. In the middle of one of these small courts a solid tower was erected which went up in the form of a pyramid with square base, having stairs on each one of its faces, and in the corners was a bastion which also tapered upward. The steps were very narrow and close, so that it was frightening to climb them; there were about thirty or forty steps in each stairway, and all were made of stone.

Near the temple or tower, at one side, there was a thick wall one and one-half meters high by two meters wide, crowned with another, close to three meters in height and also two meters in width. This had many openings through which the ropes used to bind the victims, who were to be sacrificed, were passed, so that they faced toward the god. This tower dominated all the courts where the people assembled and all could see the image of Tohil.

At the other side of the temple was the ball-court which Ximénez describes as a large pool with very large sides of stone, with their coronations or pyramids which surrounded it; they were very wide and could hold many people in them to watch the ball games which were the entertainment of the kings and the rest of the lords. All of this building, on the side opposite the houses, was closed by a wall made of stone which was called *tzalam-coxtum,* a name given to all those buildings because, in addition to serving as a place for ceremonies, they were also castles and forts for defense against their enemies, and for this reason they were built on the hilltops.

Fuentes y Guzmán (*Historia de Guatemala,* Book VII, Chap. X) describes the palaces of Utatlán with a wealth of detail and imagination, but does not give a clearer idea of the temple or place of worship, with the exception of information relative to the existence of "the fourth step," of a smooth stone of two and three-quarter yards (2.50 meters) and five feet wide (more or less, 1.50 meters), on which dismal and unhappy place they sacrificed the men, and, "with a wide knife of *chay* [obsidian] they opened the breast [of the victim] and tore out the beating heart to offer it to the god."

Then their empire grew. They were very numerous[2] when they held their council in their great houses. They reunited, but later divided, because dissensions had arisen and jealousies grew up amongst them over the price for their sisters and their daughters, and because they no longer drank together.[3]

This, then, was the reason why they divided and why they turned against each other, and they threw the skulls of the dead, they hurled them around among each other.

Then they divided into nine families, and having ended the dispute over the sisters and the daughters, they carried out the plan of dividing the kingdom into twenty-four great houses, as they did. It is a long time since they came here to their town, and finished the twenty-four great houses, there in the City of Gumarcaah, which was blessed by the Bishop. Later the city was abandoned.[4]

There they increased, there they installed their splendid thrones and royal seats, and they distributed their honors among all the lords. The nine lords of Cavec formed nine families; the lords of Nihaib formed another nine; the lords of Ahau-Quiché formed another four; and the lords of Zaquic formed another two families.

They became very numerous, and many also followed each of the lords; these were the first among their vassals, and each of the lords had large families.[5]

We shall tell now the names of the lords of each of the great houses. Here, then, are the names of the lords of Cavec. The first

[2] *E qui chic e pu tzatz.*

[3] *Rumal xa mavi chi tzacon c'uquiya chi qui vach*, in the original. They no longer gathered to eat and drink as they did in Izmachí when they arranged the weddings of their daughters and sons.

[4] Don Francisco Marroquín, the first Bishop of Guatemala, who arrived in the country in 1530 and governed the diocese until his death in 1563. The historian Ximénez (*Historia de ... Chiapa y Guatemala*, I, 115) fixes the time of the blessing of the new Spanish city which was substituted for the ancient capital, saying that the Bishop gave it the name of Santa Cruz of the Quiché "when, in the year 1539, he was in that Court, and blessing the place, fixed and raised the standard of the Faith." The site of Utatlán was abandoned when the city was moved to the plains near by, where it is today still located and serves as the capital of the department of the Quiché.

[5] *Tzatz, tzatz.*

of the lords was Ahpop,[6] [then] Ahpop-Camhá,[7], Ah-Tohil,[8] Ah-Gucumatz,[9] Nim-Chocoh-Cavec,[10] Popol-Vinac-Chituy,[11] Lolmet-Quehnay,[12] Popol-Vinac Pa-Hom Tzalatz,[13] and Uchuch-Camhá.[14]

These, then, were the lords of Cavec, nine lords, each one of which had his great house, which afterward will appear again.

Here then are the lords of Nihaib. The first was Ahau-Galel, then Ahau-Ahtzic-Vinac, Gale-Camhá, Nima-Camhá, Uchuch-Camhá, Nim-Chocoh-Nihaibab, Avilix, Yacolatam, Utzam-pop-Zalclatol, and Nimá-Lolmet-Ycoltux, the nine lords of Nihaib.[15]

And as for those of Ahau-Quiché, these are the names of the lords: Ahtzic-Vinac, Ahau-Lolmet, Ahau-Nim-Chocoh-Ahau, and Ahau-Hacavitz, four lords of Ahau-Quiché, in the order of their great houses.

And the house of Zaquic had two families, the Lords Tzutuhá and Galel Zaquic. These two lords had only one great house.[16]

[6] The king.

[7] The assistant to the monarch, the one designated to succeed him.

[8] The priest of Tohil.          [9] The priest of Gucumatz.

[10] The Great chosen one of Cavec. "They were three, the Great chosen," says Ximénez (*La Historias del Origin . . . etc.*), "like the fathers of all the Lords of the Quiché." There was a Great [one] chosen by each one of the principal clans.

[11] The counsellor *Chituy*, minister of the treasury.

[12] The agent, or accountant, and collector of tributes.

[13] The counsellor of the long ball-court.

[14] The majordomo, according to Brasseur de Bourbourg.

[15] In this enumeration, which agrees with the original manuscript, the ten names of the lords of the House of the Nihaib appear. Brasseur de Bourbourg reduces the number to nine, combining the names of Yacolatam-Utzam-pop-Zaclatol.

[16] These were the two large branches of the Zaquic-Cotuhá, according to the *Título de los Señores de Totonicapán*. The honors and functions of the Court were divided among the lords of each family, according to its category. First was the Ahpop, or king, after whom in the legal order of succession, the Ahpop Camhá followed. Writing about the middle of the sixteenth century, Las Casas (*Apologética Historia de las Indias*, Chap. CCXXXIV, p. 616) says: "That supreme king had certain principal men of counsel, who had charge of justice and advised about what should be done in all business affairs. It is said today by the Indians who saw it, that they were like the Oidores which are in Guatimala in the Royal Audience. They saw the tributes which were collected from the kingdom and they divided and sent to the king what was assigned for the support of his person and estate."

In this way [the number] of the twenty-four lords was completed and the twenty-four great houses came into being. Thus the grandeur and power of the sons of the Quiché grew, when they built the town of the ravines out of stone and mortar.[1]

Then the small tribes and the great tribes came before the king. The Quiché increased when their glory and majesty waxed, when they raised the house of their gods and the house of their lords. But it was not they who worked, or constructed their houses either, or made the house of the gods, for they were [made] by their sons and vassals, who had multiplied.

And they were not cheating them, nor robbing them, nor seizing them by force, because in reality each belonged to the lords, and many of their brothers and relatives[2] had come together and had assembled, to hear the commands of each of the lords.

The lords were really loved and great was their glory; and the sons and the vassals held the birthdays of the lords in great respect[3] when the inhabitants of the country and the city multiplied.[4]

But it did not happen that all the tribes delivered themselves up, and neither did the country and towns [the inhabitants of them] fall in battle, but instead they increased, because of the marvels of the lords, King Gucumatz and King Cotuhá. Gucumatz was truly a marvelous king. For seven days he mounted to the skies and for seven days he went down into Xibalba; seven days he changed himself into a snake and really became a serpent; for seven days he changed himself into an eagle; for seven days he became a jaguar; and his appearance was really that of an eagle

---

[1] *Zivan-tinamit*. Gumarcaah also was surrounded by ravines.

[2] *Tzatz naipuch c'atz qui chac x-uxic*, literally, "and many were their older and younger brothers."

[3] *Nimatalic xouatal puch u quih r'alaxic ahauab*. Here all the translators have been at loss because of not having read, nor understood, the direct meaning of the words *u quih r'alaxic*, the day of the birth of a person.

[4] *Ah zivan, ah tinamit.*

and a jaguar. Another seven days he changed himself into clotted blood and was only motionless blood.

The nature of this king was really marvelous, and all the other lords were filled with terror before him. Tidings of the wonderful nature of the King were spread and all the lords of the towns heard it. And this was the beginning of the grandeur of the Quiché, when King Gucumatz gave these signs of his power. His sons and his grandsons never forgot him. And he did not do this in order to be an extraordinary king, he did it as a means of dominating all the towns, as a means of showing that only one was called upon to be chief of the people.[5]

The generation of the wonderful king called Gucumatz was the fourth generation, and Gucumatz was also the Ahpop and the Ahpop-Camhá.

They left successors and descendents who reigned and ruled, and begot children, and did many things. Tepepul and Iztayul whose reign was the fifth generation of kings[6] were begotten; and in the same way, each of the generations of these lords had succession.

## CHAPTER 10

Here are the names of the sixth generation of kings. There were two great kings, the first was called Gag-Quicab, and the other, Cavizimah, and they performed heroic deeds and aggrandized the Quiché; for surely they were of marvelous nature.

Here is the destruction and division of the fields and the towns of the neighboring nations, small and large. Among them was that, which in olden times, was the country of the Cakchiquel, the present Chuvilá,[1] and the country of the people of Rabinal,[2]

[5] Xa u qutbal rib rumal xere hu qui zic u holom amac, in the original.
[6] R'oo le ahau x-uxic, in the original.
[1] "In the nettles," a name which the Mexicans translated as Chichicastenango, with identical meaning, which is the name it still bears today.
[2] The town of Rabinal.

Pamacá,³ the country of the people of Caoqué,⁴ Zaccabahá⁵ and the towns of the peoples of Zaculeu,⁶ of Chuvi-Miquiná,⁷ Xela-huh,⁸ Chuva-Tzac,⁹ and Tzolohché.¹⁰

These [peoples] hated Quicab. He made war on them and certainly conquered and destroyed the fields and towns of the people of Rabinal, the Cakchiquel, and the people of Zaculeu; he came and conquered all the towns, and the soldiers of Quicab carried his arms to distant parts. One or two tribes did not bring tribute, and then he fell upon all the towns and they were forced to bring tribute to Quicab and Cavizimah.

They were made slaves, they were wounded, and they were killed with arrows against the trees [to which they had been tied] and for them there was no longer any glory, they no longer had power. In this way came about the destruction of the towns, which were instantly razed to the ground.¹¹ Like a flash of lightning which strikes and shatters the rock, so, in an instant were the conquered people filled with terror.

Before Colché, as a symbol of a town destroyed by him, there is now a pile of stones, which look almost as if they had been cut with the edge of an ax. It is there on the coast, called Petatayub,¹²

³ Today it is Zacualpa, near the mountains of Joyabaj.

⁴ The Caoqué nation, probably represented by the present towns of Santa María and Santiago Cauqué.

⁵ The present San Andrés Saccabajá.

⁶ "White earth," a fort of the Mam near the ancient town of Chinabjul, today Huehuetenango.

⁷ "Over the hot water," today Totonicapán, a Mexican name with the same meaning, as Atotonilco in the state of Jalisco, Mexico.

⁸ Xelahuh-Quieh, "under the ten deer or chiefs," the ancient Culahá of the Mam, today Quezaltenango.

⁹ "In front of the fort," the present Momostenango.

¹⁰ "The willow," the present Chiquimula, a short distance from Santa Cruz Quiché.

¹¹ *Chi hixtahic u chi uleu*, literally, "destroyed level with the ground."

¹² The coast of Petatayub is evidently the litoral of the Pacific where the Guatemalan town of Ayutla stands today, on the border of Mexico. The *Títulos de las Casa de Ixcuín-Nihaib* mention among the conquests of the Quiché in that region, the lands washed by the Samalá, Uquz (Ocós), Nil, and Xab rivers, which are still known by these same names. *Ayutl* in Náhuatl is the turtle. The pre-

and it may be clearly seen today by people who pass, as proof of the valor of Quicab.

They could neither kill him nor overcome him, for, in truth, he was a brave man, and all the people rendered tribute unto him.

And all the lords, having gathered in council, went to fortify the ravines and the towns, having conquered the towns of all the tribes. Then spies went out to observe the enemy and they founded something like towns in the occupied places. "Just in case by chance the tribes might return to occupy the town," they said, when they reassembled in council.

Then they went out to [take up] their positions. "These shall be like our forts and our town, our walls and defenses, here shall our valor and our manhood be proved," said all the lords, when they went to take up the position assigned to each clan in order to fight the enemy.

And having received their orders they went to the places that had been founded in the land of the tribes. "Go there, for now it is our land. Do not be afraid, if there are still enemies who come to kill you, come quickly and let me know, and I will go to kill them!" said Quicab, when he took leave of all of them in the presence of the Galel and the Ahtzic-Vinac.[13]

Then the bowmen and the slingers, as they were called, set out. Then the grandfathers and the fathers of all the Quiché nation took their [battle] positions. They were on each one of the mountains, and they were like guards—of the mountains; they were guarding [with] their bows and slings; they were the sentinels of the war. They were not of different origin, nor did they have a different god, when they went. They went only to fortify their towns.

---

Columbian name of this coast was Ayotlán, and thus it appears in the *Anales de Cuauhtitlán*. Anáhuac Ayotlán was the name of all the region of Tehuantepec, washed by the Pacific Ocean, which Sahagún calls the coast of the turtles, and which later was called Soconusco. It is curious to observe that the Aztec word *ayotl* has the double meaning of "turtle" and "gourd," the same as the word *coc* in the native languages of Guatemala.

[13] The Ahau-Galel was the chief of the House of Nihaib and the Ahtzic-Vinac, the chief of the House of Ahau-Quiché.

Then all the people of Uvilá went out,[14] those of Chulimal, Zaquiyá, Xahbaquieh, Chi-Temah, Vahxalahuh, and the people of Cabracán,[15] Chabicac-Chi-Hunahpú, and those of Macá,[16] those of Xoyabah[17] and those of Zaccabahá,[18] those of Ziyahá,[19] those of Miquiná,[20] those of Xelahuh, [21] and those of the coast. They went to observe the war and to guard the land, when they went by order of Quicab and Cavizimah, [who were] the Ahpop and the Ahpop-Camhá, and the Galel and the Ahtzic-Vinac, who were the four lords.

They were sent in order to watch the enemies of Quicab and Cavizimah, names of the kings, both of the House of Cavec, of Queemá, name of the lord of the people of Nihaib, and of Achac-Iboy, the name of the lord of the people of Ahau-Quiché. These were the names of the lords who sent them, when their sons and vassals went to the mountains, to each one of the mountains.

They went at once[22] and they took captives; they brought their prisoners into the presence of Quicab, Cavizimah, the Galel, and the Ahtzic-Vinac. The bowmen and slingers made war, taking captives and prisoners. Some of the defenders of the positions were heroes, and the lords gave [them gifts] and lavished rewards upon them, when they came to deliver up all their captives and prisoners.

Later they gathered in council by order of the lords, the Ahpop, the Ahpop-Camhá, the Galel, and the Ahtzic-Vinac, and they decided and said, that those who were there first should have the rank of representing their families. "I am the Ahpop! I am the Ahpop-Camhá! Mine shall be the rank of the Ahpop; meanwhile

[14] Chuvilá, or Chichicastenango. In the manuscript of these *Historias del origen de los Indios*, as well as in the *Títulos de la Casa Ixcuín-Nihaib*, the inhabitants of this town are called Ah-Uvilá.

[15] Now Cabricán, a town in the department of Quetzaltenango.

[16] Pamacá Zacualpa, a town in the department of the Quiché.

[17] The present Joyabaj.

[18] Today it is called San Andrés-Saccabajá.

[19] Ziyahá, or Zihá, the ancient name of the town known today as Santa Catarina Ixtlahuacán.

[20] Totonicapán.

[21] Quezaltenango.

[22] *X-be na cu nabe*, in the original.

thou, the Ahau-Galel, shall have the rank of Galel," said all the lords when they held council.[23]

Those of Tamub and of Ilocab did likewise; equal in position were the three clans of the Quiché when for the first time they named their sons and vassals captains, and ennobled them. This was the result of the council. But they were not made captains here in Quiché. The mountain where the sons and vassals were made captains for the first time has its name, when all were sent, each one to his mountain, and all were reunited. Xebalax and Xecamax are the names of the mountains where they were made captains and they received their commands. This happened in Chulimal.

In this manner was the naming, the promotion, and distinction of the twenty Galel, of the twenty Ahpop, who were named by the Ahpop and the Ahpop-Camhá and by the Galel and the Ahtzic-Vinac. All of the Galel-Ahpops received their rank: eleven Nim-Chocoh, Galel-Ahau, Galel-Zaquic, Galel-Achih, Rahpop-Achih, Rahtzalam-Achih, Utzam-Achih were the names which the warriors received when their titles and distinctions were conferred upon them, as they were on their thrones and on their seats, being the first sons and vassals of the Quiché nation, their spies, their scouts, the bowmen, the slingers, the walls, doors, forts, and bastions of the Quiché.

Those of Tamub and Ilocab also did thus; they named and ennobled the first sons and vassals who were in each place.

This, then, was the origin of the Galel-Ahpops, and of the titles which are now preserved in each one of these places. This is the way their titles were created, by the Ahpop and the Ahpop-Camhá, by the Galel and the Ahtzic-Vinac they were created.

[23] Brasseur de Bourbourg confesses that the translation of this passage is very difficult, and observes that Ximénez omitted it altogether. The passage becomes easier to understand by re-establishing the punctuation to agree with the original, which Brasseur de Bourbourg has altered in his transcription. The original should be read as follows: In *Ahpop, in Ahpop-Camhá; Ahpop chire caleb vech, oc; chicu ave, at Ahau-Galel, Galel ri calem x-ch'uxic x-e cha cut ronohel ahauab*, etc.

W e shall now tell of the House of the God. The house was also given the same name as the god. The Great Edifice of Tohil was the name of the Temple of Tohil, of those of Cavec. Avilix was the name of the Temple of Avilix, of the people of Nihaib; and Hacavitz was the name of the Temple of the God of the people of Ahau-Quiché.[1]

Tzutuhá, which is seen in Cahbahá, is the name of a large edifice in which there was a stone which all the lords of Quiché worshiped and which was also worshiped by all the tribes.[2]

The people first offered their sacrifices before Tohil, and afterward went to pay their respects to the Ahpop and the Ahpop-Camhá. Then they went to present their gorgeous feathers and their tribute before the king. And the kings whom they maintained were the Ahpop and the Ahpop-Camhá, who had conquered their towns.

Great lords and wonderful men were the marvelous kings Gucumatz and Cotuhá, the marvelous kings Quicab and Cavizimah. They knew if there would be war, and everything was clear before their eyes; they saw if there would be death and hunger, if there would be strife. They well knew that there was a place where it could be seen, that there was a book which they called the *Popol Vuh*.[3]

[1] The houses or temples of the Quiché gods were destroyed after the abandonment of the city. The stones and other materials taken from the ruins of Utatlán were used to construct the buildings of Santa Cruz, the neighboring city founded by the Spaniards. There was scarcely left, among the ruins of the ancient Quiché capital, any remains of the place of sacrifice, or the Temple of Tohil.

[2] *Tzutuhá*, "Flowery Water" or "fountain." *Cahbahá*, "house of sacrifices" or "sacrificing place." The name of this place is very similar to that of the well-known town which is today called San Andrés Saccabajá, located a short distance from Santa Cruz Quiché. The *Título de los Señores de Totonicapán* says that the Quiché tribes were for some time in Tzutuhá, and says further that "there they also found a stone similar to the one which Nacxit had given them."

[3] *Xax qu'etaam vi qu cut ilbal re, qo vuh Popol Vuh u bi cumal*. Through error, Brasseur de Bourbourg writes *qo qutibal re* here. My translation agrees with that of Ximénez, which says: "and there was a place where they could see everything, and a book of all, which they called Book of the Community."

But not only in this way was the estate of the lords great, great also were their fasts. And this was in recognition of their having been created, and in recognition of their having been given their kingdoms.[4] They fasted a long time and made sacrifices to their gods. Here is how they fasted: Nine men fasted and another nine made sacrifices and burned incense. Thirteen more men fasted, and another thirteen more made offerings and burned incense before Tohil. And while before their god, they nourished themselves only with fruits, with *zapotes, matasanos,* and *jocotes.* And they did not eat any *tortillas.* Now if there were seventeen men who made sacrifice, or ten who fasted, the truth is they did not eat. They fulfilled their great precepts, and thus showed their position as lords.

Neither had they women to sleep with, but they remained alone, fasting. They were in the House of God, all day they prayed, burning incense and making sacrifices. Thus they remained from dusk until dawn, grieving in their hearts and in their breasts, and begging for happiness and life for their sons and vassals as well as for their kingdom, and raising their faces to the sky.

Here are their petitions to their god, when they prayed; and this was the supplication of their hearts:

"Oh, Thou, beauty of the day! Thou, Huracán; Thou, Heart of Heaven and of Earth! Thou, giver of richness,[5] and giver of the daughters and the sons! Turn toward us your power and your riches; grant life and growth unto my sons and vassals; let those who must maintain and nourish Thee multiply and increase; those who invoke Thee on the roads, in the fields, on the banks of the rivers, in the ravines, under the trees, under the vines.

"Give them daughters and sons. Let them not meet disgrace, nor misfortune, let not the deceiver come behind or before them. Let them not fall, let them not be wounded, let them not fornicate, nor be condemned by justice. Let them not fall on the descent or

---

[4] *Are locbal tzac, locbal abauarem cumal.* The fast of the Quiché was absolute, according to the text. It was a general practice among the Mexicans, but less strict, for they made a light meal during the day and another at night.

[5] *Ganal raxal,* "abundance of riches." *Diccionario Cakchiquel.*

on the ascent of the road. Let them not encounter obstacles back of them or before them, nor anything which strikes them. Grant them good roads, beautiful, level roads. Let them not have misfortune, nor disgrace, through Thy fault, through Thy sorceries.

"Grant a good life to those who must give Thee sustenance and place food in Thy mouth, in Thy presence, to Thee, Heart of Heaven, Heart of Earth, Bundle of Majesty. And Thou, Tohil; Thou, Avilix; Thou, Hacavitz, Arch of the Sky, Surface of the Earth, the Four Corners, the Four Cardinal Points. Let there be but peace and tranquility[6] in Thy mouth, in Thy presence, oh, God!"[7]

Thus [spoke] the lords, while within, the nine men fasted, the thirteen men, and the seventeen men. During the day they fasted and their hearts grieved for their sons and vassals and for all their wives and their children when each of the lords made his offering.

This was the price of a happy life, the price of power, the price of the authority of the Ahpop, of the Ahpop-Camhá, of the Galel and of the Ahtzic-Vinac. Two by two they ruled, each pair succeeding the other in order to bear the burden of the people of all the Quiché nation.

One only was the origin of their tradition and [one only] the origin of the manner of maintaining and sustaining, and one only, too, was the origin of the tradition and the customs of those of Tamub and Ilocab and the people of Rabinal and the Cakchiquel, those of Tziquinahá, of Tuhalahá and Uchabahá. And there was but one trunk [a single family] when they heard there in Quiché what all of them were to do.

But it was not only thus that they reigned. They did not

[6] *Xa ta zac, xa ta amac.* "Only may there be peace in your presence."–Ximénez.

[7] Bishop Las Casas has also included in his *Apologética Historia* (Chap. CLXXVIII, p. 468) a prayer which he says the Indians of Guatemala recited during the human sacrifices, the essence of which is identical to the prayer given here. It says: "Lord God, remember us who are Thine; grant us health, give us children and prosperity so that thy people shall increase and serve thee; give us water and good weather so that we may maintain ourselves and that we may live; hear our petitions, receive our prayers help us against our enemies; give us ease and rest."

squander the gifts of those whom they sustained and nourished, but they ate and drank them. Neither did they buy them; they had won and seized their empire, their power, and their sovereignty.

And it was not at small cost, that they conquered the fields and the towns; the small towns and the large towns paid high ransoms; they brought precious stones and metals, they brought honey of the bees, bracelets, bracelets of emeralds and other stones, and brought garlands made of blue feathers,[8] the tribute of all the towns. They came into the presence of the marvelous kings Gucumatz and Cotuhá, and before Quicab and Cavizimah, the Ahpop, the Ahpop-Camhá, the Galel and the Ahtzic-Vinac.[9]

It was not little what they did, neither were few, the tribes which they conquered. Many branches of the tribes came to pay tribute to the Quiché; full of sorrow they came to give it over. Nevertheless, the [Quiché] power did not grow quickly. Gucumatz it was, who began the aggrandizement of the kingdom. Thus was the beginning of his aggrandizement and that of the Quiché nation.

And now we shall name the generations of the lords and give their names; again we shall name all of the lords.

## CHAPTER 12

Here, then, are the generations and the order of all the rulers which began with our first grandfathers and our first

[8] *X-ul puch raxón cubul chactic.* The *raxón* (*Cotinga*) shared with the quetzal, *guc,* the honor of adorning with its feathers the gods and the kings; the beautiful sky blue feathers of the *raxón* were joined and then they were called *pixoh raxón,* "sewed feathers," an expression which Zúñiga (*Diccionario Pokonchí-Castellano*) explains, by saying that "the feathers are interwoven and [fasten] with knots of a very fine thread, with great skill, and there are some garlands of these blue feathers which they wear in their dances, and which they wear around their temples and forehead." *Cubul chactic* are these garlands of feathers sewed, as Zúñiga says, or stuck into a framework of light wood.

[9] In the *Títulos de la Casa de Ixcuín-Nihaib* there is an interesting account of the conquests of the Quiché kings, and of the tribute which the conquered nations had to pay them.

fathers, Balam-Quitzé, Balam-Acab, Mahucutah, and Iqui-Balam, when the sun appeared, and the moon and the stars were seen.

Now, then, we shall give the beginning of the generations, the order of the kingdoms, from the beginning of their lineage, how the lords entered into power, from their accessions to their deaths; [we shall give] each generation of lords and ancestors, as well as the lord of the town, all and each of the lords. Here, then, the person[1] of each one of the lords of the Quiché shall be shown.

Balam-Quitzé, the root of those of Cavec.

Qocavib, second generation [of the line] of Balam-Quitzé.[2]

Balam-Conaché, with whom the title of Ahpop began, third generation.[3]

Cotuhá [I] and Iztayub, fourth generation.[4]

Gucumatz and Cotuhá, [II] first of the marvelous kings, who were of the fifth generation.[5]

[1] Literally, "the face," *u vach.*

[2] The text in this place does not mention Qocaib, the son of Balam-Quitzé as the immediate successor of the latter. Nevertheless, Chapter 6 of this part refers to the return from the East of Qocaib, Qoacutec, and Qoahau and their arrival at Hacavitz, and it says literally that the three princes, who belonged to each of the three large divisions of the Quiché nation, "assumed again their rule of the tribes." It is possible that there may be an error in copying here, and that the name which was in the original Quiché manuscript, now lost, may have been that of Qocaib and not Qocavib.

[3] Balam-Conaché, son of Qocavib and of the wife of his brother Qocaib, was legitimatized by the latter, and ruled in union with Beleheb-Qeh, 9 Deer, according to Chap. 7 of Part IV.

[4] Cotuhá, a man whom the *Título de Totonicapán* says the Quiché found in the field hunting quail, and that having invited him to join them, he occupied the place of Iqui-Balam, who had died. Cotuhá ruled in company with Ixtayul, Náhuatl name which means "heart of flint." This was the son of Balam-Conaché.

[5] *U xe naual ahau.* The root or beginning of the sorcerer kings, the marvelous kings, as Ximénez calls them. This Cotuhá was the second king of this name and was the father of Quicab, according to the *Título de Totonicapán.* In the time of these kings, the capital was moved to Gumarcaah, and the twenty-four families or great houses of the nobility were organized. The *Título* expressly declares that the nine large branches of the House of Cavec "came out from the House of the Prince Qocaib." Gucumatz and Cotuhá went to conquer the towns of the Pacific Coast, and, according to the *Título de Ixcuín-Nihaib,* "that chief [Gucumatz] being happy, and to please his soldiers, became an eagle and plunged into the sea, making a demonstration of his conquest." Chapter 9 of this part also speaks of the metamorphosis of this king.

Tepepul and Iztayul, of the sixth order.[6]

Quicab and Cavizimah, of the seventh order of succession to the kingdom.[7]

Tepepul and Iztayub, eighth generation.

Tecum and Tepepul, ninth generation.[8]

Vahxaqui-Caam[9] and Quicab, tenth generation of kings.

Vucub-Noh and Cauutepech, the eleventh order of kings.[10]

Oxib-Queh and Beleheb-Tzi, the twelfth generation of kings. These were those who reigned when Donadiú came, and who were hanged by the Spaniards.[11]

Tecum and Tepepul, who paid tribute to the Spaniards, they left sons, and the former were the thirteenth generation of kings.[12]

[6] *Tepetl pul*, words in the Mexican language which mean "hill of stones."

[7] *Gag-Quicab*, "of many arms," Ximénez interprets it. It may be that "of the hands of fire." Cavizimah, who adorns himself with points like lances or arrows (*itz* in Náhuatl), according to Ximénez. Quicab and Cavizimah were the great conquerors who subdued all the peoples of the interior of Guatemala, as Chapter 10 of this part relates in detail.

[8] Ximénez says that in the time of these kings, the Cakchiquel (previously subdued by Quicab) rebelled. According to the *Annals of the Cakchiquel*, the Quiché were overcome by them in Iximché, and their kings were made prisoners and they were obliged to surrender their gods.

[9] Eight Vines. As Brasseur de Bourbourg observes, it is the translation of the Mexican name *Chicuey Malinalli*, tenth day of the Aztec calendar. During the reign of these princes, according to Ximénez, it happened that a Cakchiquel Indian, whom the Quiché remember in their dance called Quiché-Vinac, and who was probably the son of the Cakchiquel king, came at night to shout insults at the Quiché king. When at last they captured him and were on the point of sacrificing him, he announced the arrival of the Spaniards in these words: "Know that a time must come when you will despair because of the disasters which will fall upon you; and this *mama caixon* ["old bitter one," a nickname directed at the Quiché king] must also die; and know that some men dressed, and not naked like us, armed from head to foot, will destroy these buildings, which will become the homes of owls and wildcats and all this grandeur of the court shall cease."

[10] *Vucub-Noh*, 7 *Noh*, a day of the calendar. *Cauutepech*, "adorned with rings," says Ximénez, because this king used to wear such ornaments.

[11] *Oxib-Queh*, 3 Deer; *Beleheb-Tzi*, 9 Dog: These are days of the calendar. The Mexicans called King Beleheb-Tzi, Chiconavi-Ocelotl, which is to say, 9 Jaguar, and from these is derived the name of Chignauicelut which the Spaniards gave him. *Donadiú*, or Tonatiuh, the sun, in Náhuatl, was the name which the Mexicans gave to the Spanish conqueror, Pedro de Alvarado, who destroyed the Quiché kingdom and burned their kings.

230

*[Handwritten manuscript facsimile in two columns — Quiché Maya and Spanish text of the Popol Vuh]*

Page 55 of the original Ximénez manuscript of the *Popol Vuh*

Don Juan de Rojas and don Juan Cortés, the fourteenth generation of kings, were the sons of Tecum and Tepepul.

These are, then, the generations and the order of the kingdom of the lords Ahpop and Ahpop-Camhá of the Quiché of Cavec.

And now we shall name again the families. These are the Great Houses of each of the lords who followed the Ahpop and the Ahpop-Camhá. These are the names of the nine families of those of Cavec, of the nine Great Houses,[13] and these are the titles of the lords of each one of the Great Houses:

Ahau-Ahpop, one Great House. Cuhá was the name of this Great House.

Ahau-Ahpop-Camhá, whose Great House was called Tziquinahá.

Nim-Chocoh-Cavec, one Great House.

Ahau-Ah-Tohil, one Great House.

Ahau-Ah-Gucumatz, one Great House.

Popol-Vinac Chituy, one Great House.

Lolmet-Quehnay, one Great House.

Popol-Vinac Pahom Tzalatz Xcuxebá, one Great House.

Tepeu-Yaqui, one Great House.

These, then, are the nine families of Cavec. And very numerous were the sons and vassals of the tribes which followed these nine Great Houses.

Here are the nine Great Houses of those of Nihaib. But first we shall give the lineage of the rulers of the kingdom. From one root only these names originated when the sun began to shine, with the beginning of light.

Balam-Acab, first grandfather and father.

[12] *Tecum*, "heaped up." This king must not be confused with the general-in-chief of the Quiché army who appeared fighting at the front of his troops against the Spaniards. The fate of King Tecum is not known, but Tepepul is King Sequechul of whom the *Libro de Cabildo* and the chroniclers of the Conquest speak, who reigned from 1524 to 1526. After the insurrection of the Indians in 1526, he was imprisoned until 1540, and in this latter year, Alvarado hanged him together with the Cakchiquel king Belehé-Qat, whom the Spaniards called Sinacán.

[13] *Are u binaam vi beleheb chinamit chi Caviquib beleheb.* The four last words are lacking in the transcription made by Brasseur de Bourbourg.

Qoacul and Qoacutec, second generation.

Cochahuh and Cotzibahá, third generation.

Beleheb-Queh [I],[14] fourth generation.

Cotuhá, [I] fifth generation of kings.

Batza, sixth generation.

Iztayul, seventh generation of kings.

Cotuhá [II], eighth order of the kingdom.

Beleheb-Queh [II], ninth order.

Quemá, so called, tenth generation.

Ahau-Cotuhá, eleventh generation.

Don Cristóval, so called, who ruled in the time of the Spaniards.

Don Pedro de Robles, the present Ahau-Galel.

These, then, are all the kings who descended from the Ahau-Galel. Now we shall name the lords of each of the Great Houses.

Ahau-Galel, first lord of the Nihaib, head of one Great House.

Ahau-Ahtzic-Vinac, one Great House.

Ahau-Galel-Camhá, one Great House.

Nima-Camhá, one Great House.

Uchuch-Camhá, one Great House.

Nim-Chocoh-Nihaib, one Great House.

Ahau-Avilix, one Great House.

Yacolatam, one Great House.[15]

Nima-Lolmet-Ycoltux, one Great House.

These, then, are the Great Houses of the Nihaib; these were the names of the nine families of those of Nihaib, as they were called. Numerous were the families of each one of the lords, whose names we have given first.

Here, now, is the lineage of those of Ahau-Quiché, who were their grandfather and father.

14 *Beleheb-Quih* in the original, through evident error. In Chapter 7 of this part the correct version of this name appears as Beleheb-Queh, 9 Queh, a day of the calendar.

15 In the original the name of Nimá-Camhá appears twice, and those of Utzampop-Zaclatol and Nimá Lolmet-Ycoltux, which appear in Chapter 8 of this Part IV are not included at all.

Mahucutah, the first man.

Qoahau, name of the second generation of kings.

Caglacán.

Cocozom.

Comahcún.

Vucub-Ah.

Cocamel.

Coyabacoh.

Vinac-Bam.

These were the kings of those of the Ahau-Quiché; this is the order of their generations.

Here now are the titles of the lords who made up the Great Houses; there were only four Great Houses.

Ahtzic-Vinac-Ahau, title of the first lord, one Great House.

Lolmet-Ahau, second lord, a Great House.

Nim-Chocoh-Ahau, third lord, a Great House.

Hacavitz, fourth lord, a Great House.

Therefore, four were the Great Houses of the Ahau-Quiché.

There were, then, three Nim-Chocoh, who were like fathers [vested with authority] of all the lords of the Quiché.[16] The three Chocoh came together in order to make known the orders of the mothers, the orders of the fathers.[17] Great was the position of the three Chocoh.

There were, then, the Nim-Chocoh of those of Cavec,[18] the Nim-Chocoh of those of Nihaib, who was second, and the Nim-Chocoh-Ahau of the Ahau-Quiché, who was third. Each one of the three Chocoh represented his family.

And this was the life of the Quiché, because no longer can be

---

[16] *Queheri e cahauixel rumal ronohel ahauab Quiché.* The Nim-Chocoh (Great Chosen or Great Counsellors) were the dignitaries charged with proclaiming and executing the decisions of the government. *E alanel,* "those who give birth," the text calls them.

[17] *E alanel, e u chuch tzih e u cahau tzih,* literally, "those who proclaim the word of the mothers, the word of the fathers."

[18] Ximénez, in his translation, supplies this line omitted in the original, surely through an error made in the transcription from the Quiché text.

seen [the book of the *Popol Vuh*] which the kings had in olden times,[19] for it has disappeared.

In this manner, then, all the people of the Quiché, which is called Santa Cruz,[20] came to an end.

[19] The sentence from this place in the original is as follows: *rumal ma-habi chi ilbal re qo nabe oher cumal ahauab*, and is evidently garbled. It is easily completed, however, by comparing it with other two sentences of the text, one from the preamble which says: *rumal ma-habi chic ilbal re Popo Vuh*, and one from Chapter 11 of Part IV which reads: *Xax qu'etaam vi qo cut ilbal re, qo vuh, Popol Vuh u bi cumal*. The author ends his work by explaining again that he had to write it because the ancient book no longer exists in which the kings read the past and the future of their people.

[20] As has been said in another place, it was Bishop Marroquín who baptized with the name of Santa Cruz the Spanish city which replaced the ancient Quiché capital.

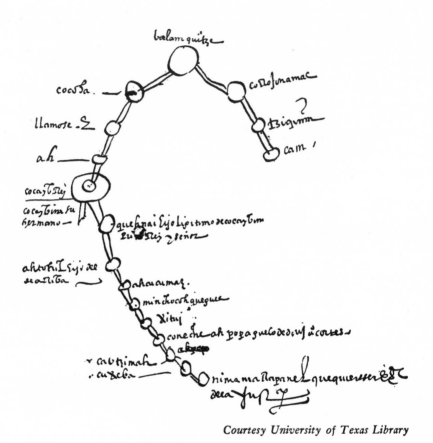

Genealogy of the Quiché Lords

# APPENDIX

## Paper Concerning the Origin of the Lords

(The following description of the origin of the Quiché lords is found in the document entitled *"Descripción de Zapotitlán y Suchitepec,"* enviada al Rey de España por el Corregidor Juan de Estrada el 22 de noviembre de 1572, the original manuscript of which is in the Latin-American Library of the University of Texas.)

The first king that these people of Utatlán had was called Balam Quisé. This king came from the part of the East and brought with him two other brothers, one called Balam Acap, the other called Mahu Cutah. These three were equal in command, and the first ones who populated the land of Rabinal. Balam Quisé, the older brother, had two sons, one called Cocohá and the other Corojón Amac. These two sons of Balam Quisé were the first ones who discovered the province of Utatlán and explored, populated, and subjected it.

Cocohá begat E. This one reigned in the place of his father, who was called Cocohá, and he it was who conquered the land of Robonal and the surrounding country. Corojón Amac, second son of Balam Quisé, brother of Cocohá, begat Tziquín. This Tziquín and E. were equal in command and they fought by night and they went by night to slay the enemy people, whom they found scattered and careless, and in order to make themselves feared, they appeared before men, by the work of the devil, as jaguars and pumas, and they flew by night through the air, spouting fire from their mouths, and in this way they did great damage, for which they were held in much fear and all the land of Robinal submitted to them. And they made the people understand that they were the sons of Tzacol Pitol, which is to say, that they were the sons of the Maker of all things.

E. [was] the real king, by virtue of being the older brother, and he begat Ah. This one also was a sorcerer and did as his forefathers had done. Tziquín begat Acan, and they were equal in command, the two first cousins between them, and they were great sorcerers.

Ah, the legitimate lord, begat Cocayb and Cocayvim. Cocayb was the heir to the kingdom through his father, and was the first one to make a republic [of his land]. This Cocayb thus subjected the eleven lords left [unconquered] by his ancestors, and he was the first who founded a town. He built and made his royal house and fort at Robinal. This one was the first one who divided the lands and made a captain and governors and captains, and he divided them into heads of wards [calpules]. He was the first one who made laws and established legal rights, and he was the first one who made them pay tribute, each one according to what he had and held, and he, who did not have wherewith to pay tribute, served with his own person or other suitable things.

This Cocayb made his brother Cocaybim general of his land, which [position] is called Ahpop, and he made him equal thus, although he did not recognize [his] right by descent [*mayorazgo*]. This latter instituted and named nine captains or governors, who governed the town and assisted him, and not one of them who was [still] young could govern, until he became of age, and he was deemed and held as apt, and if he was not [of age], one of those nearest to his family and parentage governed until he was of age.

This Cocabim, the second brother, because of the absence of

his brother, who had wandered away from his house, had a son by his sister-in-law, and his brother Cocayb being about to return [from his wanderings] and in view of the penalties, which had been fixed by his law, before he left, that of hanging, and since he had had a son by his brother's wife, the child's grandmother kept him in hiding, and being of age his uncle and stepfather gave him the position of his father, to be one of the Ahpop [a principal officer of the kingdom]. In this way the kingdom was bestowed upon this Cocayb without any one else being allowed to govern or to be king.

This Cocayb begat Quehnay and other five sons, which were appointed governors by this king and from then on until the Spaniards came, the kings had this name of Quehnay, because it is [regarded] among the natives like Caesar.

From the second brother, who was called Cocaybim, succeeded all those who were called Ahpop until there came a successor, who was called Conaché, grandfather of Don Juan Cortés, who is now living. This Conaché died in the battle which the Adelantado Don Pedro de Alvarado fought on the plains of the town of Quezaltenango, which belongs to the Royal Crown.

# BIBLIOGRAPHY

Alexander, Hartley Burr
   1920. *Mythology of All Races*, Vol. XI, *Latin American*, Chap. V, "Central America." Boston.
*Anales de Cuauhtitlán*
   1885. *"Noticias históricas de México, o Codex Chimalpopoca,"* in *Anales del Museo Nacional de Arqueología, Historia y Etnografía*, Appendix. Mexico.
Avendaño y Loyola, Fr. Andrés de
   1696. *"Relación de las dos entradas que hize, a la conversión de los gentiles Ytzaes y Cehaches (Petén Itzá),"* Mérida 6 de abril de 1696. MS in the Edward E. Ayer Collection, Newberry Library, Chicago. Partly translated into English and included in Means, "History of the Spanish Conquest of Yucatán and of the Itzás," *Papers* of the Peabody Museum of American Archaeology and Ethnology, Vol. VII. Cambridge, Mass., 1917.
Baldwin, J.
   1871. *Ancient America*. New York.
Bancroft, Hubert Howe
   1883. *The Native Races of the Pacific States*. 5 vols. San Francisco.
   1890. *History of Central America*. 3 vols. San Francisco.
Bandelier, Adolf F.
   1878. "On the Sources of the Aboriginal History of Spanish America," in American Association for the Advancement of Science *Proceedings*, Vol. XXVII (August), 328.
   1880. "On the Distribution and Tenure of Lands and the Customs with Respect to Inheritance among the Ancient Indians," in *Peabody Museum, Eleventh Report*, 391.
   1881. "Notes on the Bibliography of Yucatán and Central Amer-

ica," in *Proceedings* of the American Antiquarian Society, Vol. I, 82–118. Worcester, Mass.

Barela, Fr. Francisco

"*Vocabulario Kakchiquel.*" MS in the National Museum of Mexico, 267 ff. There is a copy of this vocabulary under the name "Varea" at the library of the American Philosophical Society of Philadelphia, made by Fr. Francisco Ceron at the Convent of San Pedro la Laguna (Lake Atitlán, Guatemala).

Basseta, Fr. Domingo de

? 1698. *Vocabulario quiché.* MS in the Bibliothèque Nationale, Paris.

Batres, Jáuregui, Antonio

1892. *Los Indios, su historia y su civilización.* Guatemala.

1915–17. *La América Central ante la Historia.* Guatemala.

Beristain de Souza, J. Mariano

1883. *Biblioteca Hispano Americana.* 2nd. ed., 3 vols. Amecameca, Mexico.

Beuchat, H.

1912. *Manuel d'Archéologie américaine.* Paris.

Brasseur de Bourbourg, Charles Etienne

1851. *Cartas para servir de introducción a la historia primitiva de las naciones civilizadas de la América septentrional.* Mexico.

1857. *Histoire des Nations Civilisées du Mexique et de l'Amérique Centrale.* 4 vols. Paris.

1861. *Popol Vuh. Le Livre Sacré et les mythes de l'antiquité américaine, avec les livres héroïques et historiques des Quichés.* Paris.

1862. *Grammaire de la langue Quichée.* Paris.

1866. *Recherches sur les ruines de Palenque.* Paris.

1868. *Quatre Lettres sur le Mexique.* Paris.

1869. *Manuscript Troano. Étude sur le système graphique et la langue des Mayas.* 2 vols. Paris.

1871. *Bibliothèque Mexico-Guatémalienne.* Paris.

Brinton, Daniel G.

1881. "The Names of the Gods in the Kiché Myths of Central America," in *Proceedings* of the American Philosophical Society. Philadelphia.

1882. *The Maya Chronicles.* Philadelphia.

1883. *Aboriginal American Authors and Their Productions.* Philadelphia.

1885. *The Annals of the Cakchiquels.* Philadelphia.

1890. *Essays of an Americanist.* Philadelphia.

1893. *The Native Calendar of Central America and Mexico.* Philadelphia.

1896. *The Myths of the New World.* 3rd. ed. Philadelphia.

Cabrera, Pablo Félix

1822. *Teatro Crítico Americano.* In Antonio del Río's *Description of the Ruins of an Ancient City, q. v.* London.

*"Calendario de los Indios de Guatemala"*

1722. In Quiché. Copied in Guatemala City in April, 1877, by Carlos H. Berendt. MS, 61 pp., in the University Museum, Philadelphia.

Capdevila, Arturo

1938. *El Popol Vuh para todos.* Guatemala.

Charencey, Comte H. de

1871. *Le Mythe de Votán, étude sur les origines asiatiques de la civilisation américaine.* Alençon.

1887. "Xibalba," in *Bulletin de la Société de linguistique de Paris,* No. 29 (April). Paris.

Charnay, Claude Joseph Désiré

1863. *Cités et ruines américaines.* With a text by M. Viollet-le-Duc. Paris.

Chavero, Alfredo

1895. *México a través de los siglos,* Vol. I. Barcelona.

*Chilan Balam de Chumayel, Book of*

1930. *Libro de Chilam Balam de Chumayel.* Translated from the Maya language into Castilian by Antonio Médiz-Bolio. San José, Costa Rica. A later edition was printed in Mexico, 1941.

1933. *The Book of Chilam Balam of Chumayel.* English translation by Ralph L. Roys. Carnegie Institution of Washington Publication No. 483. Washington, D. C.

Chimalpahin

1889. *Annales de Domingo Francisco de San Anton Muñon Chimalpahin Quauhtlehuanitzin,* Sixth and Seventh Relations (1258–1612). Published and translated from the original manuscript by Remi Siméon. Paris.

Claasen, Oswald

1933. *Die Ahnen des Mondes. Eine indianische Edda.* Krefeld.

Cogolludo, Fr. Diego López de

1688. *Historia de Yucatán.* Madrid.

1867. *Historia de Yucatán.* 3rd. ed. Mérida.

Coto, Padre Tomás
> *Vocabulario de la lengua Cakchiquel vel Guatemalteca.* MS in the American Philosophical Society, Philadelphia.

Del Río, Antonio
> 1822. *Description of the Ruins of an ancient city discovered near Palenque, in the kingdom of Guatemala in Spanish America, translated from the original manuscript Report of Captain Don Antonio del Río.* Followed by *Teatro Crítico Americano,* by Pablo Félix Cabrera. London.

*Diccionario de Motul*
> 1929. *Diccionario de Motul, Maya Español.* Attributed to Fr. Antonio de Ciudad Real. Mérida.

Finger, Charles J.
> 1924. *Tales from Silver Lands.* Garden City, New York.

Franciscanos, M. R. P.
> 1787. *"Vocabulario de la lengua quiché compuesto por el apostólico celo de los M. R. P. Franciscanos de esta santa provincia del dulcissimo nombre de Jesus del arzobispado de Guatemala."* Probably made at Sacapulas. MS in the Peabody Museum, Cambridge, Mass. There is a copy in The New York Public Library.

Fuentes y Guzmán, Francisco Antonio de
> 1882. *Historia de Guatemala, o Recordación Florida.* 2 vols. Madrid.
> 1932–33. *Recordación Florida.* Edited by the Sociedad de Geografía e Historia de Guatemala. 3 vols. Guatemala.

García de Palacio, Diego
> 1576. *"Relación hecha por el Licenciado Palacio al Rey D. Felipe II en la que describe la provincia de Guatemala."* In *Colección de documentos inéditos de Indias,* Vol. VI, 5–40. Madrid, 1866. Also in Squier, *Collection of Rare and Original Documents,* Vol. I, New York, 1860.

Gavarrete, Francisco
> 1868. *Geografía de la República de Guatemala.* 2nd. ed. Guatemala.

Genêt, Jean
> 1927. *Esquisse d'une civilisation oubliée.* Paris.
> 1929. *Histoire des peuples Shoshones-Aztèques.* Paris.
> 1934. *Revue des Études Maya-Quichées,* Vol. I. Paris.

Genêt and Chelbatz
1927. *Histoire des peuples maya-quichés.* Paris.
Girard, Rafael
1948. *Esoterismo del Popol Vuh.* Mexico.
Gordon, George Byron
1915. "Guatemalan Myths," in *Museum Journal,* Vol. IV, No. 3 (September), 103. University of Pennsylvania. Philadelphia.
Guzmán, Fr. Pantaleón de
1704. "*Compendio de nombres en lengua cakchiquel,*" MS in E. G. Squier's Collection. There is a copy of this vocabulary at the library of the University Museum in Philadelphia.
Helps, Sir Arthur
1855-61. *The Spanish Conquest.* 4 vols. London. This gives in the Appendix a brief synopsis of the *Popol Vuh,* the first one made in English.
Herrera y Tordesillas, Antonio de
1601-15. *Historia general de los hechos de los castellanos en las islas y tierra firme del mar Oceano.* 5 vols. Madrid. A modern edition was printed in Madrid in 1934.
Imbelloni, José.
1940. "*El Génesis de los pueblos proto-históricos de América.*" First section, "*La Narración Guatemalteca,*" *Boletín de la Academia Argentina de Letras,* Vol. VIII, No. 32 (October-December), 539-628.
1948. "*¿Qué significa 'Popol Vuh'? Intitulación y función del manuscrito de Chichicastenango,*" in *Actes du XXVIIIe. Congrés International des Americanistes,* pp. 393-405. Paris.
*Isagoge Histórica Apologética de las Indias Occidentales,* 1711
1892. 1st ed. Guatemala.
1935. 2nd. ed. by Sociedad de Geografía e Historia de Guatemala.
Ixtlilxochitl, Fernando de Alva
1891. *Obras Históricas.* Ed. by Alfredo Chavero. 2 vols. Mexico.
Krickeberg, Walter
1928. *Märchen der Azteken und Inkaperuaner, Maya und Muisca, übersetz, eingeleitet und erläutert.* Jena.
Landa, Fr. Diego de
1864. *Relación de las cosas de Yucatán.* Paris.
1937. *Yucatán before and after the Conquest, by Friar Diego de Landa.* Translated with notes by William Gates. Baltimore.

1941. *Landa's Relación de las cosas de Yucatán.* A translation. Edited with notes by Alfred Tozzer. Cambridge, Mass.

Las Casas, Fr. Bartolomé de
1909. *Apologética Historia de las Indias.* In *Nueva Biblioteca de Autores Españoles. Historiadores de Indias.* Vol. I. Madrid.

Le Plongeon, Augustus
1886. *Sacred Mysteries among the Mayas and the Quichés, etc.* New York.

Lehmann, Walter
1909. *Methods and Results in Mexican Research.* Translated by Seymour de Ricci. Paris.
1911. *"Der Kalender der Quiché-Indianer Guatemalas,"* in *Anthropos,* Vol. VI, pp. 403–10.

Lehmann Nitsche, Robert
1926–27. *"Mitología Centroamericana,"* *Anales Sociedad de Geografía e Historia de Guatemala,* Vol. II, No. 4, pp. 408–14.

Lothrop, Samuel Kirkland
1936. *Zacualpa. A Study of Ancient Quiché Artifacts.* Carnegie Institution. Washington, D. C.

Mackenzie, Donald A.
1941. *Myths of Pre-Columbian America.* London.

Maudslay, Alfred Percival
1897. *Archaeology.* A section of *Biología Centrali-Americana,* edited by Du Cane Godman and Osbert Salvin. London.

Maudslay, A. C. and A. P.
1899. *A Glimpse at Guatemala and Some Notes on the Ancient Monuments of Central America.* London.

*Memorial de Tecpán Atitlán*
1873–74. *Memorial de Tecpán Atitlán, escrito por Don Francisco Hernández Arana Xahilá y continuado por Don Francisco Díaz Xebutá Queh.* Translated into Spanish from the unpublished French translation of Brasseur de Bourbourg by Don Juan Gavarrete. In *La Sociedad Económica de Guatemala.* Reprinted several times in Spanish. Translated into English (*see* Brinton, 1885).

Mencos F., Agustín
1890. *"Fray Francisco Ximenez,"* *La Revista.* Guatemala.
1937. *Literatura guatemalteca en el período de la Colonia.* Guatemala.

246

Mexican and Central American Antiquities, Calendar Systems, and
    History
  1904. *Bureau of American Ethnology Bulletin 28.* Washington.
Milla, José
  1879–82. *Historia de la América Central.* 2 vols. Guatemala.
  1937. *Historia de la América Central.* 2nd. ed., 2 vols. Guatemala.
Molina, Alonso de
  1571. *Vocabulario de lengua mexicana.* Mexico.
Morley, Sylvanus Griswold
  1946. *The Ancient Maya.* Stanford University, Calif.
Müller, Friedrich Max
  1867. *Chips from a German Workshop.* 2 vols. London.
  1878. *Ensayo sobre la historia de las religiones.* Madrid.
Núñez de la Vega, Francisco
  1702 *Constituciones Diocesanas del Obispado de Chiapa.* Rome.
Ordóñez y Aguiar, Ramón de
  1907. *Historia de la Creación del Cielo y de la Tierra.* MS of the
    eighteenth century published by Nicolas León, professor of
    ethnology in the National Museum of Mexico, and included
    in his *Bibliografía Mexicana del Siglo XVIII*, Sec. 1, Part 4.
    Mexico.
Pohorilles, Noah Elieser
  1912. *"Der Bedeutung mythischer Namen in den alten und neuen
    Welt,"* in *Anthropos*, Vol. VII, pp. 995–1013.
  1913. *Das Popol Wuh. Die mytische Geschichte des Kicé-Volkes
    von Guatemala nach dem Original-Texte übersetz und
    bearbeitet.* Leipzig.
*Popol Vuh*
  1855. *"Ueber die vorcolumbische Geschichte von Guatemala,"* in
    *Das Ausland*, No. 27 (July 6). Berlin.
  1857. *Las Historias del origen de los Indios.* See Ximenez.
  1861. *Popol Vuh. Le livre sacré.* See Brasseur de Bourbourg.
  1862. *"Popol Vuh, Le Livre Sacré,"* etc., by L. de la Cressonière,
    Lausanne, March 31, 1862. In *Nouvelles Annales des Voy-
    ages, de la Géographie, de l'Histoire et de l'Archéologie*,
    Sixth series, eighth year, pp. 87–116. Paris.
  1872–73. *El Popol Buj. Versión española de la traducción de
    Brasseur de Bourbourg comparada con la de Ximénez, con
    notas tomadas de ambos comentadores y concordancias con
    las Santas Escrituras, por D. Juan Gavarrete. Colección de*

*documentos históricos reunidos en la parte etnográfica del Museo Nacional.* In *La Sociedad Económica de Guatemala,* Vol. III, Nos. 1–27. Guatemala.

1894–96. *El Popol Vuh.* A reprint of the 1872–73 translation. In *El Educacionista, Revista de Instrucción Pública,* Nos. 3–24. Guatemala.

1905. *El Popol Vuh o libro sagrado de los antiguos votánides. Documento de capital importancia para el estudio de la historia precolombina de estos países. Precedido de un estudio preliminar por el Dr. Santiago I. Barberena.* 3 vols. San Salvador. It contains Gavarrete's Spanish version of the French translation by Brasseur de Bourbourg.

1905. "The Popol Vuh or Book of the Holy Assembly. The Significance of the Popol Vuh," in *The Word* (October and November). A monthly magazine devoted to philosophy, science, religion, Easter thought, occultism, theosophy, and the brotherhood of humanity. New York.

1905. *The Popol Vuh or Book of the Holy Assembly.* Translated by Kenneth S. Guthrie. In *The Word,* beginning with the December issue. New York.

1906–1907. *El Popol Vuh (o libro sagrado de los antiguos votánides).* A Spanish translation from the French version of Brasseur de Bourbourg. In *Revista del Archivo y Biblioteca Nacional de Honduras.* Tegucigalpa.

1907. "The Story of the Calabash-tree in the Popol Vuh," by C. V. Hartman, in *Journal of American Folk-lore,* Vol. XX, No. 77, pp. 148–50.

1913. *Einleitung in das Popol Vuh,* by Wolfgang Schultz. Leipzig.

1914. "*Le Popol Vuh et l'État de Xibalba,*" by Comte H. de Charencey, in *Journal de la Société des Américanistes de Paris,* Vol. XI (n. s.), No. 1, pp. 366–68.

1918. *A Short Work on the Popol Vuh and the Traditional History of the Ancient Americans by Ixtlilxóchitl.* Kansas City, Mo.

1919–21. *El Popol Vuh. A reprint from El Educacionista,* 1894–96. In the *Revista Centro-América,* published by the Oficina Internacional Centro-Americana, Vols. XI, XII, and XIII. Guatemala.

1923. "*El Popol Vuh, su importancia y trascendencia,*" by Ricardo Mimenza Castillo, in *Tierra,* Nos. 9, 11, and 13. Mexico.

1923. *El Popol Vuh, o Libro Sagrado de los antiguos votánides, etc. Tomado de la edición centroamericana de 1905.* Mérida.

1926. *Popol Vuh, Libro Sagrado del Quiché.* Spanish version from the French translation by Brasseur de Bourbourg. Ed. by the Biblioteca Nacional. San Salvador.

1926. "*El Popol Vuh. El monumento literario de los pueblos maya-quiché,*" by Jorge Lardé, in *El Salvadoreño* (July 12). San Salvador.

1927. "*El Popol Buj,*" by Antonio Batres Jáuregui, in *Anales Sociedad de Geografía e Historia de Guatemala,* Vol. IV, No. 1 (September), 25–29.

1929–31. "*Popol Vuh.*" A reprint of the Quiché book. In *El Teósofo,* Nos. 13–17 (July, 1929) and Nos. 22–25 (July, 1931).

1932. "*Traducciones del Popol Vuh,*" by J. M. González de Mendoza (*Noticia bibliográfica*), in *El Libro y el Pueblo* (August). Mexico.

1933. "*La Creación del mundo según el Popol Vuh,*" by Gabriel Porras Troconis, in *Anales Sociedad de Geografía e Historia de Guatemala,* Vol. X, No. 1 (September), 21–31.

1934. "*Sobre el Popol Vuh,*" by Rafael Heliodoro Valle, in *Investigaciones Lingüísticas,* Vol. II, pp. 331–32. Mexico.

1934. "*Leyendo el Popol Vuh,*" by David Vela, in *El Imparcial.* Guatemala.

1935. "*Popol Vuh,*" by A. G. J., in *Anales Sociedad de Geografía e Historia de Guatemala,* Vol. XI, No. 4 (June), 459–64.

1940. "*El Génesis de los pueblos proto-históricos de América. Primera Sección. La Narración Guatemalteca,* by José Imbelloni, in *Boletín de la Academia Argentina de Letras,* Vol. VIII, No. 32 (October-December), 539–628. Printed in book form in Ediciones Coni, Buenos Aires, 1943.

1941. "*Pop-ol Vug,*" by Rafael E. Monroy, in *Anales Sociedad de Geografía e Historia de Guatemala,* Vol. XVII, No. 1, pp. 26–29.

1943. *Estampas del Popol Vuh* (with 10 colored lithographs), by Carlos Mérida. Mexico.

1944. *El Popol Vuh. Advertencia y Selección de Ermilo Abreu Gómez. Biblioteca Enciclopédica Popular,* No. 34. Mexico.

1944. *Popol Vuh o el Libro del Consejo* (modernized edition taken from the translation of Raynaud). With notes by Luis M. Baudizzone. Buenos Aires.

249

1944. *"Popol Vuh,"* by Rafael E. Monroy, in *Anales Sociedad de Geografía e Historia de Guatemala,* Vol. XIX, No. 2 (December), 418-26.

1944-46. *"Popol Vuh"* (a reprint of the 1905 edition), in *Revista Yikal Maya Than,* Vol. V. to Vol. VIII. Mérida.

1945. *"Popol Vuh.* A New Translation of the Sacred Book," by S. Linné (a commentary on Schultze Jena's translation), in *Ethnos,* No. 4, pp. 165-81. Ethnographic Museum of Sweden, Stockholm.

1946. *"Antigua tradición del pueblo quiché. De cómo al descender el aliento divino se creó un mundo, idea contenida en las dos palabras 'Popol Vuh,' "* a lecture by Rafael E. Monroy, in *Anales Sociedad de Geografía e Historia de Guatemala* (June), 419.

1948. *"¿ Qué significa 'Popol Vuh? Intitulación y función del manuscrito de Chichicastenango,"* by José Imbelloni, in *Actes du XXVIIIe. Congrés International des Américanistes,* pp. 393-405. Paris.

1949. *Problemas etnológicos del Popol Vuh: 1. Procedencia y lenguaje de los Quichés,* by Antonio Goubaud Carrera, in *Antropología e Historia de Guatemala,* Vol. I, No. 1 (January).

*See also* Girard, Capdevila, Pohorilles, Raynaud, Recinos, Schuller, Schultze Jena, Spence, *and* Villacorta and Rodas.

Prowe, Herman

1929. *"Vestigios de ciencias en los documentos antiguos de los indios de Guatemala,"* in *Anales Sociedad de Geografía e Historia de Guatemala* (June), 419.

Raynaud, Georges

1893. *Les manuscrits précolombiens.* Paris.

1918. *Les créations et les guerres des dieux, d'après une Bible centro-américaine.* École pratique des Hautes-Études, section on religious sciences. Paris.

1925. *Les dieux, les héros et les hommes d'l'ancien Guatémala d'après le Livre du Conseil (Popol Vuh).* Paris.

1927. *Los dioses, los héroes y los hombres de Guatemala antigua o el Libro del Consejo. Popol Vuh de los indios quichés.* Translated by Miguel Angel A turias and J. Manuel González de Mendoza. Paris.

1928. *Anales de los Xahil de los indios cakchiqueles.* Translated from the French version edited by Professor Raynaud, director of studies on the religions of pre-Columbian America in the School of Advanced Study of Paris, by the graduate students of the same, Miguel Angel Asturias and J. Manuel González de Mendoza. Paris.

1937. *Anales de los Xahil.* 2nd. ed. Guatemala.

1939. *El Libro del Consejo.* A reprint of the 1927 edition in *Biblioteca del estudiante universitario.* Mexico.

1947. *Anales de los Xahil.* A reprint in the *Biblioteca del estudiante universitario.* Mexico.

Recinos, Adrián

1947. *Popol Vuh. Las historias antiguas del Quiché.* Translated from the original text with an introduction and notes. Mexico.

1950. *Memorial de Sololá. Anales de los Cakchiqueles.* Translated from the original MS with an introduction and notes. Mexico.

Remesal, Fr. Antonio de

1619. *Historia de la Provincia de San Vicente de Chiapa y Guatemala.* Madrid.

1932. A 2nd. ed. of the above, published by the Sociedad de Geografía e Historia de Guatemala. 2 vols. Guatemala.

Rivera Maestre, Miguel

1832. *Atlas Guatemalteco, en ocho cartas formadas y grabadas en Guatemala de orden del gefe del Estado, Ciudadano Mariano Gálvez.* Guatemala.

Rodas N., Flavio, and others

1938. *Simbolismos de Guatemala,* by Flavio Rodas N. and Ovidio Rodas Corzo. Guatemala.

1940. *Chichicastenango. The Kiché Indians. Their History and Culture, Sacred Symbols of Their Dress and Textiles,* by Flavio Rodas N., Ovidio Rodas Corzo, and Laurence F. Hawkins. Guatemala.

*See also* Villacorta and Rodas.

Rodríguez Cabal, Juan

1935. *Apuntes para la vida del M. R. Padre presentado y predicador general Fr. Francisco Ximénez.* Guatemala.

Roys, R. L.

1931. *The Ethno-Botany of the Maya.* Middle American Research

Series, Publication No. 2, Department of Middle American Research, Tulane University. New Orleans.

Román y Zamora, Fr. Jerónimo
1897. *Repúblicas de Indias, Idolatría y Gobierno en México y Perú antes de la Conquista, ordenadas por Fr. Jerónimo Román y Zamora, Cronista de la Orden de San Agustín. In Colección de Libros raros o curiosos que tratan de América.* 2 vols. Madrid.

Sáenz de Santa María, Carmelo
1940. *Diccionario Cakchiquel-Español.* Guatemala.

Sahagún, Fr. Bernardino de
1829. *Historia general de las cosas de Nueva España.* 3 vols. Mexico.
1938. The above reprinted in 5 vols. Mexico.

Salazar, Ramón A.
1897. *Historia del desenvolvimiento intelectual de Guatemala. La Colonia.* Guatemala.

Sapper, Carl
1893. *"Beiträge zur Ethnographie der Republik Guatemala,"* in *Petermanns Mitteilungen,* Vol. 39. Gotha.
1895. *"Die Gebräuche und religiösen Anschauungen der Kekchi-Indianer,"* in *Intern. Archiv für Ethnogr.,* Vol. VIII. Leyden.

Scherzer, Karl von
1856. *Mitteilungen über die Handschriftlichen Werke des Padre Francisco Ximénez in der Universitäts-Bibliothek zu Guatemala.* Vienna.
1856. *Die Indianer von Santa Catarina Istlavacan (Frauenfuss). Ein Beitrag zur Kultur-Geschichte der Urbewohner Central-Amerikas.* Vienna.
1864. *Aus dem Natur un Völkerleben in tröpischen Amerika. Skizzenbuch* of Dr. Karl V. Scherzer. Leipzig.

Schuller, Rudolph
1919–20. *"Zur sprachlichen Verwandschaft der Maya-Quitzé mit den Carib-Arauac,"* in *Anthropos,* Vol. XIV, XV. Vienna.
1929. *"El Huracán, dios de la tormenta, y el Popol Vuh,"* in *Archivos del folklore cubano,* Vol. IV, No. 2 (April-June), 113–18.
1931. *"Der Verfasser des Popol Vuh,"* in *Anthropos,* Vol. XXVI, Nos. 5, 6 (September, December).
1935. *"Das Popol Vuh und das Ballspiel der K'icé Indianer von Guatemala, Mittelamerika,"* in *Intern. Archiv für Ethnogr.,* Vol. XXXIII, pp. 105–16. Leyden.

Schultze Jena, Leonhard

1933. *Leben, Glaube und Sprache der Quiché von Guatemala.*
*Indiana I.* Jena.

1943. *Popol Vuh. Das heiliges Buch der Quiché Indianer von*
*Guatemala.* Stuttgart, Berlin. Verlag von W. Kolhammer. In
the collection *Quellenwerke zu alten Geschichte Amerikas*
*Aufgezeichnet in den Sprachen der Eigeborenen,* Ibero Am-
erikanisches Institut, Berlin.

Seler, Eduard

1902–23. *Gesammelte Abhandlungen zur Amerikanischen Sprach-*
*und Altertumskunde.* 5 vols. Berlin.

1904. "The bat god of the Maya race," in *Bureau of American*
*Ethnology Bulletin 28.* Washington, D. C.

1913. *"Der Bedeutungswandel in den Mythen des Popol Vuh. Eine*
*Kritik,"* in *Anthropos,* Vol. VIII, pp. 382–88.

Silva, Pedro

1875–93. *Vocabulario Maya-Quiché-Cakchiquel, que se habla en*
*la Laguna de Atitlán, Distrito de Sololá.* Compiled by Pedro
Silva. MS, 206 ff., in the National Museum of Mexico.

Spence, Lewis

1908. *The Popol Vuh. The Mythic and Heroic Sagas of the Kichés*
*of Central America.* London.

1928. "The Popol Vuh: America's oldest book," in *The Open*
*Court,* Vol. XLII, pp. 641–58. Chicago.

1930. *The Magic and Mysteries of Mexico.* Philadelphia.

1930. *An Introduction to Mythology.* New York.

Standley, Paul C.

1930. *Flora of Yucatán.* Field Museum of Natural History, Publication No. 279; *Botanical Series,* Vol. III, No. 3. Chicago.

Standley, Paul C., and Julian A. Steyermark

1946. *Flora of Guatemala.* Field Museum of Natural History
*Botanical Series,* Vol. 24, Part IV Chicago.

Stephens, John Lloyd

1841. *Incidents of Travel in Central America, Chiapas, and Yuca-*
*tán.* New York.

Stoll, Otto

1884. *Zur Ethnographie der Republik Guatemala.* Zurich.

1888. *Die Maya-Sprachen der Pokom-Gruppe.* Part I: *Die Sprache*
*der Pokonchi-Indianer.* Vienna.

1889. *"Die Ethnologie der Indianerstämme von Guatemala,"* In-

*tern. Archiv für Ethnogr.*, Supplement to Vol. I, pp. 1–112. Leyden.

1896. *Die Maya Sprachen der Pokom-Gruppe.* Part II: *Die Sprache der K'e'kchi-Indianer.* Leipzig.

1938. *Etnografía de la República de Guatemala.* Translated by Antonio Goubaud Carrera. Guatemala.

Teletor, Pbro. Celso Narciso

1943. *"Toponimia de Rabinal,"* in *Anales Sociedad de Geografía e Historia de Guatemala* (December).

*Título de los Señores de Totonicapán* (1554)
*Titre Généalogique des Seigneurs de Totonicapán*

1885. A document written in Quiché, translated into Spanish in 1834 by Father Dionisio-José Chonay, curate of Sacapulas; translated into French from the Spanish version by the Comte de Charencey and published in Spanish and French. Alençon.

*Títulos de Ixcuin-Nehaib*

1876. *"Titulos de los antiguos nuestros antepasados, los que ganaron estas tierras de Otzoyá antes que viniera la fe de Jesucristo, entre ellos, en el año de mil y trescientos,"* in *La Sociedad Económica de Guatemala.* Also in *Anales Sociedad de Geografía e Historia de Guatemala* (September, 1941).

Torquemada, Fr. Juan de

1943. *Monarquía Indiana.* 3rd. ed. Mexico.

Trübner, Nicolaus

1856. "The New Discoveries in Guatemala," in *The London Athenaeum*, No. 1472 (January 12), 42–43.

1856. "Central American Archaeology," in *The London Athenaeum*, No. 1492 (May 31), 683–85.

Varea, Fr. Francisco de

1699. *Calepino en lengua cakchiquel.* MS in the American Philosophical Society, Philadelphia. This is a copy of the original MS of Father Francisco Barela in the National Museum of Mexico.

Vázquez, Fr. Francisco

1714–16. *Chrónica de la Provincia del Santissimo Nombre de Jesus de Guatemala.* 2 vols. Guatemala.

1937–44. 2nd. ed. of the above by the Sociedad de Geografía e Historia de Guatemala. 4 vols. Guatemala.

Vela, David

1943–44. *Literatura Guatemalteca.* 2 vols. Guatemala.

Villacorta C., J. Antonio

1936. *Memorial de Tecpán-Atitlán. Anales de los Cakchiqueles.* Guatemala.

1938. *Prehistoria e Historia Antiqua de Guatemala.* Sociedad de Geografía e Historia de Guatemala. Guatemala.

Villacorta C., J. A., and Flavio Rodas N.

1927. *Manuscrito de Chichicastenango. El Popol Buj. Estudio sobre las antiguas tradiciones del Pueblo Quiché.* The Quiché text and a Spanish translation. Guatemala.

Villagutierre y Sotomayor, Juan de

1701. *Historia de la conquista de la provincia del Itzá.* Madrid.

1933. 2nd. ed. of the above by the Sociedad de Geografía e Historia de Guatemala. Guatemala.

*Vocabulario de las Lenguas Quiché y Kakchiquel*

MS in the Americana Collection of Brasseur de Bourbourg, No. 65, Bibliothèque Nationale, Paris.

Wauchope, Robert

1949. "*Las edades de Utatlán e Iximche,*" in *Antropología e Historia de Guatemala,* Vol. I, No. 1 (January).

Winsor, Justin

1884–89. *Narrative and Critical History of America.* Edited by Justin Winsor, librarian of Harvard University. 8 vols. Vol. I, *Aboriginal America.* Boston and New York.

Ximénez, Fr. Francisco

1857. *Las Historias del Origen de los Indios de esta Provincia de Guatemala, traducidas de la lengua Quiché al castellano . . . por el R. P. F. Francisco Ximénez. . . . Publicado por la primera vez y aumentado con una introducción y anotaciones por el Dr. C. Scherzer. Vienna. En casa de Carlos Gerold e hijo, Libreros de la Academia Imperial de Ciencias.* Some copies show a different title page and the following printer's mark: "En casa de Trubner and Co., 60 Paternoster Row, London."

1926. *Las Historias del Origen de los Indios.* A reprint of the Vienna edition. San Salvador.

1929–31. *Historia de la Provincia de San Vicente de Chiapa y Guatemala.* 3 vols. Edited by the Sociedad de Geografía e Historia de Guatemala.

(M.S.) *"Primera Parte de el Tesoro de las lenguas Cacchiquel, Quiché y Tzutuhil"* en que las dichas lenguas se traducen en la nuestra española. 2 vols. 204 ff. MS in the Bancroft Library, Berkeley, Calif.

(MS.) *Arte de las tres lenguas, Cacchiquel, Quiché y Tzutuhil.* 93 ff. MS in the Newberry Library, Chicago.

(MS.) *Empiezan las historias del origen de los indios de esta provincia de Guatemala.* 112 ff. MS in the Newberry Library, Chicago.

(MS.) *Historia Natural del Reino de Guatemala.* MS in the Sociedad de Geografía e Historia de Guatemala.

Zorita, Alonso

1892. *Breve y Sumaria Relación de los Señores de la Nueva España.* In *Nueva Colección de documentos para la historia de Mexico,* Vol. III. Reprinted in *Biblioteca del estudiante universitario.* Mexico.

1909. *Historia de la Nueva España. In Colección de Libros y documentos referentes a la Historia de América,* Vol. IX. Madrid.

# Index

257

quinahá or Zutuhil, 171 n., 182 n.; its inhabitants send a petition to the King of Spain, 120 n.

Avendaño y Loyola, Fr. Andrés de: describes the books of the Maya, 10; says the Itzá worshiped Itzamná Kauil, 94 n.

Avilix, god of Balam-Acab: 175, 225

Avilix, the mountain: 71

Ayer, Edward E.: acquires the MS of the *Popol Vuh, xii*, 34, 45, 60

Ayotlán, name of the coast of Soconusco: 221 n.

Bacabs, the four supporters of the sky: 80 n.

Balam-Acab: one of the founders of the Quiché nation, 62, 71, 73, 167–70, 175, 183; founder of the House of Nihaib, 171

Balam-Conaché, Quiché king: 210 n., 212, 229

Balami-ha: the House of the Jaguars, place of punishment of Xibalba, 117, 149; name of a tribe, 171

Balam-Quitzé: first man and Quiché chief, 62, 71, 73, 74, 167–70, 237; head of the House of Cavec, 171; given his god, 175; asks for fire for his people, 176; bids farewell to his sons, 204, 206

Ball game: ball-court and playing gear, 109 n., 111; Hunahpú and Xbalanqué find the playing implements of their fathers, 135; description of the game by Sahagún, 143 n.; first game played at Xibalba, 143; second and last game, 152, 153; ball-court of Chichén Itzá, 144 n.

Bancroft, Hubert Howe: his opinion of the *Popol Vuh*, 16; buys part of Brasseur de Bourbourg's collection, 45

Bancroft Library (University of California): 34, 45

Bandelier, Adolf: on the influence of the Book of Genesis on the Quiché account of the creation, 18–19; estimates value of *Popol Vuh*, 19

Barela, Fr. Francisco: 84 n., 154 n., 156 n., 209 n.

Basseta, Fr. Domingo: 55, 88 n., 118 n.

Beebe, Colonel: translates the *Popol Vuh* into English, 60

Beleheb-Tzi, Quiché king burned by Alvarado: 230

Belehé-Qat, Cakchiquel king hanged by Alvarado: 232.n.; *see also* Sinacán

Beristain de Souza, Mariano: 27

Bitol, the Maker, name of God: 78

Bolonpel Uitz, Nine Hills, starting point of the Maya who emigrated to Yucatán: 67

Brasseur de Bourbourg, C. E.: thinks Quiché MS copied from ancient books, 21; claims to have been the first to show the existence of Ximénez' work, 39; arrives in Guatemala in 1855, xi, 41; gets and translates into French the Quiché and Cakchiquel MSS, xi, 42; publishes the *Popol Vuh xii*, 42, 45, 55; other works, 45; criticizes the Ximénez translation, 53; estimate of his own translation, 56

Brinton, Daniel G.: acquires the Cakchiquel MS and publishes it with an English translation, 45; opinion of translations of the *Popol Vuh*, 60, 66; on the calendar, 107–108 n.

Cabauil, generic name of God in Quiché: 54, 94 n.

Cabauil-Pom, the incense of the gods: 187

Cabracán, earthquake: name of one of the sons of Vucub-Caquix, 95, 104; name of a Quiché town, 223

Cabrera, Félix: on the works of Ximénez, 38

Caculhá, the lightning: 82

Cahá-Paluna, wife of Balam-Quitzé: 170, 183

Cahbahá, seat of a great temple: 225

Cakchiquel: origin and wanderings, 61–70; those of the red tree, 70; capital in Iximché, 171 n.; steal the fire from the Quiché, 179; name of their god, 180, 190; origin of their name, 182; their language different from Quiché, 190

Camalotz (Camazotz), the bat: a monster which cut off the heads of men, 90; decapitates Hunahpú, 150

Campeche, Mexican state: 64

*Camucú*, farewell song of the chiefs of the Quiché nation: 189, 204

Cáncer, Fr. Luis: 43 n.

Canek, chieftain of Petén-Itzá: 67

Cano, Fr. Agustín: on the tree that gives blood, 122 n.

Canté, yellow tree: 128 n.

Caquixahá, wife of Iqui-Balam: 170, 183

Carchah: ancient town, site of a ball-court, 112; settlement of the Quiché and Cakchiquel, 112–13 n.

Cardinal points: 80 n.

Cauutepech, Quiché king: 230

for fire, 177; their men disappear, 193, 194; fight against the Quiché, 196; send their daughters to tempt Tohil, 196; defeated, 200–203

Vucub-Camé, lord of Xibalba: 109

Vucub-Caquix, the arrogant: 37, 93, 94; his destruction by Hunahpú and Xbalanqué, 96–99

Vucub-Hunahpú, brother of Hun-Hunahpu: 107; sacrificed by the Lords of Xibalba, 117, 163

Vucub-Noh, Quiché king: 230

Vucub-Pec, Vucub-Zivan: 62, 174

Xan, a mosquito: 135, 140

Xbalanqué: *see* Hunahpú and Xbalanqué

Xbaquiyalo, wife of Hun-Hunahpú: 108

Xecotcovach: destroys the wooden men, 90

Xelahuh: *see* Quetzaltenango

Xenacoj, parish in the valley of Sacatepéquez: 32

Xibalba, underground region inhabited by evil people: 53, 54, 68, 109; the road to, 109, 113, 114, 139; punishments of, 117; messenger from Xibalba comes before the Quiché, 177

Xibalba, Lords of: 68, 109–11; sacrifice Hun-Hunahpú and Vucub-Hunahpú, 117; send for Hunahpú and Xbalanqué, 136; death of, and destruction of their empire, 159–60

Xibalba ocot, a Maya dance: 109n.

Xic, lord of Xibalba: 109, 111n., 115

Xicalanco, old trade center, temporary station of the Guatemalan tribes: 65, 65, 68, 69

Ximénez, Fr. Francisco: discovers the MS of the *Popol Vuh*, xii, 4–6; speaks of the books found in Petén, 11; horoscope of the children, 11; finds the original histories of the Quiché court, 14–15; biography and notice of his works, 30–49; translations of the *Popol Vuh*, 50, 55; on the antiquity of the Quiché kingdom, 73; describes the city of Utatlán, 216n.

Xiquiripat, lord of Xibalba: 109, 110n.

Xmucané, the grandmother, creator of man: 79, 87, 88, 173; mother of Hun-Hunahpú and Vucub-Hunahpú, 107, 113; makes man from yellow and white corn, 167

Xmucur, the turtledove, guard of Hunahpú and Xbalanqué: 131

Xóchitl, flower, name of the twentieth day of the Mexican calendar: 78–79n.

Xpiyacoc, the grandfather, companion of Xmucane: 79, 87, 88, 107, 173

Xpuch, and Xtah, maidens who tried to tempt Tohil: 197

Xpurpuvec: *see* Purpuvec

Xquic, daughter of a lord of Xibalba, mother of Hunahpú and Xbalanqué: 119ff.

Xtoh, Xcanil, Xcacau, godess of agriculture: 125

Xtzul, centipede, an ancient dance: 156

Xulpit, people of the region of Laguna de Términos, hostile to the Cakchiquels: 64, 67

Xulú, diviner: *see* Pacam

Xuxulim-ha, House of Cold, place of punishment of Xibalba: 117, 148

Yaqui, Mexican tribe which accompanied the Quiché, the sacrificers: 62, 65, 69, 70, 170n., 174, 189

Yaxcanul, volcano of Santa María: 95

Yolcuat-Quitzalcuat, god of the Yaqui: 189

Yucatán: the East in the Quiché legend, residence of Quetzalcoatl, 3, 9, 10, 13, 54, 62, 63, 64, 65; invaded by the Itzá and by the Tutul Xius, 67, 167n., 207

Yzumpán: *see* García Calel Yzumpán

Zaccabahá: the present S. Andrés Saccabajá, 221, 225

Zacahá, 69, 171

Zacualpa, Quiché town: 221n.

Zaculeu, fortress of the Mam: 221

Zakikoxol, the spirit of the mountain: 84n.

Zaqui-Nim-Ac, Zaqui-Nimá-Tziís: names given to the Creator, 78; old man and old woman who help to kill Vucub-Caquix, 97

Zaquic, a royal house of Quiché: 217, 218

Zaquitoc, knife made of flint, used in the sacrifices; the pine of Xibalba: 116, 121, 145

Zibaque, a kind of rush from which the woman's flesh was made: 90n.

Zipacná, son of Vucub-Caquix: played with the mountains, 95, 99; kills the four hundred youths, 101; destroyed by Hunahpú and Xbalanqué, 102–104

Zorita, Alonso de: saw the paintings

of the Indians, 12, 209n.; meets the last kings of Quiché, 22; saw the temples of Utatlán, 215n.

Zotzi-há: House of Bats, 117, 149; royal house of the Cakchiquel, 190n.

*Zotzil*, bat, symbol of the Cakchiquel kings: 179, 190n.

Zutuhil, a tribe established on the shores of Lake Atitlán: 62, 71, 73, 210

Zuyva, Tulán-Zuiva: cradle of the Toltec, Maya, and Quiché, 62; town on the Laguna de Términos where the Cakchiquel were defeated, 62, 64, 66, 189

Zúñiga: author of the *Diccionario Poconchí*, on the feather work of the Indians, 228n.

UNIVERSITY OF OKLAHOMA PRESS

NORMAN